新编英汉笔译教程 （第2版）

张林影　主编

U0360841

清华大学出版社

北京

内 容 简 介

本教材由14章构成，简单介绍了翻译的定义、标准、分类、策略、方法及过程，分析了英汉两种语言、文化之间的差异及其对翻译的影响，重点介绍了词类转换、增词法、重复法、省略法、正反转换法，定语从句、名词性从句、状语从句译法，以及被动语态和长句译法等常用翻译技巧与方法，所讲内容构成了一个完整的体系。教材坚持理论与实践相结合的原则，每个翻译技巧或方法都会结合一定数量的翻译案例来进行阐述。大部分章节后都配有翻译练习题，结合考级选材，注重能力培养。

本教材适合高等院校翻译、英语等专业的本科生、研究生使用，亦可作为职场人士和翻译爱好者的参考用书。

图书在版编目 (CIP) 数据

新编英汉笔译教程 / 张林影主编 . -- 2 版 . -- 北京：
清华大学出版社，2024. 9. -- ISBN 978-7-302-67124-4

Ⅰ . H315.9

中国国家版本馆 CIP 数据核字第 2024X8B329 号

责任编辑：刘远菁
封面设计：常雪影
版式设计：方加青
责任校对：马遥遥
责任印制：沈 露

出版发行：清华大学出版社
      网　　址：https://www.tup.com.cn，https://www.wqxuetang.com
      地　　址：北京清华大学学研大厦 A 座　　　邮　　编：100084
      社 总 机：010-83470000　　　　　　　　邮　　购：010-62786544
      投稿与读者服务：010-62776969，c-service@tup.tsinghua.edu.cn
      质 量 反 馈：010-62772015，zhiliang@tup.tsinghua.edu.cn
印 装 者：北京嘉实印刷有限公司
经　　销：全国新华书店
开　　本：185mm×260mm　　印　　张：15　　　字　　数：328 千字
版　　次：2016 年 11 月第 1 版　2024 年 9 月第 2 版　印　　次：2024 年 9 月第 1 次印刷
定　　价：59.00 元

产品编号：102397-01

作者简介

　　张林影，女，牡丹江师范学院副教授，硕士研究生导师，省级一流本科课程"英汉笔译"和省级研究生精品课程"旅游文化翻译"负责人。发表学术论文三十余篇，出版专著两部，教材一部。专著《当代西方主要翻译理论及其在文体翻译中的应用研究》获得黑龙江省高校人文社科优秀成果一等奖和黑龙江省外语学科优秀科研成果一等奖；教材《新编英汉笔译教程》获得黑龙江省教育科学规划"十三五"期间高等教育优秀成果二等奖。主持黑龙江省哲学社会科学年度规划项目四项，黑龙江省高等教育教学改革项目两项，以及黑龙江省教育科学规划重点项目、黑龙江省经济社会发展重点项目等厅级项目十余项；获得黑龙江省外语学科优秀科研成果一、二、三等奖各一项，黑龙江省高等教育教学改革优秀成果二等奖两项，牡丹江市优秀科研成果一等奖一项。主持黑龙江省研究生课程思政高质量建设项目和智慧树全国共享课"旅游文化翻译"。主讲课程"英汉笔译"获评黑龙江省课程思政示范课程，同时入选黑龙江省首批课程思政优秀教学案例。

前　言

　　笔者从事翻译教学十七载，讲授过"英汉笔译""应用翻译""翻译理论与实践""文体与翻译"等近十门翻译课程，期间收集了大量的典型翻译案例并总结出不少翻译实践经验。本教材第1版于2016年出版，受到广大师生好评，被十几所高校用作教材，印刷7次，并获得黑龙江省"十三五"期间教育科学优秀成果二等奖。本教材所依托的"英汉笔译"课程于2015年获评校级精品课，2020年获评校级课程思政示范课程和校级一流课程，2021年获评省级一流课程，2022年入选省级课程思政优秀案例，2024年获评省级课程思政示范课程。笔者依托"英汉笔译"课程和本教材于2020年获得课程思政教学名师称号、校首届教师教学创新大赛二等奖，并于2023年获得全国高校英语教师教学基本功大赛二等奖，此外，笔者所在的团队于2024年获评省级课程思政示范教学团队。

　　翻译人才的培养应适应社会经济发展的需求，因此，翻译教材的编写要紧跟时代步伐。2020年《普通高等学校本科外国语言文学类专业教学指南》(以下简称2020《指南》)指出，要培养时代需要、国家期待的外语专业人才，将立德树人、坚定文化自信和培养家国情怀等纳入外语专业人才培养目标。按照2020《指南》要求，并结合笔者自身的教学实践，在保留原版教材框架结构的基础上，新版教材增加了一些具有时代特点的翻译案例和翻译练习题，进一步完善了原版教材的内容。

　　《新编英汉笔译教程(第2版)》与时俱进，精选典型翻译案例，重视知识更新；结合考级选材，专注能力培养；融入思政元素，注重价值塑造。全书共分14章，除了简单介绍中外翻译理论和知识外，还通过英汉两种语言、文化的对比和大量译例分析，介绍英汉翻译方法和技巧，所讲翻译技巧构成了一个完整的体系，可以帮助学生掌握翻译的基本原理、方法和技巧。本教材坚持理论与实践相结合的原则，每个翻译技巧都会结合一定数量的案例进行阐述，每个章节后都配有相应翻译技巧的句子和语篇翻译练习，目的是使学生通过练习了解英汉两种语言的差异，找出英汉互译的规律，从而熟练掌握英汉常用翻译技巧，培养翻译能力。正如"一千个读者眼中就会有一千个哈姆雷特"，翻译没有绝对的"标准译文"。本教材中提供的译文仅供参考。此外，本教材还充分利用翻译课程文化内涵丰富的特点，深入挖掘思政元素，将精选的经典励志美文用于章节段落翻译练习，对学生开展德育教育；翻译案例和章节练习中适当融入中国元素，在培养学生翻译能力的同时使学生理解当代中国，提高其用英语讲好中国故事的能力。

相比于第1版，第2版教材做了如下更新与调整：

1. 对原教材部分章节的内容进行了调整和删减。

2. 对原教材的部分文字表述进行了修订，替换、删除了部分翻译案例，同时添加了一些案例。

3. 对部分章节的配套练习进行了替换和增减，并对参考译文的文字表述进行了适当修改。

4. 将翻译专业资格考试历年真题部分内容融入教材，结合考级选材，注重能力培养。

5. 融入中国元素，使学生在掌握翻译技巧的同时为讲好中国故事奠定基础。

本教材是黑龙江省高等教育教学改革一般项目"翻译教学中习近平新时代中国特色社会主义思想'三进'研究"(SJGY20220604)、黑龙江省教育科学"十四五"规划2023年度重点课题"课程思政背景下英语翻译教学中'三进'实施路径研究"(GJB1423130)、黑龙江省教育学会一般课题"东北抗联精神融入高校翻译课程思政教学研究"(23GJYBB195)和黑龙江省课程思政示范课程"英汉笔译"的阶段性成果。

本教材适合高等院校英语、翻译等专业的本科生、研究生使用，亦可作为职场人士和翻译爱好者的参考用书。由于笔者水平有限，书中肯定会存在一些不足，诚切希望各位专家、学者和广大读者批评指正，多提宝贵意见。反馈邮箱：wkservice@vip.163.com。

本教材免费提供配套电子课件，授课教师扫描下方二维码并填写相关验证信息即可下载。

目　录

第1章
翻译概述

学习翻译时究竟应该学些什么?

首先,学习翻译时应该学习翻译的基本知识,如翻译的定义、翻译的标准、翻译的分类、过程、主要翻译方法与策略;了解翻译理论和实践的发展历史和翻译研究的主要流派。

其次,学习翻译时应该学习常用翻译技巧,如直译、意译、词类转换、增词法、重复法、省略法、正反转换法等;了解不同文体的特点,掌握相应的翻译方法。

通过学习翻译了解英汉两种语言与文化之间的差异,加深对两种语言、文化的理解,提高自身双语与文化的转换能力和跨文化交流能力,坚定文化自信,培养家国情怀和国际视野。

1.1 翻译的定义

　　随着全球化时代的到来，各国之间的交流日益深入，翻译活动越来越受到重视。翻译是使用不同语言的民族之间沟通思想的纽带，是国际合作、文化交流、文明互鉴的桥梁。从经济发展的角度讲，翻译为各国之间开展经济合作提供了机会。经济合作是在交际中进行的，翻译是企业实现对外交流与合作的关键点。离开翻译，跨文化沟通就很难进行，沟通不成，就无法开展经济合作。从文化传播角度讲，翻译促进了文化交流，推动了文化多元化发展。翻译为讲不同语言的人提供了相互沟通和了解的机会，促进了不同社会制度、不同地域民族、不同文化背景的国家/地区和人民间的沟通与交流。通过翻译和介绍国外优秀文化，对本国传统文化产生积极的、革命性的影响，从而创造出更优秀的新文化。没有翻译，中国文化就无法走出去，国外文化也无法传播到中国，文明的交流与互鉴就无从谈起。诺贝尔文学奖获得者莫言曾说："翻译的工作特别重要，我之所以获得诺奖，离不开各国翻译者的创造性工作。有时候，翻译比原创还要艰苦。我写《生死疲劳》，初稿只用了43天。瑞典汉学家陈安娜，整整翻译了6年。"由此可见，翻译的重要性再怎么强调也不过分。

　　翻译使我们可以从其他语言文化中汲取有益成分，丰富我们自己的语言，活跃我们的思想，开发我们的智力，开阔我们的视野，从而将语言文化、人类文明推向一个更高的层次和发展阶段。翻译既是一门艺术，也是一门科学，既有跨文化性，又有交际性，涉及两种不同的语言文化。既然翻译如此重要，那么到底什么是翻译呢？学者们给翻译下过很多定义，但由于各自的视角不同，目前为止尚未形成统一的定义。有人将翻译视为一门科学，因为翻译有自身的规律可循；有人将翻译看作一门艺术，因为翻译是译者对原文再创造的过程；还有人将翻译视为一门手艺，因为源语的信息需要用地道而恰当的目的语再现。列维在《翻译是一个抉择过程》中提到，翻译的过程就是译者不断做出决策的过程，它是译者主体能动性的一种体现。翻译好比下棋，在走棋过程中需要对每一步的多种可能的走法做出选择，在做选择时应当考虑诸多因素。

　　《现代汉语词典》将翻译定义为"把一种语言文字的意义用另一种语言文字表达出来"。根据《剑桥语言百科全书》，"翻译"这个中性术语是指将一种语言（"源语"）里的词句的意思转变为另一种语言（"目的语"）的意思所发生的一切行为，不论其手段是说话、写字，还是做手势。《牛津英语词典》(*Oxford English Dictionary*)对翻译的定义是：to turn from one language into another (从一种语言转换成另一种语言)；《韦氏新国际英语词典第三版》(*Webster's Third New International Dictionary of the English Language*)对翻译的定义是：to turn into one's own or another language (转换成本族语或另一种语言)。广义的翻译指语言与语言、语言变体与语言变体、语言与非语言等的代码转换和基本信息的传达。狭义的翻译是一种语言活动，是指把一种语言表达的内容忠实地用另一种语言表达出来。

文艺学派对翻译的定义：从文艺学的角度解释翻译，认为翻译是艺术创作的一种形式，强调语言的创造功能，讲究译品的艺术效果。西塞罗(106BC—43BC)提出，译者不必逐字死译，直译是缺乏技巧的表现。译者必须照顾译语读者的语言习惯，用符合译文读者的语言来打动读者或听众；翻译要传达的是原文的意义和精神，而不是原文的语言形式；因为文学作品的翻译就是再创作，翻译文学作品的译者必须具备文学天赋或素质；由于各种语言的修辞手段"彼此有相通之处"，在翻译中做到风格对等是完全可能的。他还主张译作应当超过原作，这与我国当代翻译家许渊冲的翻译"竞赛论"和"优势论"观点相似。英国著名翻译理论家泰特勒(Tytler，1791)将翻译定义为：A good translation is one in which the merit of the original work is so completely transfused into another language as to be as distinctly apprehended and as strongly felt by a native of the country/region to which that language belongs as it is by those who speak the language of the original work. (优秀的翻译应该把原作的优点完全地移注到另一种语言之中，以使译入语所属国家/地区的本地人能明白地领悟、强烈地感受，如同使用原作语言的人所领悟、所感受的一样)。所以文学翻译是"传达作者的全部意图，即通过艺术手法影响读者的思想、感情"。茅盾(1954)将文学翻译定义为："文学翻译是用另一种语言，把原作的艺术意境传达出来。"

文艺学派强调翻译是艺术意境的再创造，将侧重点放在文学的翻译上，因而并未顾及非文学作品的翻译。英国诗人、翻译理论家约翰·德莱顿(John Dryden，1631—1700)认为，翻译是一门艺术，译者必须具有艺术家的气质——具有敏锐的艺术鉴赏力和丰富的表现力，才能把握和再现原作的艺术特征。

语言学派则从另一个视角定义翻译。英国著名的翻译理论家约翰·卡特福德(John Catford)用现代语言学视角诠释翻译问题，他对翻译的定义如下：翻译是把一种语言(源语)的文本材料转换成另一种语言(目标语)中对等的文本材料，把寻求对等视作翻译研究和实践的中心问题，对翻译的不同语言层次进行描写、研究。他在1965年出版的《翻译的语言学理论》(*A Linguistic Theory of Translation*)一书中定义了"转换"这一概念，认为转换意味着"在从源语到目的语的过程中偏离了形式上的对等"，他将转换分为层次转换和范畴转换，从不同的视角为译者提供了翻译指导。巴尔胡达罗夫(Barhudalov)认为，翻译是把一种语言的言语产物(即话语)在保持内容(也就是意义)不变的情况下改变为另外一种语言的言语产物(区分语言(langue)和言语(parole))；费道罗夫(Federov)指出，翻译就是用一种语言把另一种语言在内容和形式不可分割的统一中所表达出来的东西准确而完全地表达出来。

1980年，我国著名翻译家张培基先生在《英汉翻译教程》一书的绪论中，从语言学的角度为翻译下了这样的定义："翻译是运用一种语言把另一种语言所表达的思维内容准确而完整地重新表现出来的语言活动。"美国翻译理论家尤金·奈达(Eugene Nida)在《奈达论翻译》(1984)中对翻译的定义是：Translating consists in reproducing in the receptor language the closest natural equivalent of the source-language message, first in terms of meaning and secondly in terms of style. (所谓翻译，是指在译语中用最切近而又自然的对等语再现原语的信息，首先在语义上，其次在文体上。)

总体而言，语言学派强调的是话语的语际转换过程或信息的转换过程。翻译是语义的翻译，不是语言形式的翻译，是运用另一种语言文字的适当方式来表达一种语言所表达的内容，而不是在另一种语言中寻找与一种语言中含义相似的某些词语或结构。也就是说，翻译必须跳出原文语言层面的束缚，必须着眼于传达原文的内容和意义。换句话说，翻译是运用一种语言把另一种语言所表达的内容和意义准确而完整地重新表达出来的语言活动。德国译学教授沃尔弗拉姆·威尔斯(Wolfram Wilss)在 *The Science of Translation*: *Problems & Methods*(1977)一书中提到：Translation is not simply a matter of seeking other words with similar meaning, but of finding appropriate ways of saying things in another language. Translating is always meaning-based, i.e. it is the transfer of meaning instead of form from the source language to the target language.(翻译不只是在另一种语言中寻找意义相似的其他词语，而是寻找表达事物的适当方式。翻译始终立足于语义，也就是说，是语义从源语到译语的转换，而不是形式的转换。)

翻译理论研究在后结构主义、后现代主义、后殖民主义以及文化研究的影响下将研究重心由研究原文内在的文本结构及原文与译文之间的对等转向对翻译活动产生重要影响的政治权利以及意识形态等外部宏观因素，开始研究诸如翻译与政治权利的关系、翻译与意识形态的关系、翻译与性别的关系、翻译与伦理学的关系等，更注重翻译过程和译作在文化和意识形态方面的影响、翻译的外部环境以及翻译行为与社会文化因素之间的关系。20世纪80年代后期翻译研究出现文化转向。

下面来看文化学派对翻译的定义。霍恩比(1988)提出，翻译研究应摒弃所谓的"科学的"态度，"文化"应取代"文本"，成为翻译研究的单位；巴斯奈特(1990)将翻译视为动态过程，认为翻译是文化与文化之间的交流，深深根植于语言所处的文化之中，她特别强调文化在翻译中的地位，认为翻译等值就是源语与译语在文化功能上的等值，但参考译文与原文的完全等值是不可能的。她指出翻译不应只关注对原文的描述，而应关注原文在目的语环境下文化功能的等值。巴斯奈特的文化翻译观表明，翻译绝非单纯的语言转换行为，而是与文化紧密相关。

文化学派将文化视为翻译单位，将翻译视为特定文化背景下的交流活动，而不是一种静态的语言转换行为。翻译不是简单的双语交际，而是文化之间的相互交流，翻译的目的是通过打破语言障碍，实现并改善文化交流。翻译的精髓是跨文化转译信息，而不是简单地进行编码和解码，其主旨是文化植入和融合。文化学派强调文化对翻译的制约作用，将翻译研究的重点从原作转向译作，从作者转向译者，从源语文化转向译语文化。

综上所述，翻译是把一种语言所表达的内容、形式、风格以及传达的文化信息用另一种语言忠实、流畅、艺术地再现出来的实践活动(语言文化活动)，以达到沟通思想情感、传播文化知识以及促进社会文明的目的。根据系统功能语言学家的观点，翻译的基本单位应该是语篇，而不是词语结构。语言的实际使用单位是语篇这样的言语单位，而不是词语结构这样的语法单位。实际使用的语篇有可能是一个句子、一个段落、一个句群，也有可能是一个词语。翻译作为语言文化交流的一种形式，其实质是用一种语言的语篇代替另一种语言与其文化意义对等的语篇。不管如何定义，翻译都要经过原文理解(understanding)、信息转换(transfer)、译文重组/表达restructuring/expression和译文检验(testing)。

1.2　翻译的标准

翻译标准是指译者在翻译实践中所遵循的原则，也指翻译批评家批评译文时必须遵循的原则。翻译标准是翻译活动必须遵循的准绳，是衡量译文质量的尺度，也是翻译工作者应该努力达到的目标。翻译标准是翻译理论的核心问题。但是，译界尚未对此形成完全一致的定论。

1.2.1　国内翻译标准

良好的中英文语言能力对于英汉翻译必不可少。但除此之外，还必须掌握常用的翻译技巧，遵循一定的翻译原则。提及国内的翻译原则时，必谈严复。严复是我国近代著名的思想家、文学家、翻译家。他在《天演论·译例言》(1898)中提出的"信、达、雅"(faithfulness, expressiveness, and elegance)三字标准被视为衡量翻译质量的重要标准，成为过去一个世纪以来我国翻译理论和实践的核心概念。"信"是指意义不违背原文，"达"是不拘泥于原文形式，尽译文语意之能事以求原意明显。"信""达"互为照应，不可分割开来。"雅"在今天看来是不可取的，因为严复所谓的"雅"，即所谓的上等文言文。"信、达、雅"的翻译标准在我国翻译史上独具意义，给译界以有益的启发，甚至成为中国人翻译西方语言文字的准绳。

1932年，梁实秋在《新月》第4卷第5号的文章《论翻译的一封信》中提倡译文应在"信"的基础之上做到"顺"，强调"信"与"顺"的统一，即译文既对原文忠实，又通顺可诵。"翻译要忠于原文，如能不但对原文的意思忠实，还对'语气忠实'，这自是最好的翻译。虽能使读者读懂而误译原文，这种翻译是要不得的。既误译原文，又要令读者'硬着头皮'去懂，这太霸道了。坏的翻译，包括下列几个条件：(一)与原文意思不符；(二)未能表达出'原文的强悍的语气'；(三)令人看不懂。三条有其一，便不是好翻译；若三者具备，便是最坏的翻译。误译、曲译、死译、硬译，都是半斤八两。"他有一段话颇有见地："国内有人说，翻译的最高境界就是让人读起来不觉得是翻译作品，这种说法自然是正确的，但要看一个翻译作品是好还是坏，是决然离不开与原文的比对的。一篇翻译是否忠实于原文，对翻译十分重要，如果这类翻译作品读来朗朗上口，文笔流畅，浅白自知，但是一比对原文发现，文不对题，言不达意，那还是好的翻译作品吗？所以翻译作品要字斟句酌，要忠于原作，而不可一味追求文笔流畅而舍本逐末。"

林语堂总结并继承前人的翻译成果，在其1933年发表的《论翻译》一文中提出了翻译的三大标准：忠实、通顺、美。他认为这不仅是翻译的标准，也是译者应有的责任。"忠实"是译者对原著者的责任，"通顺"是译者对中国读者的责任，"美"是译者对艺术的责任。具备这三种责任心，然后可谓具有真正译家的资格。他提出，"忠实"的程度可以大致分为四等，即"直译""死译""意译""胡译"。

1935年，鲁迅在其《题未定草(一至三)》中指出："只求易懂，不如创作，或者改作，将事改为中国事，人也化为中国人。如果还是翻译，那么，首先的目的，就在博览外国的作品，不但移情，也要益智，至少是知道何地何时，有这等事，和旅行外国，是很相像的：它必须有异国情调，就是所谓洋气。其实世界上也不会有完全归化的译文，倘有，就是貌合神离，从严辨别起来，它算不得翻译。凡是翻译，必须兼顾着两面，一当然力求其易解，一则保存着原作的丰姿，但这保存，却又常常和易懂相矛盾：看不惯了。"可见鲁迅在强调信的前提下，是坚持信、顺兼顾的翻译方法的。也就是说，译文既要信又要顺(both faithful to the source language and smooth in expression)。这与我国当代翻译理论家张培基等人在其《英汉翻译教程》中所提出的"忠实""通顺"标准有异曲同工之妙。

1951年，傅雷在《高老头·重译本序》中提出"神似"说。他指出，以效果而论，翻译应当像临画一样，所求的不在形似而在神似。假如为了传达异国文字的特性而去破坏本国文字的结构与特性，等于"两败俱伤"，所以，如果假定理想的译文仿佛是原作者的中文写作，那么原文的意义与精神，译文的流畅与完整，都可以兼筹并顾，不至于再有以辞害意，或以意害辞的弊病了。傅雷在1963年1月6日致罗新璋函中指出，译事第一要求将原作(连同思想、感情、气氛、情调等)化为我有，方能谈到移译。

1954年，茅盾在《为发展文学翻译事业和提高翻译质量而奋斗》的报告中将中国古典美学中的意境引入翻译，把传达原作的艺术意境作为翻译的根本任务，提出了著名的"艺术创造性翻译"思想，这是对他翻译实践的最高经验总结。

1964年，钱钟书在发表于《文学研究集刊》上的《林纾的翻译》一文中指出：文学翻译的最高标准是"化"。把作品从一国文字转变成另一国文字，既能不因语文习惯的差异而露出生硬牵强的痕迹，又能完全保存原有的风味，那就算得入于"化境"。17世纪有人将这种造诣的翻译比为原作的"投胎转世"(the transmigration of souls)，躯壳换了一个，而精神姿致依然故我。换句话说，译本对原作应该忠实得以至于读起来不像译本，因为作品在原文里绝不会读起来像经过翻译似的。这段表述既体现了文学翻译的最高标准"化"，也体现了文学翻译的理想境界"化境"。钱钟书表示，一方面，"能不因语文习惯的差异而露出生硬牵强的痕迹"，另一方面，"又能完全保存原有的风味"；或者一方面，"躯壳换了一个"，另一方面，"精神姿致依然故我"。

许渊冲先生在文学翻译的求美之路上，于1979年在《外语教学与研究》第2期发表的题为《意美、音美、形美》一文中提出了"三美"原则。文章开篇写道："有个外国作家说过：'散文是井然有序的文字；诗是井然有序的绝妙好词。'我觉得'绝妙好词'就是具备意美、音美、形美的文字。毛泽东诗词是具备意美、音美、形美的艺术高峰。翻译毛泽东诗词要尽可能传达原诗的三美。"许渊冲把审美、传达美当作他诗歌翻译的主要任务。许先生在具体讨论"三美"之前，提出"三美的基础是三似：意似、音似、形似。意似就是要传达原文的内容，不能错译、漏译、多译"。这里必须指出，美学取向的翻译原则多适用于文学翻译，以此指导翻译实践，的确产生了不少精彩的文学译作。但是，该原则对于一些人而言显得过于"高深"和"抽象"，也不太适合用来指导非文学作品的翻译实践。

1984年，罗新璋在《我国自成体系的翻译理论》一文中指出：主张"神似"的傅雷所追求的是"原文的意义与精神，译文的流畅与完整"。很显然，"躯壳换了一个"就是追求"译文的流畅与完整"，"精神姿致依然故我"就是保存"原文的意义与精神"。罗新璋也认为："译本……读起来不像译本"，与傅雷所说"仿佛是原作者的中文写作"，有异曲同工之妙；"而精神姿致依然故我"，含义上似乎比"神似"又多所增进，但追本溯源，也就是获致原作精神的"神似"。

朱光潜提倡信顺统一。朱先生认为："直译和意译的分别根本不应存在。"语言跟思想有一致性，语言变了，思想也必然要变。要使译文尽可能"信"，就要尽可能保留原文的结构形式；而若完全按照原文的结构形式组织中文——直译，就可能产生不顺的译文。因此，"理想的翻译是文从字顺的直译"。直译、意译的方法都不能过度使用。好的直译必然包含意译的成分，好的意译又必然包含直译的成分。朱先生(1988)曾说：

"直译不能不是意译,而意译也不能不是直译。"总之,理想的翻译要"信""顺"统一。一篇通顺的原文,如果译得不"顺",那么"信"也不复存在。但是,这毕竟是两个方面。好的译文要"信""顺"兼顾,不可偏废。

1994年,刘重德在综述历代名家论翻译原则学说的基础上,参考严复和泰特勒两家的观点后,提出了"信、达、切"的翻译标准:信于内容;达如其分;切合风格。刘先生指出,在翻译实践中,我们应该严格根据"信、达、切"三字原则的要求,对于选词炼句,要有像杜甫"语不惊人死不休"、贾岛"两句三年得"和严复"一名之立,旬月踟蹰"那样推敲琢磨、一字不苟的精神,力求使译文不仅达意,而且传神,以保存原作的丰姿和风格。

无论是"神似""化境"还是"信、达、切"等,都旨在修补、更新、完善我国大翻译家严复提出来的"信、达、雅"的翻译标准,可始终没有哪一种新提法能取而代之。因为"信、达、雅"言简意赅,主次突出,全面系统,完整统一。"信、达、雅"这条标准看似简单,在实践中却很难真正做到,常会遇到顾此失彼的问题。在这个意义上说,这条标准仍具有相对的意义。原作品本身就很难令人满意,更何况是翻译,永远不会十全十美。我们来对比一下元朝作家马致远创作的散曲《天净沙·秋思》的三个英译本。

原文:

天净沙·秋思

枯藤老树昏鸦,

小桥流水人家,

古道西风瘦马。

夕阳西下,

断肠人在天涯。

马致远的这首曲作共28个字。以景托情,寓情于景,全曲无一秋字,但通过多种景物的并置,在景情的交融中构成一种凄凉悲苦的意境,准确地传达出旅人凄苦的心境。语言凝练简洁,词语之间和分句之间未使用任何连接形式,文字流畅自然,分句间丝丝入扣,话了而句终,意尽则语绝,体现了重意合的语义型句子特征。这些词看似没有关联,但都旨在烘托最后一句"夕阳西下,断肠人在天涯",每个意象都做到情与景的自然统一。原作中,前三句通篇运用的是名词和形容词,没有一个动词,也没有各景物间相对关系和位置的信息,它们所呈现的形态等内容都没有清晰的介绍,而是凭借读者的想象来合理组织这些意象,给读者留下无限的想象空间,于是产生了不同的英译本。

译文一:

Tune: Sunny Sand

Autumn Thoughts

Over old trees wreathed with rotten vines fly evening crows;

Under a small bridge near a cottage a stream flows;

On ancient road in the west wind a lean horse goes.

Westward declines the sun;

Far, far from home is the heartbroken one.

——许渊冲(译)

译文二：

Autumn

Crows hovering over rugged trees wreathed with rotten vine—the day is about done.

Yonder is a tiny bridge over a sparkling stream, and on the far bank, a pretty little village.

But the traveler has to go on down this ancient road, the west wind moaning, his bony horse groaning, trudging towards the sinking sun, farther and farther away from home.

——翁显良(译)

译文三：

Tune to "Sand and Sky"

—Autumn Thoughts

Dry vine, old tree, crows at dusk.

Low bridge, stream running, cottages.

Ancient road, west wind, lean nag.

The sun weltering,

And one with breaking heart at the sky's edge.

——施文林(译)

许渊冲先生的译文句式工整，流畅通顺，韵律和谐自然，最大限度地保留了原作的意象和形式。但对个别景物的翻译需要考虑不同文化背景所承载的文化内涵的差异，如汉语中的"西风"意味着深秋或冬季将至，天气变冷，树叶凋零，人们由此联想到悲凉的景象。而在英国，西风吹来的时候，正是春天来临、万物复苏的季节。文化的差异导致对原文主调的理解出现了偏差，该译文虽然再现了音美、形美，但却未能完全做到达意。

翁显良的译文舍去了原作经典的景物词汇组合形式，采用了完整的句式组合，用更直接、更具体的语言将原文意境展现给目标语读者，使译文读者能够很好地领会原作的精神，理解该曲的意境，但该译文显然是在牺牲了原作韵律和节奏的基础上做到的传意，顾其义而丢其神，已不再是诗歌的形式，失去了原作的音美、形美。

施文林(Wayne Schlepp)采用"意象叠加"和"意象并置"的写作手法，即把不同时间、空间的两个可见意象并置排列，借以启发和引起全新的感受。总体来讲，施文林的译文在形式和意义方面比较贴近原文。但美中不足之处是原作的韵律在该译文中未能得以体现，译文没有明显的韵脚；再者，译文虽给西方读者一种新鲜感和异国情调，但由于文化背景的不同，西方读者未必能领会曲中的意境和所表达的旅人凄苦的心境。

由此可见，要达到完全的"信、达、雅"或"等值(效果)"，只能是一种美好的理想或愿望，能达到七八成或八九成之忠实，已是十分不错的了，因为任何一种文字都有其声音之美，有其意义之美，有其传神之美，有其文气、文体、形式之美，翻译者常会顾其义而丢其神，得其神而忘其体，难以把义、神、气、体、音之美完全兼顾，同时译出。

1.2.2　国外翻译标准

国外的翻译标准主要是指西方翻译理论家对翻译提供的标准。在西方，较早的翻译标准是18世纪末英国著名翻译理论家亚历山大·泰特勒(Alexander Tytler，1747—1814)在《论翻译的原则》(*Essay on the Principles of Translation*)一书中提出的著名的翻译三原则。这是以作者和读者为取向的翻译原则(the author-and-reader-oriented translation principle)，既考虑了作者又考虑了读者，比较全面。泰特勒翻译三原则具体内容如下：

(1) 译文应完全复写出原作的思想(A translation should give a complete transcript of the ideas of the original work.)

(2) 译文的风格和笔调应与原文的性质相同(The style and manner of writing should be of the same character as that of the original.)

(3) 译文应和原作同样流畅(A translation should have all the ease of the original composition.)

在国外的译论中，多数翻译标准集中反映在一个"等"字上。"等"指的是原作与译作之间的对等或等值。引证最多的是等值标准和等效标准。运用语言学成果科学、严正地提出等值概念论体系，是从20世纪下半叶开始的。其代表作有费道罗夫(Federov)的《翻译概念》，该书研究了等值翻译所运用的语言模式，从传统语言学模式发展到结构主义语言学模式，最后发展到各种模式的综合运用。等值标准不但要求译文与原文思想内容等值，而且要求语言形式上的等值。

尤金·奈达根据认知经验因素将功能对等分为最小对等和最大对等。最小对等可以表述为"译文的读者对译文应该理解，能够想象出原文读者如何理解和欣赏原文"。任何低于这种对等程度的内容都是不可接受的。最大对等可以表述为"译文的读者应该能够以与原文读者理解原文基本相同的方式理解和欣赏译文"。"最大限度的定义意味着源语言和目标语言之间高度的语言文化对应，以及异常有效的翻译，以便产生与原文读者体验非常接近的反应能力"(奈达，1993)。由此可见，奈达强调原语读者和目标语读者之间的感受对等、反应对等。等效标准所追求的目标是：译文读者能和原文读者同样顺利地获得相同或基本相同的信息，包括原文精神、具体事实、意境风格等。

彼得·纽马克(Peter Newmark)在总结、借鉴前人研究理论的基础上，于1981年在其第一部著作《翻译问题探讨》(*Approaches to Translation*)中提出了著名的语义翻译和交际翻译。语义翻译要求译者在目的语语义和句法结构允许的情况下，尽可能切近、准确地呈现原文的语境意义，追求的是语义准确但不一定达到适当的交际效果。语义翻译以原文的形式和原作者的原意为中心。不同于语义翻译，交际翻译不考虑使用场合。交际翻译的重点是根据目的语的语言、文化和语用方式传递信息，使译文不论是在内容上还是在语言形式上都能为读者所接受，而不是尽量忠实地复述原文的文字。

基于行为理论和跨文化交际理论，弗米尔(Vermeer)在其1978年出版的《普通翻译理论框架》一书中首次提出翻译目的论，并在《翻译行为中的目的与委托》(*Skopos and Commission in Translational Action*，1989)中对"目的论"的基本内容进行了概述，提出了翻译的三个原则：目的原则(skopos rule)、连贯原则(coherence rule)和忠实原则(fidelity rule)。弗米尔指出，目的原则是所有翻译活动必须遵循的首要原则，翻译应能在译入语情境和文化中，按译入语接受者期待的方式发生作用。连贯原则指译文必须符合语内连贯(intra-textual coherence)的标准，即译文具有可读性和可接受性，能够使接受者理解并在译入语文化及使用译文的交际语境中有意义。忠实原则指原文与译文之间应该存在语际连贯(inter-textual coherence)。这相当于其他翻译理论所谓的忠实于原文，但与原文一致的程度和形式取决于译文的目的和译者对原文的理解。

现代人已经把翻译的标准概括为言简意赅的四个字——"忠实，通顺"。忠实指的是忠实于原文。译者必须准确而又完整地把原文的思想及内容表达出来，不可擅自增删或变意，要绝对尊重原文作者在叙述、说明和描写过程中所反映的思想、观点、立场及个人感情，决不可凭着个人好恶去肆意歪曲，要"保存着原作的丰姿"；通顺指的是译文的语言必须合乎规范、通俗易懂。译者应该使用大众化的现代语言，力求译文朴实、通畅、清新、生动。

1.3 翻译的分类、策略、方法及过程

1.3.1 翻译的分类

既然可以从不同的角度对翻译进行定义，那么同样可从不同的视角对翻译进行分

类。一般来讲，我们可以从五种不同的视角对翻译进行分类。

(1) 从译出语和译入语的角度进行分类，翻译可分为本族语译为外语和外语译为本族语。

(2) 按照涉及的语言符号进行分类，翻译可分为语内翻译(intralingual translation)、语际翻译(interlingual translation)和符际翻译(intersemiotic translation)。语内翻译指在同一语言内部进行的翻译，也就是用同语言的一种变体替代另一种变体，如方言与普通话之间的转换，文言文与白话文之间的转换等。语际翻译是不同语言之间进行的对应，即把外族语译成本族语，或把本族语译成外族语，是发生在不同语言之间的翻译活动，诸如英汉互译、英法互译等。符际翻译是把一种非语言的符号译成另一种语言符号，或把一种语言符号译成另一种非语言符号。这里的非语言符号指手势、图画(应包括自然界的画面)、数学符号、音乐符号等。换而言之，即用非语言符号解释语言符号，或用语言符号解释非语言符号。如英语与计算机代码间的翻译，数学符号、音乐符号、手势语、旗语等与言语间的翻译，都属于符际翻译。

(3) 按照翻译的手段进行分类，翻译可分为人工翻译(human translation)和机器翻译(machine translation)。人工翻译又可以分为口译(interpretation)和笔译(translation)。口译又可以进一步分为连续传译(consecutive interpretation)和同声传译(simultaneous interpretation)。连续传译又称为交替传译、即席翻译，用于会议发言、宴会致辞、商务谈判、学术研讨、游览参观等场合，发言人讲完部分或全部内容之后，由口译人员进行翻译；同声传译通常发生在正式的大型会议上，如顶级国际大型会议、经济论坛、政府组织的正式会议等，译员利用专门设备，不间断地边听边译，传译行为几乎与发言人讲话同步进行。

(4) 按照翻译对象的性质和题材进行分类，翻译可分为文学翻译(literary translation)和非文学翻译(non-literary translation)。文学翻译主要包括小说、戏剧、散文和诗歌等文学作品的翻译；非文学翻译涉及的范围比较广，如科技、商务、法律、政治、新闻和旅游等应用文体的翻译。

(5) 按照翻译的处理方式来进行分类，翻译可分为全译(full translation)、节译(abridged translation)、摘译(partial translation)和编译(translation plus editing)。全译是指完整地将源语译为目的语的翻译活动，即对原文文本的语篇和内容进行完整的翻译，这也是翻译实践中最为常见的方式。节译是指挑选某种特定需要的、受他人指定的或译者本人最感兴趣的部分，将其译为目的语。节译所选部分须为相对完整的段落或篇章，且语义完整。摘译是指根据译文使用者的需要，仅对原文文本的某些部分进行选择性地翻译。摘译是指把文章的要点和主要内容翻译出来，不一定完全忠于原文，但内容要相对完整，译文应概括出整篇文章的内容。编译则是指在对原文文本进行完整的或有选择性的翻译的同时，对译文内容进行进一步的加工、取舍、调整、扩展或重组。编译不是严格地按照原文逐字逐句地进行翻译，而是选择性地进行翻译，再加上译者本人的思想观点和创作。不同类型的文本有着不同的翻译要求，学习过程中应注意它们的共性和个性。

1.3.2 翻译策略与方法

策略是指适合具体情况的做事原则和方式方法，是可以实现目标的方案集合。"策略"虽与"方式方法"有关，但强调的是宏观的原则和基本的方案，另外，采用什么"方法"不是任意决定的，而是"基于事先确定的原则或方案"。可见，"方法"是"策略"之内的一个范畴。因此，翻译策略(translation strategy)是指翻译活动中，为实现特定的翻译目的所依据的原则和所采纳的方案集合。

1 异化与归化翻译策略

文化意象的翻译一直都是翻译中的一个棘手问题。文化意象的处理策略也历来是译界很有争议的一个话题。在涉及文化因素的翻译中，异化与归化作为常用的翻译策略，是对立统一而又共生并存的。完全归化和完全异化都不是恰当的翻译策略。

1) 异化与归化翻译策略的提出

美国语言学家、翻译理论家尤金·奈达(Eugene Nida，1984)曾说过：就真正成功的翻译而言，译者的双文化能力甚至比双语能力更重要。翻译作为一种文化活动，既是特定政治、经济、社会、文化和历史条件下的产物，也是译者主观的选择。译者所持的人生观、价值观、政治理想、文化态度、文化立场在其对翻译文本、翻译策略的选择上都发挥着非常重要的作用。

"归化""异化"翻译策略的提出可追溯到19世纪初。1813年，德国著名的翻译理论家施莱尔马赫(Schleiermacher，1813) 在《论翻译的方法》中对"归化"和"异化"两种翻译策略进行了阐述，但其只是对两个概念进行一般意义上的区分。 1995年，美国著名的解构主义翻译理论家韦努蒂 (Venuti) 在《译者的隐形》中提出了"异化法(foreignization)"和"归化法(domestication)"的概念。尤金·奈达是"归化"策略的推崇者，他对西方翻译标准中的"等值观"进行了全面的阐释，并以语言学理论为基础，对"动态对等"进行了论述，最终提出了"功能对等(functional equivalence)"和"读者反应论(theory of reader's response)"的观点。韦努蒂则是"异化"原则的倡导者，他从解构主义视角提出了"异化"翻译观。

"异化"以源语文化为归宿(source culture oriented)，采取对应于作者所使用的源语表达方式，译文保留源语文化的异域性(foreignness)色彩，保留源语与译语的语言文化差异，译者向源语文化读者靠拢。"归化"则是以目标语文化为归宿(target culture oriented)，使译文顺应译语文化的规范和标准，译者向目标语文化读者靠拢。韦努蒂(1995)认为，"归化"策略是"采取民族中心主义的态度，使外语文本符合译入语的文化价值观，把原作者带入译入语文化"；"异化"策略则是"对这些文化价值观的一种民族偏离主义的压力，接受外语文本的语言及文化差异，把读者带入外国情景"。由此可见，译者对"归化""异化"翻译策略的选择，体现了自身的文化立场。韦努蒂认为，如果在将弱势语言文本翻译成强势语言文本的过程中采用"归化"翻译策略，其结果就是弱势语言文本所包含的"异化"成分被扼杀。这样的译文不仅不能体现异族文化的"异"之所在，还会误导译入语读者，使他们陶醉于本族文化之中不能自拔，不利于文化的传播。所以韦努蒂确信"将'异化'翻译策略应用于外译英过程中将有利于民主的地缘政治关系，成为对抗种族主义、我族中心主义、文化帝国主义和文化自恋情绪的一种方式"。

2) 异化和归化策略在翻译中的应用

异化策略有利于促进文化间的相互了解。在翻译过程中，对于地域差异、民俗文化差异、历史文化差异、语义联想差异等各种差异，在不影响理解的前提下，译者要秉持"异化为主，归化为辅"的原则，尽量使用"异化"策略，对于无法通过"异化"策略进行翻译的内容，则采取"归化"策略进行处理。

"异化"翻译策略的优势在于可以更好地促进文化交流，为目标语注入新鲜血液，丰富目标语的语言表达，并为目标语读者了解异域文化创造条件。请看下面的例子：

原文：Unless you've an ace up your sleeve, we are dished.

译文：除非你有锦囊妙计，否则我们输定了。

译文从目的语读者角度出发，套用汉语成语"锦囊妙计"，采取目的语读者所习惯的语言表达方式来翻译原文中的"an ace up one's sleeve"。这一译法在语义层面上似乎达到了"传真"，却掩盖了源语文化与目标语文化之间客观存在的差异，扭曲了原文所传递的文化信息，导致"文化失真"和"文化误读"。英语表达"an ace up one's sleeve"原意是指在16世纪的西方，人们的衣服没有口袋，赌徒往往把王牌"A"藏在袖子里以便作弊。"锦囊妙计"一词出自中国四大名著之一的《三国演义》第五十四回，指诸葛亮给刘备的封在"锦囊"中应对东吴的三条妙计。以上两则成语故事有着截然不同的文化背景和内涵，因而引起的语义联想不同。如果硬要套用汉语成语去翻译，势必误导目标语读者，使其误认为西方也有善出"锦囊妙计"的诸葛亮式的人物。鉴于此，这句话最好还是采取"异化"策略进行翻译：除非你袖中藏有王牌，否则我们输定了。

历史文化是在特定历史发展进程中所形成的文化。各民族的历史发展不同，因而形成了各自独特的历史文化。在各民族的历史文化中都有特定的人物和事件可以体现该民族鲜明的历史文化色彩。例如，英语中用"to meet one's Waterloo"(遭遇滑铁卢)来形容一个人遭遇了惨败。该典故源于滑铁卢战役。1815年，在比利时的小镇滑铁卢，拿破仑率领法军与英国、普鲁士联军展开激战，法军惨败。这场战役被称为滑铁卢战役，是战争史上著名的战役，最终决定了拿破仑及其帝国的命运，对欧洲有着深远的影响。此前拿破仑一直打胜仗，直到在滑铁卢大败，就开始走下坡路了，之后被囚禁。所以 "to meet one's Waterloo" 的引申义就是一个人失败的地方或是让一个人就此失败的一件事情。汉语中有个与此寓意相似的典故——"败走麦城"。该典故是指三国时期蜀国名将关羽被打败后退兵麦城一事。曾经有译者套用英语典故 "to meet one's Waterloo" 来翻译汉语典故 "败走麦城"。两个表达虽然喻义相同，都是指惨遭失败，但分别来源于不同的历史事件，若直接套用目标语中现成的表达进行翻译，就会丢掉原文的文化色彩。可以采用异化翻译策略，将其译为 "The failure of Guan-yu, a famous general of the Shu Kingdom of the Three Kingdoms Period"，这样更有利于目标语读者了解中国的历史文化，推动中华文化更好地走向世界。

异化翻译策略虽然有很多优点，但其运用也会受两个因素的制约：一是译入语语言文化规范的限度，二是译入语读者接受能力的限度。所以在运用异化翻译策略的时候，既要考虑译入语语言文化规范许可的限度，也要考虑译入语读者所能接受的限度，若超出限度，将导致译文晦涩难懂。为了避免这种情况的发生，译者需要进行适当的归化处理。

例如，英语表达 "go Dutch" 带有浓厚的文化色彩。如果译者运用异化翻译策略将 "Let's go Dutch." 译成 "让我们去荷兰人那里吧"，读者就会不知所云。我们先了解一下这一表达的由来：16—17世纪的荷兰是海上商品贸易和早期资源共享主义的发迹之地，荷兰商人终日奔波，具有很强的流动性，请客过后也许请客者与被请者再也不会相遇。为了彼此都不吃亏，各自付费便成为最好的选择，于是衍生出聚时交流信息、散时各自付费的风俗习惯。又因为荷兰人普遍都很精明，凡事都要分清楚，所以出现了与 "荷兰人(Dutch)" 相关的俗语表达 "Let's go Dutch."，可采用异化翻译策略将其译为 "让我们各付各的(或AA制)"。

出于对读者接受能力的考虑，英国翻译家霍克斯(Hawkes)将《红楼梦》里刘姥姥的话 "谋事在人，成事在天" 译成了 "Man proposes, God disposes"。这样翻译的结果虽然易于理解，但没有考虑源语宗教背景和深层文化信息。源语中刘姥姥是佛教徒，在译入语中却变成了基督教徒。出于对这一问题的考虑，杨宪益先生在翻译此书时将该句译为 "Man proposes, Heaven disposes"。此外，称呼同样被赋予了文化色彩。在《红楼梦》中，贾府里的小辈常称贾母为 "老祖宗"，杨宪益将其译为 "Old Ancestress"，霍克斯则将其译为 "Grannie"。"Grannie" 自然是英美人惯用的称呼，特点在于亲切。"Old Ancestress" 虽不是正式称呼，但含有敬意，属于中国文化色彩。

不同民族的人由于地理位置、生活环境、宗教信仰、风俗习惯及思想表达方式不同，对同一事物的看法在许多情况下是不一致的。如果仅采用异化翻译策略，就不能把原文所表达的思想准确地反映出来，从而引起译入语读者的误解，导致翻译失败。因此，在某些情况下，只能牺牲原文的某些文化特色，根据上下文采用归化翻译策略，以保持原文内容的完整性。例如，对于句子"The man is the black sheep of his family."，如果采用异化法将其译成"这个人是家里的黑羊"，便会令读者感到莫名其妙，不知所云，因为大多数中国人并不知道西方文化中喻体"黑羊"是指魔鬼的化身。如果译者采用归化翻译策略将这句话译为"这个人是败家子"，其喻义就一目了然。翻译西方人士难以理解的汉语文化时亦如此。例如，若把"力壮如牛"翻译成"as strong as a cow"，西方人士也会感到难以接受，不如借用英语中现成的表达，将其译为"as strong as a horse"。

由于文化差异，英汉两种语言中有些词的形象意义不同，但其文化内涵及交际意义相同或相似。为了不使译文比原文逊色，在翻译时可运用替换原喻体的方法，采用归化翻译策略。例如："The spirit is willing, but the flesh is weak."(心有余而力不足)，如果采用异化策略译成"精神上愿意，肉体上太弱"，不仅形式上有失精练，意思也不明确，因此应采用归化翻译策略，使得表达非常精练、到位；a lion in the way如果采用异化策略译为"拦路狮"，中国读者将会不知所云，而如果运用归化策略，用"虎"替换原喻体"狮子"，将其译为"拦路虎"，其喻义会一目了然。

2 直译与意译翻译方法

方法是为达到某种目的而采取的途径、步骤、手段等，其英文表述为"a particular way of doing something"，因此，翻译方法是指翻译活动中，为达到特定的目的所采取的特定途径、步骤、手段。翻译方法体现的是翻译中的一种概括性的处理方式，而非具体的、局限的处理办法。采用什么翻译方法不是任意决定的，而是基于事先确定的翻译原则或标准。直译和意译一直是翻译史上比较有代表性的、翻译活动中经常使用的两种翻译方法，也是译界极具争议的问题。在对其进一步探讨之前，应先对两者进行界定。

1) 直译与意译的界定

古今中外很多学者对直译和意译进行了界定，林林总总，莫衷一是。茅盾(1934)指出：直译并非一定是"字对字"，一个不多，一个也不少……"直译"的意义就是不要歪曲了原作的面目，要能表达原作的精神。朱光潜(1946)在《谈翻译》一文中写道："所谓'直译'是指依原文的字面翻译，有一字一句就译一字一句，而且字句的次第也不更动。'直译'偏重对于原文的忠实。"1982年，周煦良在《翻译三论》一文中写道，直译可以分为三类：第一类是译音而不译意，如democracy译为"德谟克拉西"，而不译为"民主"；第二类是照字面译，如crocodile tears译作"鳄鱼的眼泪"，而不译作"虚伪的眼泪"；第三类是不按照中国语言习惯和词序而按照原文的结构或词序的翻译，如"'你来了，'她说"。周建人(1959)为《外语教学与翻译》写了一篇文章，题目是《关于'直译'》。他在文中写道："直译既不是'字典译法'，也不是死译、硬译，它是要求真正的意译，要求不失原文的语气与文情，确切地翻译过来的译法。换一句话说，当时所谓直译是指真正的意译。"

朱光潜(1946)在《谈翻译》一文中写道：所谓"意译"是指把原文的意思用中文表达出来，不必完全依原文的字面和次第。"意译"偏重译文语气的顺畅。范仲英(1994)是这样定义意译的：意译从意义出发，只要求将原文大意表达出来，不注意细节，译文自然流畅即可。范仲英的定义侧重点在于译文表达的"自然流畅"。但是译文的"自然流畅"并不意味着译者可以对原文内容"随意删改，或添枝加叶。译者必须深入钻研原文，达到融会贯通，方能抓住要点，起到画龙点睛的作用"。孙致礼(2003)认为意译法不拘泥于原文的表现形式，而应以传达原文的深层意思为主旨。这里的重点在于传达原文的精神主旨，为此原文的表现形式是可以牺牲的。

国外也有很多学者对意译进行过界定。英国剑桥大学乔治·斯坦纳教授在1975年发表的《通天塔——文学翻译理论研究》(*After Babel: Aspects of Language and Translation*)一书中写道："翻译的正确道路，既不应是直译，也不应是模仿，而应是意译(paraphrase)。"所谓意译，就是"译者有一定限度的自由，他要时刻看到作者，这样就不至于迷失方向，但他主要是紧跟作者的意思而不死抠字眼，他可以对作者的意思加以引申，但不能改变"。英国翻译理论家卡特福德(1965)认为，意译的"等值关系可以在上下层次间变动，但趋向于较高的层次，有时是在比句子更大的单位间进行"。按等值关系(equivalence)发生的层次，可将翻译划分为逐字译、直译和意译三种，其中逐字译是建立在单词层次上的等值关系，意译则不受限制(unbounded)，而直译介于两者之间。翻译理论家巴尔胡达罗夫(1975)将意译界定为"超出必要层次，使内容不变并遵守译入语规范"的翻译。这里巴尔胡达罗夫也使用了层次这一概念，在这一点上他和卡特福德类似，但在语言层次的具体划分上巴尔胡达罗夫比卡特福德更为深入。不过，巴尔胡达罗夫还强调意译不能改变原文的内容，同时需要遵守译入语的规范，也就是说，意译不是不受任何限制的发挥。2004年，沙特尔沃斯(Shuttleworth)和考伊(Cowie)指出，意译指"侧重于使目标文本读起来自然流畅，而不是完整保留原语文本措辞的翻译类型"。这两位学者认为意译和意对意翻译(sense for sense translation)的含义是完全相同的，目的都是译出符合译入语文化的语言和文本规范的译文，使译文读起来没有"外国味"，从而满足译入语读者的需要。

综上所述，所谓的直译就是译文与原文须保持"形似"，即按照原文的形式将原文内容在目标语中表达出来。意译就是译文与原文保持"神似"，传达原文的意义和精神，即不拘于原文在词序、语序、语法结构等方面的形式，不照搬原文句型或修辞格。

2) 直译与意译之争

在中外译论史上，直译与意译一直是长期争论的话题。中外翻译史对翻译理论的研究无不源于对直译与意译的讨论。两种翻译方法的目的都是忠实地传达原作的思想内容，再现原作的艺术效果。由于理解不同，认识不同，译界的学者们对两种翻译方法各持己见。有对两种翻译方法都持肯定态度的，也有肯定其中一种方法，否定另一方法的，还有对两种方法都持否定态度的。

"直译与意译之争，在我国自有翻译之时起就已存在"(罗新璋，1984：4)。我国的佛经翻译始于直译。佛经译家支谦提出的"因循本旨，不加文饰"的主张，可视为我国早期的直译说。鸠摩罗什 (343—413) 追求"善美"，是"文"派的代表。玄奘 (602—664) 认为既要不违佛陀教旨，又要实现大法流布，译人须"谠而不文，辩而不质"。玄奘在"文"与"质"之间寻求折中与调和。佛经翻译"文""质"之争本质上与"直""意"之争无异。玄奘的译文严谨，多用直译，善参意译，被梁启超等后人称为直译与意译结合的最好典范。严复早期的译文偏重意译。同一时期，尤为突出的意译派代表非林纾莫属。林纾本人并不懂外文，翻译全靠合作者口述，根据自己的理解对一些情节加以修改，甚至改写，其译作完全是二次创作，却翻译了共计一千二百万字的一百八十多部欧美小说。林语堂提出取消直译与意译的区分，认为翻译的标准只能有一个，即翻译就是翻译，本来无所谓什么译。直译在英文中是literal translation，只是句栉字比的翻译，其最大的成功是一字不增一字不减地移译原文的全部内容，而忽略了文笔及风格。意译对应的英文单词是paraphrase，不是translation，不能说是翻译。因此直译是"死译"，"死译"的病虽然不亚于曲译，但流弊较少，因为死译最多令人看不懂；意译是"曲译"，曲译却愈看得懂愈糟。因此，他又称直译只是"形似"的翻译，应该还有"意似"与"神似"两种"高标准的翻译"，但他又说翻译只有一个"信"的标准。傅雷的"神似论"及钱钟书的"化境论"是解放后极具代表性的翻译理论。两人都是意译的支持者，但钱钟书的"化境论"比傅雷的"神似论"更进了一步。瞿秋白则主张直译，鲁迅在这方面有过之而无不及。

与国内译界遥相呼应，在西方，直译与意译之争也是翻译界论战的焦点。芒迪(2007)认为直译与意译之分始于公元前1世纪的西塞罗与公元4世纪晚期的圣哲罗姆，由此形成了数世纪以来直至今日所有重要译论的基石。圣哲罗姆 (347—420)将直译与意译视为一种"互补"关系，在翻译实践中有时意译，有时直译。美国翻译理论家尤金·奈达(Eugene Nida)提出的"形式对等"(formal equivalence)与"动态对等"(dynamic equivalence)，美国当代翻译学家朱莉安·霍斯(Juliane House)的显性翻译(overt translation)与隐性翻译(covert translation)，德国学者厄恩斯特·奥古斯特·格特(Ernst August Gutt)的直接翻译(direct translation)与间接翻译(indirect translation)，以色列翻译家吉迪恩·图里(Giden Toury)的适当性(adequacy)与可接受性(acceptability)，英国翻译理论家彼得·纽马克(Peter Newmark)提出的语义翻译(semantic translation)与交际翻译(communicative translation)以及美国翻译理论家劳伦斯·韦努蒂(Lawrence Venuti)提出的异化法(foreignization)和归化法(domestication)在本质上和直译与意译是一致的。

直译并非一定是对原文"字对字"的逐字翻译，而是指翻译时尽量保持原作的语言形式，包括用词、句子结构、比喻手段等，同时要求语言流畅易懂。意译也不意味着译者可以随意对原文内容进行删改，或添枝加叶，而是从原文的意义出发，只要求将原文大意表达出来，不注意细节，译文自然流畅即可。意译不注重原作形式，包括句法结构、用词、比喻以及其他修辞手段。很多人称直译和意译为传统的翻译方法。"直译"和"意译"作为实际翻译中具体用到的方法，是可以并存的。但如果把它们当中的任何一种奉为翻译的原则，用来统率翻译实践，显然会成大问题。采取"意译"，便于译者跳出短语、小句或句子结构的约束而在宏观上更好地把握文义，这尤其适合充满神韵并需要"二度创作"的文学翻译，在这种情况下，译者便拥有了更大的自由和展示才能的空间，也更有可能确保译文"可读性好"。

3) 直译与意译在翻译中的应用

许渊冲(1978)在《翻译中的几对矛盾》一文中也谈到了直译与意译的问题，他说："直译是把忠实于原文内容放在第一位，把忠实于原文形式放在第二位，把通顺的译文形式放在第三位的翻译方法。意译却是把忠实于原文的内容放在第一位，把通顺的译文形式放在第二位，而不拘泥于原文形式的翻译方法。"最后他得出五点结论，这些结论归纳成两点就是：译文能以和原文相同的形式表达和原文相同的内容时，可以直译，不能表达时就意译；原文的表达形式比译文精确、有力时，可以直译，译文的表达形式比原文精确、有力时，可以意译。

直译是很重要的翻译方法，可以传达原文意义，体现原文风格，在翻译中，广为译者采用。下面的例子采用的就是直译的翻译方法：

They say a person needs just three things to be truly happy in this world: someone to love, something to do, and something to hope for.

话说，人生在世满足三点就是真正幸福：有所爱，有所为，有所盼。

但是直译也具有一定的局限性，如果不顾及两种语言的差异，一味地直译，就会出现硬译、死译和误译现象。每一个民族的语言都有自己的词汇、句法结构和表达方法。当原文的思想内容与译文的表达形式有矛盾，不宜采用直译法处理时，就应采用意译法。当然，意译法不是任意翻译。意译要求译文能正确表达原文的内容，但可以不拘泥于原文的形式。例如：

她怕碰一鼻子灰，话到了嘴边，她又把它吞了下去。

如果我们将"碰一鼻子灰"直译为"have one's nose rubbed in the dust/knock one's nose into ashes"，目标语读者读后肯定会一头雾水。在此情况下，我们可以采用意译法，使译文能清楚、准确地传达原作的意思。所以，该句可以译为： She was afraid of being snubbed, so she swallowed the words that came to her lips.

再如：Do you see any green in my eyes?

这句话若按照原文直译为"你在我眼里看到绿色了吗？"，读者将会不知所云，所以需要采用意译法将原文字里行间的意思表达出来，译文为：你以为我是好欺骗的吗？

再看下面的例子:

She kept her hands clasped on mine a moment longer than was necessary.

她紧握着我的手,比必要的时间长一点。(直译) (×)

她紧握着我的手,没有马上松开。(意译)(√)

The girl is a dead shot.

这位姑娘是死射手。(直译) (×)

这位姑娘是神枪手。(意译)(√)

After the failure of his last novel, his reputation stands on slippery grounds.

他的上部小说失败之后,声誉站在滑动的场地上了。(直译) (×)

他的上部小说失败之后,声誉一落千丈。(意译)(√)

He went west by stage coach and succumbed to the epidemic of gold and silver fever in Nevada.

他乘公共马车到了西部,患了内华达州的金银发烧流行病。(直译) (×)

他乘公共马车到了西部,卷入了内华达州的淘金热和淘银热。(意译)(√)

更多直译与意译的例子如表1-1所示。

表1-1　直译与意译举例

直译与死译	意译与乱译
当原文结构和汉语结构一致时,可完全直译。但如果原文结构与汉语结构不一致,直译就变成了死译。例如: In some automated plants, electronic computers control the entire production line. 在某些自动化工厂,电子计算机控制整个生产线。(直译)(√) Manganese has the same effect on the strength of steel as silicon. (manganese 锰; silicon 硅) 锰有同样的影响在钢的强度上像硅。(直译但不符合汉语表达方式=死译)(×) 锰像硅一样会影响钢的强度。(√) bull's eye 牛眼睛(直译)(×)靶心(√) cold wave 寒冷的波浪(直译)(×)寒潮(√) a black sheep 黑羊(直译)(×)害群之马(√) a white lie 白色的谎言(直译)(×)善意的谎言(√) a baby kisser 亲吻婴儿者(直译)(×)政客(√) Queen's English 女王的英语(直译)(×)标准英语(√) the apple of one's eye 眼睛里的苹果(直译)(×)掌上明珠(√) China policy 中国政策(直译)(×)对华政策(√) 采用直译的中国核心术语翻译: 社会主义核心价值观 the core socialist values 中国特色社会主义 socialism with Chinese characteristics "两个一百年"奋斗目标 Two Centenary Goals 中国梦 the Chinese Dream	意译指在翻译过程中不拘泥于原文的形式,以达意为主。意译强调神似,但不能歪曲原文,否则会变成乱译。例如: She was born with a silver spoon in her mouth. 她出身富贵之家。(√) You are talking through your hat again. 你又在胡说八道了。(√) You should keep your nose out of this. 你别管闲事。(√) Good to begin well, better to end well. 要善始善终。(√) Life sometimes seems too hard and difficult to understand but no matter what obstacles are standing in your way right now you have the power to overcome them. Sometimes your strength lies in stubbornness and determination but even more often it is hidden in your ability to go around obstacles and learn from the previous mistakes. Be strong as a fire that crushes everything in its way and like water that finds a way around any obstacle with gentle determination and a peaceful flow.

直译与死译	意译与乱译
中国式现代化道路 a unique Chinese path to modernization 社会主义现代化强国 a great modern socialist country 中华民族伟大复兴 the great rejuvenation of the Chinese nation 全过程人民民主 whole-process people's democracy 中国式现代化 Chinese modernization 共同富裕 common prosperity 一带一路倡议 the Belt and Road Initiative 中国空间站 China Space Station	有时生活既艰难，又难懂，但无论你面对着怎样的障碍，都要记住你有跨越它们的能力。有时候力量源自你的固执和决绝，但更多的时候，吸取以前的教训，聪明地绕过障碍是你潜在的更大力量。要像火一样勇猛无畏，歼灭一切眼前障碍；更要像水一样具有柔中带刚的力量，安静地绕过挫折，获得胜利。（√）

有些英语习语直译过来后不能为汉语读者所理解，甚至可能造成误解，但又没有相应的汉语表达可以套用，这时可采用意译法。也就是说舍去原有喻体，将其基本含义和表达色彩呈现给译文读者。例如：

Every tub must stand on its own bottom.

人贵自立。

Love lives in cottages as well as in courts.

爱情不分高低贵贱。

Every dog has his day.

凡人皆有得意时！

Insecurity, unemployment, and the "rat race" of the American life place heavy strains on marriage and the family.

社会不稳定、失业率上升、生活竞争激烈，这些都给美国人的婚姻和家庭带来了沉重的压力。

几十年来，在我国翻译界一直存在着关于直译法和意译法的争论。事实上，上面已经谈到，直译和意译都只是在一定条件下所能运用的。两种方法都有其限度，若超出了限度，则过犹不及：直译会变成令人不解或不可读的死译或硬译，而意译则会变成随意发挥或随意伸缩的胡译、乱译，根本不可能产生完美的译品。

不同的语言各有其特点和形式，在词汇、语法、惯用法、表达方式等方面有相同之处，也有相异之处。所以翻译时必须采取不同的手段，或意译或直译，量体裁衣，灵活处理。直译和意译的最终目的都是忠实表达原作的思想内容和文体风格，殊途同归，互不矛盾。译者必须善于把两者结合起来，用两条腿走路，两者缺一不可。例如：

Ruth was upsetting the other children, so I showed her the door.

鲁斯一直在扰乱别的孩子，我就把她撵了出去。

前一部分是直译，后一部分是意译。如把后者so I showed her the door 直译为"我把她带到门口"或"我把门指引给她看"，都不能确切表达原意。再如：

This was the last straw. I was very young: the prospect of working under a woman constituted the ultimate indignity.

我忍无可忍了。我当时很年轻，要我在一个女人手下工作，这对我简直是最大的侮辱。

对第一个句子"This was the last straw."的翻译采用的是意译法，对第二个句子"I was very young"的翻译使用的是直译法，而对冒号后面的部分"the prospect of working under a woman constituted the ultimate indignity."的翻译则又采用了意译法。这是典型的直译与意译并用。

有些长句的翻译需要综合运用直译与意译翻译方法。例如：

But a broader and more generous, certainly more philosophical, view is held by those scientists who claim that the evidence of a war instinct in men is incomplete and misleading, and that man does have within him the power of abolishing war.

该句的主句部分可采用意译的翻译方法，从句部分可采用直译法。由此得出的译文为："一些科学家的观点更开阔，更富有普遍性和哲理性。他们指出，有关人类战争本能的证据尚不完全，而且容易引起误解，事实上，人类自身具有消除战争的能力。"

No child wants to feel like the outsider, although many do. They want recognition, appreciation, engagement, and acceptance—much like adults.

这段话的结构并不复杂。若仅采用直译法，其译文为：没有一个孩子愿意感觉自己像个局外人，尽管很多孩子愿意。他们想要认可、欣赏、参与和接受——就像成年人一样。该译文未能准确传达原文意思，且行文不通顺。若能灵活处理，综合运用直译与意译，根据上下文语境进行适当地增译、转换词性，就能恰到好处地传达原文的神韵，由此得出如下译文：没有哪个孩子想被排除在外，尽管很多孩子都有这种遭遇。他们渴望被认可、被欣赏、被接受，渴望参与进来，这一点和成人很像。

一般来说，如果直译能够晓畅达意，则应坚持直译；如果直译不能完全达意，则要采取一些补偿措施，做一些必要的添加、删除，甚至采用意译方法。在翻译过程中，我们要学会灵活机动，哪个方法效果好，就采用哪个方法，不可将就。要摆脱不合理的条条框框，以最巧妙、最精确的方式传达原文内容，决不可随意脱离或替换原文的意思。

1.3.3　翻译过程

翻译过程是正确理解原文和创造性地用另一种语言再现原文的过程，是译者理解原文并把这种理解恰当地传递给读者的过程。翻译过程由三个相互关联的环节组成：理解、表达和校核。下面将对这三个环节进行讨论。

1 理解

理解可分为广义的理解和狭义的理解。广义的理解指对原文作者、原文产生的时代背景、原文内容，以及读者对该作品的反应的理解。狭义的理解仅指对原文的理解，这种理解主要包括对原文语义系统、背景与专业知识的理解，涉及对原文的语法分析、语义分析、语体分析、语境分析和语用分析等。准确理解是翻译成功的先决条件和重要步骤。

理解原文是整个翻译过程的第一步。这是最关键、也是最容易出问题的一步。理解是表达的前提，是译文这座大厦的地基。地基没打扎实，大厦迟早是要倒塌的。若不能准确而透彻地理解原文，就谈不上精确地表达。许多译文里含糊不清、语焉不详的地方，正是译者没有透彻理解原文的地方。多数的误译都源于译者对原文的理解错误。脱离了正确的理解，译者就无法准确传达原作的意思，翻译活动就从根本上失去了应有的意义。

正确理解原文并不像我们想象的那么容易。在翻译过程中，在最难料到会出理解问题的地方，往往会出问题。例如：

The secretary and accountant of the company was present.

公司的秘书和会计在场。(×)

公司的秘书兼会计在场。(√)

该案例看似很简单，但非常容易出现误译。在英语中，当两个名词共用一个冠词时，表示的是同一人或同一物。上述案例中的两个名词（"secretary"和"accountant"）共用同一冠词"the"，且系动词was是单数，因此秘书和会计应为同一人，由此得出的译文为"公司的秘书兼会计"，而非"公司的秘书和会计"。

英语中的"cousin"一词可以对应汉语中的同辈表亲(或堂亲)，如堂兄(或弟、姊、妹)或表兄(或弟、姊、妹)。当上下文中缺少必要的确证材料时，反而需要某种程度的"模糊"，这实际上是一种"精确"。请看下面的例子：

Three cousins of the French President were also to receive diamonds.

法国总统的三位表亲后来也接受了一些钻石。

就性别而言，three cousins有4种可能性：三男、三女、两男一女、一男两女。从年龄来说，有最大、其次、最小3种排列。从血统来说，有堂、表2种可能性。因此，总计有4×3×2=24种可能性。这还不包括远房堂表兄弟姐妹。傅雷在《贝姨》译序中说"一表三千里"，可见cousin所指之广，所以只好译得模糊一点。

普通读者根据其原有知识水平以及阅读的实际目的，对一个文本的理解可深可浅，可多可少。他可以绕开一些费解之处，而仍能大体明白作者在说什么。译者就没有这种自由。他必须完全弄明白原作的每个细节，弄明白每个字句在上下文里的确切意思。他必须比任何读者都细心周到，绝不能马马虎虎、不求甚解，如此，才能译得毫不含糊。

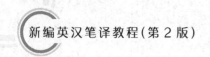

例如：

原文：The market for the (tea) company's products consisted of young people, women between the ages of 18 and 49, and older people who wanted a warm drink that was caffeine-free.

原译：这家公司产品的市场由年轻人、18至49岁之间的妇女和想喝不含咖啡因的热茶的老人组成。

分析：该译文至少存在两处错误。首先，18至49岁的妇女≠年轻人；其次，只有"老人"才喝"热饮"。造成上述误译的原因包括语法方面以及逻辑方面的理解问题。原文中"women between the ages of 18 and 49"实际是"young people"的同位语，对其进一步解释和限定，因此，根据上下文，"18至49岁的女性"=年轻人。这些人既然都买该公司的产品(茶叶)，理应都喜欢喝热茶，因而该句中的定语从句是同时限定或修饰这两类人的。所以，在正确理解原文的基础上得出修改后的译文：该(茶业)公司的销售对象为喜欢喝无咖啡因热茶的18至49岁年轻女性及年长的顾客。

原文：结合3个病历，分析新型冠状病毒感染在河北地区的病机。另外，亦当注重顾护脾胃，注重中西医协作，优势互补，多角度发挥中医药作用。

原译：The pathogenesis of COVID-19 in Hebei were analyzed in combination with three cases in clinical practice. In addition, the spleen and stomach should be protected during the treatment and importance should be attached to the collaboration between traditional Chinese medicine and western medicine to complement each other's advantages and play the role of traditional Chinese medicine from multiple angles.

分析：同一个词语在不同语境下会有不同含义，翻译过程中要关注语境。译前一定要准确理解原文，挖掘字里行间的意思，在此基础上进行翻译，而不是按照字面意思直译。医学文体中经常出现"结合临床(其他结果)""结合病历"和"中西医结合"等表述，但并不是所有"结合"都翻译为"combine (in combination with/combined)"。《朗文当代英语大辞典》(*Longman Dictionary of Contemporary English*)对"combine"的解释为：

(1) If you combine two or more different things, or if they combine, they begin to exist or work together.

(2) to have two or more different features or qualities at the same time.

(3) If two or more different substances combine, or if you combine them, they mix or join together to produce a new single substance.

由此可见，"combine"一词通常为把两者或以上内容放在一起的意思。但"结合临床(其他结果)"其实是指"参考"临床其他结果，而不是真的把现在的检查结果跟其他检查结果放在一起，因此其译文应为"refer to"。

上文中提到的"结合3个病历"也不是把"病机"跟3个病历放在一起。这里的"结合"指的是在这"3个病历"的基础上做分析，译为"based on"更合适。在后文的"中西医协作"中，确实是把"中医"和"西医"放在一起，应使用"combined with"。原译文第二句话将原文按照字面意思进行直译，句子冗长，且为中式英语。做汉英翻译时，要有意识地将汉语的"意合"特征"形合化"，在处理逻辑关系时，应将原文的逻辑关系显性化，增补连接词或将其改为主从结构，使译文符合译入语的语言习惯。由此得到如下修改后的译文：

The pathogenesis of COVID-19 in Hebei was examined based on the three cases in clinical practice. The spleen and stomach should be protected during the treatment. Therefore, traditional Chinese medicine can be combined with western medicine to complement each other, giving play to the role of traditional Chinese medicine from multiple angles.

在理解过程中，还应留心原文表达所暗含的意义，即注意说话者真正的用意(implied meaning)，有时若只从字面上理解，可能会背离原意。如果公司老板对一位上班经常迟到的雇员说"You are late for the last time."，他的意思不是表面上的"你这是最后一次迟到了(下次不能再迟到了)"，而是"你被解雇了(即不可能再迟到了)"。

美国中文学者阿基里斯•方(Achillis Fang)在谈到理解原文之难时指出："所有关于翻译问题的研究都认为这是理所当然的事，即译者已经领会原作的语言和思想。然而我们从经验里懂得：领会并非易事，汉语翻译尤其如此。"

为了做到准确理解，务必勤查词典。初习翻译者往往会高估自己的外语水平。在开展翻译活动时经常望文生义，不求甚解。发现一段话中的词语基本都认识，草草通读一遍，便以为已经理解了原文，想当然地去翻译。殊不知自以为认识的某些词语，其实只是"泛泛之交"，译者只知其常见意义，对于这些词在当前语境下的意思，他们并不清楚。结果误解了原文的含义，影响了译文的质量。用自己所熟知的词义去翻译某个词语时如果发现译文读起来晦涩难懂，不符合逻辑，就应该意识到该词语在此处的确切含义并非自己想当然的含义，这时一定要查词典，以便准确理解原文，从而根据上下文精准翻译。例如：

I would be poor before I got money in this way.

在我以这种方式得到钱之前，我会很穷。(×)

我宁愿过穷日子也不愿用这种方式挣钱。(√)

分析：我们熟知的"before"一词的含义为"在……以前"，但如果用该词义去翻译上述句子，得到的译文"在我以这种方式得到钱之前，我会很穷"读起来不通顺。这时就要去查证一下，看看"before"除了可以译为"在……以前"之外是不是还有其他不常见的含义。查字典后我们发现，该词还有"(宁可……而)不愿"的意思，相当于"rather than"，因此，该句应译为"我宁愿过穷日子也不愿用这种方式挣钱"。

2 表达

表达是理解的深化和体现，是保证译文成功的又一关键步骤。表达时应避免死译、硬译、翻译腔、过分表达和欠表达。在这一过程中，译者要充分考虑目的语读者的阅读习惯，恰到好处地再现原文的思想内容和语体色彩，使译文既忠实于原作又符合译入语的语法和表达习惯。要做到这一点，译者就必须在选词用字、组词成句、组句成篇上下工夫，灵活运用各种翻译方法与技巧。能直译时尽量直译，不能直译时则考虑意译，恰当使用各种翻译技巧。例如：

You have unique gifts and talents that no one else in this world has. Sometimes we feel that we need to be someone else in order to fit in, be a better mother or wife, or portray an image that we believe everyone else will love. No matter how hard you try to be someone else, you will never be good enough. You will do the best and be the happiest only if you stop living by someone else's standards and start using your unique potential to shine like a light in this world.

你拥有这世上独一无二的天赋。有时我们会觉得：为了更好地融入这个世界，我们得扮成别人，比如当个称职的妈妈、妻子，或扮演我们认为人人都会喜欢的形象。然而，无论你多努力，也永远当不了完美的"别人"。只有抛开别人的标准，挖掘自己的潜力，绽放自己的光芒，你才能成为最优秀、最快乐的自己。

分析：原文第一句话是一个复杂句，包含一个定语从句。该译文并未按照原文的句子框架将第一句话直译为"你拥有世界上其他人所没有的独特天赋和才能"，因为"unique"(独一无二的)已经表达了"no one else has"的含义，所以翻译时应采用省略法，省去原文中的"no one else has"，将第一句话译为"你拥有这世上独一无二的天赋"。第二句话包含一个宾语从句和一个限制性定语从句。宾语从句中有三个并列的不定式结构，可采取顺译法。定语从句比较短，且与先行词关系较为密切，可以译为前置定语。第三句和第四句分别包含一个让步状语从句和一个条件状语从句，翻译时应按照汉语的表达习惯，先译状语从句，再译主句。

In times of stress, like living through a global pandemic, it's natural to fall back on soothing habits—gardening, playing video games, or lighting up a cigarette.

面对压力时，例如在全球新冠疫情之下，人们会自然而然地借助一些习惯来舒缓身心，例如种植花草、打电子游戏或抽烟。

分析：此为2022年11月CATTI英语三级笔译实务真题中节选的一句话。原文虽然较长，但是结构并不复杂，为简单句，翻译时采取顺译法即可。

表达时还应注意避免翻译腔、过分表达和欠表达。翻译腔是指译文不符合汉语语法和表达习惯，佶屈聱牙，晦涩难懂。过分表达是指译文画蛇添足，增加了原文没有的东西；而欠表达则是省略或删减原文的内容。翻译时应尽量避免这类错误。

例如：

The study found that non-smoking wives of men who smoke cigarettes face a much greater than normal danger of developing lung cancer. The more cigarettes smoked by the husband, the greater the threat faced by his non-smoking wife.

原译：这项研究发现抽烟男子的不抽烟妻子罹患肺癌的危险比一般人大得多，丈夫烟抽得越多，其不抽烟的妻子面临的威胁越大。

改译：这项研究表明，妻子不抽烟，但丈夫抽烟，妻子得肺癌的危险性比一般人大得多。丈夫抽的烟越多，妻子受到的威胁也就越大。

分析：原译文死抠原文形式，翻译腔严重。将原文宾语从句中的主语"non-smoking wives of men who smoke cigarettes"照搬下来，直译为"抽烟男子的不抽烟妻子"，不符合汉语表达习惯。翻译过程中应该根据原文的含义，并考虑到目标语读者的阅读习惯，将名词短语"non-smoking wives"和定语从句"who smoke cigarettes"分译为两个句子，同时根据上下文省略第二句中重复的成分"non-smoking"。

3 校核

校核是对理解和表达质量的全面检查，可以纠正译文中的错误，绝非多余之举。优秀的译者总是十分重视校核的作用，且总是利用这一良机来克服自己可能犯下的错误，初学翻译的人更应该如此。

1) 校核的目的

(1) 检查译文是否存在失误、遗漏或不妥；

(2) 检查译文是否自然、精确、简练；

(3) 检查理解和表达是否需要进一步深化；

(4) 对译文语言做进一步推敲、落实。

2) 校核注意事项

(1) 校核译文在人名、地名、日期、方位、数字等方面有无错漏；

(2) 校对译文的段、句或重要的词有无错漏；

(3) 修改译文中译错的和不妥的句子、词组和词；

(4) 力求译文中没有冷僻的词汇或陈腔滥调，力求译文段落、标点符号正确无误。

校核通常至少进行两遍。第一遍着重校核内容，对照原文校对，检查有无疏漏、误译的地方。第二遍着重润饰文字，脱离原文审校，检查有无生硬、拗口的地方。如果时间允许，应把已校核两遍的译文对照原文通读一遍，进行最后一次检查、修改，务必使所有的问题都得到解决，译文才能定稿。

综合练习

一、请翻译以下段落，注意灵活使用本章介绍的翻译策略和方法。

A decade ago, when asked about popular pastimes, many people would say going to KTV or amusement parks. However, young people now spend their free time at health clubs, or getting Tuina, or even a foot massage to experience traditional Chinese medicine (TCM) practices, such as acupuncture and moxibustion. A 2023 survey conducted by China Youth Daily, involving 1,000 respondents in China, revealed that 93.3 percent of them had tried various TCM diagnostic and treatment methods. "Many young people in their 20s come to me for neck and back pains, as well as dry eye syndrome, all of which are usually associated with the elderly," said Ma Huifang, a professor at Beijing University of Chinese Medicine, who is also a TCM doctor. "I have witnessed such diseases becoming more common among a younger age group due to unhealthy lifestyles and increased pressure." When faced with the choice between Western medicine and TCM, young people often prefer TCM therapies "due to its efficacy" for these diseases, according to Ma. The impact of TCM on young people's lives is noteworthy, with many not only incorporating TCM practices into their daily lives, but also learning TCM skills to treat themselves and others.

参考译文

要说十年前流行的娱乐活动，很多人会提到 KTV 或游乐园。现在有很多年轻人喜欢在休息时间去"养生馆"，体验推拿、足底按摩、针灸、艾灸等传统中医疗法。《中国青年报》2023 年对 1000 名中国受访者进行的一项调查显示，93.3% 的受访者尝试过各种中医诊断和治疗方法。"很多二十多岁的年轻人来找我治疗颈椎、背部疼痛以及干眼症，这些通常是老年人多发的症状。""由于不健康的生活方式和压力的增加，一些以往在老年人群中多发的疾病已经越来越常见于青年人群。"北京中医药大学教授、中医师马医生说道。马医生还表示，相较于西医，中医疗法往往更受年轻人喜欢，"因为它对这些疾病有功效"。中医对年轻人生活方式的影响值得关注，许多年轻人不仅将中医养生思路融入日常生活，还学习使用中医技能为自己和他人治病。

二、请思考以下问题，并对本章所学内容进行反思和总结。

1. 应该如何定义翻译？

2. 翻译应该遵循哪些标准？

3. 如何看待直译与意译？

4. 如何看待异化与归化？

5. 翻译过程包括哪些环节？

第2章

英汉语言对比与翻译

吕叔湘先生曾经指出："只有比较才能看出各种语文表现法的共同之点和特异之点。拿外语跟汉语进行比较，可以启发我们注意被我们忽略过去的现象。"

汉语和英语的对比研究始于一百多年前的《马氏文通》，是我国第一部汉语语法书，是在比较和模仿拉丁文法的基础上写成的。

世界上每一种语言都有自己的语法，否则，人们将不能进行翻译实践和翻译理论的研究。而通过分析和对比英汉两种语言，译员必将更加深刻地体会到译事之艰辛。

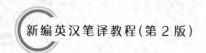

2.1 英汉语言宏观对比与翻译

2.1.1 综合语与分析语

英语和汉语属于不同的语系：

英语属于印欧语系(Indo-European Family, including English, Portuguese, French, German, etc.)。

汉语属于汉藏语系(Sino-Tibetan Family, including Chinese, Siamese, Burmese, etc.)。

汉语是世界上最古老的语言之一，英语是世界上使用最广的语言之一。

英语是一种拼音(alphabetic)文字，单词有重音、次重音等，句子可以有不同的语调(intonation)。

汉语是一种表意(ideographic)文字，音节有四种声调(tone)变化，语调也很丰富。

1 综合语

综合语即综合型语言，这种语言主要通过本身的形态变化来表达语法意义。(A synthetic language is characterized by frequent and systematic use of inflected forms to express grammatical relationships.)

2 分析语

分析语即分析型语言，这种语言中的句法关系并非主要通过词本身的形态来表达，而是通过虚词、词序等手段来表示。(An analytic language is characterized by a relatively frequent use of function words, auxiliary verbs, and changes in word order to express syntactic relations, rather than of inflected form.)

3 形态变化

英语形态变化，即词的形式变化，主要包括构词形态和构形形态。

1) 构词形态

构词形态即起构词作用的词缀变化(affixation)，包括大量的前缀(prefix)和后缀

(suffix)。

英语通过词形变化，改变词性，用这些词灵活组句，可以表达一个几乎相同的意思；汉语则不能。

例如，汉语语句"他前进的速度令人诧异！"在英语中对应的表达多达10种：

(1) He moved astonishingly rapidly.

(2) He moved with astonishing rapidity.

(3) His movements were astonishingly rapid.

(4) His rapid movements astonished us.

(5) His movements astonished us by their rapidity.

(6) The rapidity of his movements was astonishing.

(7) The rapidity with which he moved astonished us.

(8) He astonished us by moving rapidly.

(9) He astonished us by his rapid movements.

(10) He astonished us by the rapidity of his movements.

2) 构形形态

构形形态即表达语法意义的词形变化。

英语的动词、助动词和情态动词常常结合起来，运用其形态变化，表示动词的时态、语态和语气。

现代英语的形态变化主要包括动词的变化(conjugation)和名词、代词、形容词及副词的变化，以及上述的词缀变化。

这些变化有：性(gender)、数(number)、格(case)、时(tense)、体(aspect)、语态(voice)、语气(mood)、比较级(degree of comparison)、人称(person)和词性(parts of speech)等。

有了这些变化，一个词可以表达几种语法意义。例如：

I *gave* him a book. 我给他一本书。

He has *given* me two books. 他已给我两本书。

His father often *gives* him books. 他爸爸常常给他一些书。

❹ 汉语词性与词序

在汉语中，如果单独来看，很难判断"学习""困难""危险"这些词是名词、动词，还是形容词。但对于下列短语，我们不难看出其词性：

"政治学习"(the study of politics)；　　"学习政治" (to study politics)；

"克服困难"(to overcome difficulties)；　"困难问题" (a difficult problem)；

"脱离危险"(to get out of danger)；　　　"非常危险" (exceedingly dangerous)。

可见汉语词性往往要通过它在句子中的词序或位置来判别。可以说，词序在汉语里是重要的语法手段。

5 汉语词序与意义

汉语的词序会影响句子的意义，试比较表2-1中的几组句子。

表2-1　句子比较

一吨煤用不了一个月	一个月用不了一吨煤
他昨天坐车到郊外	他昨天到郊外坐车
一会儿再说	再说一会儿

6 汉语词尾变化

汉语也有一些词尾变化。如词尾"X子"可以指人(孩子、瞎子、胖子)；也可以指物(箱子、刷子、椅子)；还可以指时间(日子等)。类似的还有"X儿""X员""X们""X者""X家""X了""X着""X过"等。但汉语词形变化比较少，所以说汉语是分析型语言。

汉语还被认为是粘着型(agglutinative)语言，词的组合依靠词素的粘着。如光(+明)→光明(+正大)→光明正大；打(+击)→打击(+犯罪+分子)→打击犯罪分子。

7 英语趋向分析型

现代英语中，名词已失去了若干"性"的形态变化；形容词也失掉了与所修饰的名词之间的性、格、时等方面的一致形式，因此，形容词与名词的搭配就不要求性、数、格方面一致了，例如，goldfish(金鱼)、history teacher(历史教师)；同时句子的词序逐渐固定下来，与汉语的句子词序基本相似：主+谓+宾，如"We drink water."(我们喝水)。

其分析型特征也体现在词序和助词(auxiliary)的组句功能上。如："He works well."是正确句子，不能颠倒词序，将其变为"Works he well."，但可以改变词序，将其变为"Well he works."以突出"well"。

又如："Does he work hard?"一定得将does置于句首，使其成为一般疑问句，若改变词序，使其变为"He does work hard."则改变了该句的功能，该句变为陈述句，强调"work hard"。

所以我们说现代英语是正在不断由综合型语言向分析型语言发展的语言。

综合练习

一、请翻译以下词组与句子，注意英语综合型语言与汉语分析型语言之间的差异。

1. two cultures taken as a whole

2. two cultures taken as wholes

3. The food was exhausted only in a few days.

4. In another twist, although this was the direction Chinese mainland was taking in the 20th century, traditional characters are now far more "in vogue" than they have been over the last few decades, a trend which is likely linked to cultural and political developments.

5. Few follow the advice of Isabella Beeton, the guru of British cooks in the 19th century, who decreed in an early edition of her book that "a good meal, if enjoyed and digested, gives the support necessary for the morning's work."

参考译文

1. 将两种文化视为一体

2. 将两种文化各自视为一个整体

3. 食物几天就吃完了。

4. 还有一个转向，就是尽管汉字简化曾经是20世纪中国大陆的趋势，但或许是受到政治和文化发展的影响，繁体字现在比过去几十年更流行了。

5. 19世纪英国烹饪大师伊莎贝拉·比顿曾在其著作的一个早期版本里说过："享用一顿美餐，能使整个上午精力充沛地工作。"这番"高见"，现在很少有人领教了。

二、请翻译以下段落，注意英语综合型语言与汉语分析型语言之间的差异。

China's domestically developed single-aisle passenger jet C919 netted 40 new orders from Tibet Airlines at the opening day of the Singapore Airshow, while its debut at an overseas air show signals the model's official entry into the global civil aircraft market, said an industry expert. Tibet Airlines signed a deal with Commercial Aircraft Corp. of China for 40 C919 aircraft in the plateau variant. The variant meets transportation requirements in high-altitude areas by shortening the fuselage and featuring high-altitude modifications. So far, the C919, comparable with the narrow-body Airbus A320 and the Boeing B737 series, has netted more than 1,100 orders from home and abroad. Two C919 and three ARJ21 regional aircraft made their debut at the Singapore Airshow. As the global air travel market continues to recover from the COVID-19 pandemic, the C919 is expected to meet growing travel demand and break the market duopoly of Boeing and Airbus.

参考译文

国产单通道客机C919在新加坡航展开幕当天收获了西藏航空的40个新订单，业内专家表示，C919国际航展首秀标志着该机型正式进入全球民用飞机市场。西藏航空与中国商飞签署协议，订购40架C919高原型飞机。该机型通过缩短机身和实施高原改装来满足高原地区的运输要求。迄今为止，与窄体飞机空客A320和波音B737系列相媲美的C919已获得一千一百多个国内外订单。此前，两架C919和三架ARJ21支线飞机在新加坡航展上首次亮相。随着全球航空旅行市场继续从新冠疫情中复苏，C919 有望满足日益增长的旅行需求，并打破波音和空客的市场双头垄断。

小结

本节从语言形态学的角度讨论汉语和英语的不同，主要关注汉语与英语在表达语法意义时的不同倾向：无论是名词的数，还是动词的时态、语态，汉语均需要用词汇的手段来表达，而英语只依赖词汇自身的形态变化。

汉译英即用目的语的形态变化来表示分析型汉语的语法意义。在这一过程中应尤其注意如何选择动词的适当形态来表达汉语中某些词汇包含的意义。

2.1.2　形合与意合

英语句法结构重形合(hypotaxis)，句中各成分常用适当的连接词结合在一起，以表示其结构关系。

汉语句法结构重意合(parataxis)，句中各成分多依靠语义的贯通和语境的映衬结合在一起，少用或不用连接词。

汉语与英语的对比如表2-2所示。

表2-2　汉语与英语对比

汉语	英语
汉语是表意文字，属分析型语言。因为汉字起源于象形文字，文字的图形表示某种意义，汉语是以意念逻辑排列为主的语言，所以汉语的句法结构重意合。汉语重意合体现在句子各成分的相互结合多依靠语义的贯通、语境的映衬和词序的排列，少用或不用连接词语，逻辑关系靠语序体现	英语是拼音文字，属综合型语言，二十六个字母是基本的文字表达符号，句子的表达靠符号按一定的语法逻辑关系排列、组合，所以说英语是一种重形式逻辑的语言，英语的句法结构重形合。英语重形合主要体现在句中各成分常用适当的连接词语体现其逻辑关系，句子显得严密紧凑
意合法(parataxis)：一个复句所包含的分句(并列分句或主从分句)或短语等顺次排列，分句与分句之间，或短语与短语之间，在意思上有联系，但不用关联词 意合(形散)强调内容和表意的完整性，常靠语意的逻辑将句子串起来，连词、介词的使用都少于英语。注重以神统形	形合法(hypotaxis)：在分句与分句之间或短语与短语之间，用关联词把关系明确表达出来。形合长句多，强调结构的完整性和形态的严谨性，结构严密紧凑，主次分明，依靠代词、介词、连词建立骨架并将句子串起来

试比较以下英汉句子。

(1) *Even if* I were to be beaten to death, I will not tell.

打死我也不说。(译成汉语后省略了连接词*Even if*)

(2) Modesty helps one go forward, *whereas* conceit makes one lag behind.

谦虚使人进步，骄傲使人落后。(译成汉语后省略了连词*whereas*)

(3) We will not attack *unless* we are attacked.

人不犯我，我不犯人。(译成汉语后省略了连词*unless*)

(4) 拿近点，我好看得清楚。

Bring it nearer *so that* I may see it better. (译成英语后增补了连接词*so that*)

(5) 发展体育文化，增强人民体质。

Promote physical culture *and* build up the people's health. (译成英语后增补了连接词*and*)

英语中也存在一些意合句子，但主要是古英语或中古英语遗留下来的谚语成语，例如：

Man proposes, God disposes.

No pains, no gains.

Easy come, easy go.

Out of sight, out of mind.

First come, first served.

Like father, like son.

Nothing venture, nothing gain.

英译汉时，往往要先分析句子的结构、形式，才能确定句子的功能、意义；汉译英时，往往要先分析句子的功能、意义，才能确定句子的结构、形式。

综合练习

一、请翻译以下几个句子，注意英语形合与汉语意合之间的差异。

1. Change is part of life and the making of character. When things happen that you do not like, you have two choices: You get bitter or better.

2. Winners do not dedicate their lives to a concept of what they imagine they should be; rather, they are themselves and as such do not use their energy putting on a performance, maintaining pretence, and manipulating others.

3. A home without love is no more a home than a body without a soul is a man.

4. 不到长城非好汉。

5. 造纸术、指南针、火药、活字印刷术被称作"中国四大发明"。

6. 中国是一个有五千年文明历史的国家，因此，有必要从历史和文化的视角来了解和认识中国。

7. 我常见许多青年的朋友，聪明用功，成绩优异，而语文程度不足以达意，甚至写一封信亦难得通顺，问其故则曰其兴趣不在语文方面。

参考译文

1. 变化是生活的一部分，可以塑造人的性格。当不喜欢的事情发生时，你有两种选择：要么痛苦不堪，要么痛快达观。

2. 胜利者不会将毕生精力浪费在想象自己应该成为什么样的人上；相反，他们本色行事——不把精力用在矫揉造作、虚伪迎合、操纵他人之类的事上。

3. 没有爱的家不能称其为家，就像没有灵魂的人不能称其为人一样。

4. He who has never reached the Great Wall is not a true man.

5. The paper-making, the compass, gun powder, and the moveable type printing are called the four great inventions of China.

6. China is a country with 5,000 years of civilization. Therefore, it is necessary to approach China from a historical and cultural perspective.

7. I have come across a great many young friends who are bright and diligent and have done exceedingly well in their studies, but are rather weak in Chinese. They can not even write a letter in correct Chinese. When asked why, they said they were not interested in the Chinese language.

二、翻译以下语篇，注意英语形合与汉语意合之间的差异。

Bruce Lee

Bruce Lee was born, according to the Chinese zodiac, during the Hour of the Loong in the Year of the Loong. His birth took place during an American tour of Hong Kong SAR's Cantonese Opera Company, in which his father was a comic actor. Known in the family as Little Loong, Lee was actually sickly and weak; he took up martial arts as a means of self-protection around his tough neighborhoods and soon became agile and versatile. A year after being named the Hong Kong Cha-Cha Champion at eighteen, he returned to the United States, where he studied philosophy and medicine.

On the side, Lee mastered every physical technique of fighting, becoming almost supernaturally good. Eventually he was most often either working out, thinking about it, or teaching others. On the street he practiced kicks on trees and pieces of litter. At the dinner table he chopped at the empty chair next to him; while watching TV he did very slow sit-ups, and even in his sleep he would kick and punch. At parties he did one-finger push-ups and would gladly remove his shirt to show off his "muscles on top of muscles". He believed that concentration was 50 percent of a workout, and "Meditation and Mental Training" always topped his daily to-do list.

参考译文

李小龙

按照中国的十二生肖，李小龙出生于龙年龙时。李小龙的父亲是香港粤剧团的一名丑角，而李小龙就是在父亲随团到美国巡演的时候出生的。虽然家里人都叫他小龙，但实际上他体弱多病。为了对付周围那些凶悍的邻居，他选择习武，以此作为自我防卫的一种方式。他很快就变得身手敏捷、武艺非凡。他18岁时还拿过香港恰恰舞冠军。一年后，他回到美国攻读哲学和医学。

此外，李小龙还精通各种格斗技巧，几近炉火纯青的地步。他最终形成了这样一种生活方式：不是自己构思、设计武术技巧，就是教别人习武。在大街上他冲着树木或废弃物练踢腿；在午餐桌上他会对着邻座的空椅砍砍劈劈；看电视时他缓慢地做仰卧起坐；甚至在睡觉的时候也要伸伸拳、踢踢腿。在舞会上他会用一个指头撑地做俯卧撑，并且很乐意脱去衬衣，展现他"无与伦比的肌肉"。他深信在体育锻炼中全神贯注是成功的一半，而"冥想与精神训练"总是列在他日程安排的首位。

小结

汉语重意合，连接成分"尽在不言中"，句群的组合讲求流洒铺排，疏放迭进。英语重形合，具有实际意义的形合连接成分一般不能省略，句群组合讲求环环相扣，严密紧凑。因此汉译英时应先从"形散神聚"的源语析出条理，然后用"以形驭意"的目的语使诸般条理各就各位。

2.1.3 主语与主题

中国传统哲学主张"天人合一""万物与我为一"，反映在语言上就是施事主体可以蕴含在行为事件的主观表现中。正如王力所说："就句子结构而论，西洋语言是法治的，中国语言是人治的。法治的不管主语用得着用不着，总要呆板地求句子形式的一律，人治的用得着就用，用不着就不用，只要能使人听懂说话人的意思，就算了。"因此在句子构造中，汉语并不把主语看成必要的成分。正因为汉语缺乏主语或主语不明显，语言学家从语言类型学的角度出发，认为汉语是主题显著(topic-prominent)的语言，而英语是主语显著(subject-prominent)的语言。例如：

这本书我花了很多心血。

I worked very hard on this book.

群众投票给干部发奖，这是我有生以来经历的第一次。

This is the first time in my life that I've experienced the masses voting on rewards for cadres.

看电视、唱歌、跳舞这类活动他都不感兴趣。

He isn't interested in things like watching TV, listening to songs, or dancing.

综合练习

一、请翻译以下句子，注意主语的灵活处理。

1. 他的话，我可不信。

2. 会上讲了什么，我一点没记住。

3. 张先生我认识。

4. 唱英文歌，他是最棒的。

5. 他会干这种事，我不相信。

6. 桌子上他放了一本书。

7. 昨天的事，多亏你帮忙。

8. 他的学识我羡慕，他的为人我鄙视。

参考译文

1. I would not believe what he said.

2. I did not remember a single point discussed at the meeting.

3. I know Mr. Zhang.

4. He is the best singer of English songs.

5. I don't believe (that) he should have done such things.

6. He put a book on the desk.

7. I owe you a lot for your help yesterday.

8. I admire his learning, but I despise his character.

二、翻译以下语篇，注意英语主语与汉语主语之间的差异。

Youth

Youth is not a time of life; it is a state of mind; it is not a matter of rosy cheeks, red lips, and supple knees; it is a matter of the will, a quality of the imagination, a vigor of the emotions; it is the freshness of the deep springs of life. Youth means a temperamental predominance of courage over timidity, of the appetite for adventure over the love of ease. This often exists in a man of 60 more than a boy of 20. Nobody grows old merely by a number of years. We grow old by deserting our ideals. Years may wrinkle the skin, but to give up enthusiasm wrinkles the soul. Worry, fear, self-distrust bows the heart and turns the spirit back to dust. Whether 60 or 16, there is in every human being's heart the lure of wonders, the unfailing childlike appetite for what's next and the joy of the game of living. In the center of your heart and my heart, there is a wireless station: so long as it receives messages of beauty, hope, cheer, courage, and power from men and from the infinite, so long are you young. When the aerials are down, and your spirit is covered with snows of cynicism and the ice of pessimism, then you've grown old, even at 20; but as long as your aerials are up, to catch waves of optimism, there's hope you may die young at 80.

—by Samuel Ullman

参考译文

青春

青春不是年华，而是心境；青春不是桃面、丹唇、柔膝，而是深沉的意志，恢宏的想象，炙热的恋情；青春是生命的深泉在涌流。青春气贯长虹，勇锐盖过怯弱，进取压倒苟安。如此锐气，二十后生而有之，六旬男子则更多见。年岁有加，并非垂老，理想丢弃，方堕暮年。

岁月悠悠，衰微只及肌肤；热忱抛却，颓废必致灵魂。忧烦，惶恐，丧失自信，定使心灵扭曲，意气如灰。无论年届花甲，抑或二八芳龄，心中皆有生命之欢乐，奇迹之诱惑，孩童般天真久盛不衰。人人心中皆有一台天线，只要你从天上人间接受美好、希望、欢乐、勇气和力量的信号，你就青春永驻，风华常存。一旦天线下降，锐气便被冰雪覆盖，玩世不恭、自暴自弃油然而生，即使年方二十，实已垂垂老矣；然则只要树起天线，捕捉乐观信号，你就有望在八十高龄告别尘寰时仍觉年轻。

——王佐良(译)

小结

英语的主谓：支配与被支配，具有明确的形式结构特征。汉语的"话题+说明"：陈述与被陈述、说明与被说明，语义上结合的汉语是主题显著(topic-prominent)的语言，建构在意念主轴(thought-pivot)上。英语是主语显著(subject-prominent)的语言。英语句子建构在主谓主轴(subject-predicate-pivot)上，主语和谓语之间存在一种形式上的一致关系。

2.1.4　表态与叙事

如果一个句子里既有叙事的部分，又有表态的部分，汉语表达往往叙事在前，表态在后。英语则恰恰相反：表态在前，叙事在后。例如：

We believe that it is right and necessary that people with different political and social systems should live side by side—not just in a passive way but as active friends.

我们认为生活在不同政治和社会制度下的各国人民应该和谐共处——不只是共处，而且要主动交往，建立友好关系，这是正确且必要的。

The visit gives me the opportunity which I have long sought, to see for myself the achievements of the Chinese people.

这次访问使我有机会亲眼看一看中国人民取得的成就，这是我向往已久的。

My parents were relieved that I was unhurt, but they were angry that I had done such a risky thing.

我没有受伤，父母感到宽慰；但我做了这么危险的事，他们又很生气。

2.1.5　树状与竹状

西文句中名物字，多随举随释，如中文之旁支，后乃遥接前文，足意成句。

——严复

英语句子"多随举随释"，枝杈蔓生，呈树状结构，分叉处由介词、关系代词连接。而汉语按时间顺序或逻辑顺序逐层展开，节节延伸，犹如竹子。

英语的词组与词组、句子与句子之间的结构关系和逻辑联系必须交代得十分清楚。英语的关系词(包括介词、关系代词、关系副词、连接词等)十分丰富，英语正是靠这些关系词的过渡和连接来从形态上维系句内和句间的各种关系的。因此英语句子结构呈树状，往往有一主干(复合句中的主句或简单句中的某主要成分)，主干上枝蔓横生：句子成分随时可加以修饰，而修饰语中的某成分又可被别的成分修饰。由此往往形成长句。

英语句子以主语和谓语动词为主干，借助关系词进行空间搭架，把各个子句有机地结合起来，构成葡萄串似的句子，主干可能很短，却硕果累累。

汉语句子一般按思维的先后顺序或事情发生的逻辑顺序，将内容在说明部分逐项交代出来，犹如竹竿，一节连一节，又如行云流水。

简而言之，英语：树状，重词形与句法。汉语：竹状，重直觉，强调意识流。例如：

In Africa I met a boy, who was crying as if his heart would break and said, when I spoke to him, that he was hungry because he had had no food for two days.

在非洲，我遇到了一个男孩，他哭得伤心极了，我问他时，他说他饿了，两天没有吃饭了。

It is a curious fact, of which I can think of no satisfactory explanation, that enthusiasm for country life and love of natural scenery are strongest and most widely diffused precisely in those European countries/regions which have the worst climate and where the search for the picturesque involves the greatest discomfort.

这些欧洲国家/地区，天气最为恶劣，那里的人们要费上一番辛苦才能寻到优美的景致。奇怪，他们恰好最热衷于乡村生活，也最喜爱天然风景，这种情形极为普遍。这是实情，可我怎么也找不出令人满意的解释来。

综合练习

一、请翻译以下句子，特别注意句子的主干和连接部分的翻译。

1. The moon is so far from the earth that even if huge trees were growing on the mountains and elephants were walking about, we could not see them through the most powerful telescopes which have been invented.

2. Upon his death in 1826, Jefferson was buried under a stone which described him as he had wished to be remembered as the author of the Declaration on Independence and the Virginia Statute for Religious Freedom and the father of the University of Virginia.

3. What parents can learn from these studies is to listen calmly without getting angry right away when their child confesses.

4. When someone feels stressed from his or her teachers or parents, your smile is like the sun breaking through the clouds; your smile can help him or her realize that all is hopeful—that there is still joy in the world.

参考译文

1. 月球离地球非常遥远，即使那边山上长着大树，有大象在跑来跑去，我们也无法用已经发明的最高倍率的望远镜看到它们。

2. 1826年杰斐逊逝世。按照他的遗愿，在其墓碑上刻有：美国《独立宣言》的起草人，《弗吉尼亚州宗教自由法令》的执笔人，弗吉尼亚大学之父，安葬于此。

3. 父母可以从这些研究中学到的是，孩子忏悔时，要冷静地倾听，不要立即发脾气。

4. 当有人感受到来自老师或父母的压力时，你的微笑就像冲破云层的太阳，能让他/她意识到一切都充满希望——世上还有欢乐。

二、请翻译以下语篇，注意英汉句子结构的差异。

What's the meaning of "dark horse"? Its someone who wins when no one expects it. Han Xiaopeng took China's first gold on snow. He became an Olympic "dark horse" last Thursday by winning the gold medal in men's freestyle aerial skiing at Turin in Italy. He made two almost perfect jumps for the highest score. Han had never won a world gold medal before, let alone in the Olympics!

"I never thought this would happen," said the 23-year-old. "I feel like I'm in a dream." It's China's second gold medal at the Turin Olympics. But more importantly, Han's gold was the country's first ever in a snow sport. In 2002, China's Yang Yang won the gold for speed skating at the winter Olympics in Salt Lake City, U.S. Just because Han's win was unexpected doesn't mean that he didn't work hard.

Han grew up in Jiangsu Province. Before he started his training on snow, he used to be an acrobat at a circus. In 1995, a coach found his talent. The coach, Yang Er'qi, said Han had the agility and courage to be a ski jumper. When Yang first took the 12-year-old to northern China, the boy couldn't swim, skate, or ski. But he wasn't afraid of the high platform and kept on training.

Han almost left the sport after hurting his knee months before the Salt Lake Games. In that Olympics he only got 24th. "I was hopeless at that time, but my family and the coach stood firmly behind me, helping me through," he recalled.

Han Xiaopeng worked so hard that he won the gold medal in the Olympics at last. Because of his success, more and more people in China are becoming interested in skiing. We are proud of him and we hope he will have another big success in the next winter Olympics.

参考译文

"黑马"是什么意思？"黑马"指的是意想不到的获胜者。上周四，韩晓鹏在意大利都灵举行的自由式滑雪男子空中技巧比赛中以两个几乎完美的跳跃获得了最高分，摘得中国雪上项目首金，成为奥运"黑马"。韩晓鹏此前从未获得过世界级比赛金牌，更不用说奥运会金牌了！

"我从没想过自己能拿金牌，"23岁的韩晓鹏说道，"像做梦一样。"这是中国在都灵奥运会上获得的第二枚金牌，但更重要的是，韩晓鹏的这枚金牌是中国雪上项目首金。2002年，中国选手杨扬在美国盐湖城冬奥会上夺得短道速滑金牌。此次韩晓鹏的夺冠出乎意料，但这并不意味着他未曾努力。

韩晓鹏在江苏省长大，在开始雪上项目训练之前，曾是马戏团的杂技演员。1995年杨尔绮教练发现了韩晓鹏的滑雪天赋。杨教练表示，韩晓鹏具备跳台滑雪运动员的敏捷和勇气。杨尔绮教练第一次把韩晓鹏带到东北时，韩晓鹏才12岁。那时他不会游泳，更不会滑冰或滑雪。滑雪大跳台很高，但他并不害怕，一直坚持训练。

就在盐湖城冬奥会的几个月前，韩晓鹏膝盖受伤了，差点告别滑雪运动。在那届冬奥会上，他只取得了这个项目的第24名。韩晓鹏回忆道："当时我都绝望了，但家人和教练坚定地站在我身后，帮我渡过难关。"

韩晓鹏非常努力，最终夺得了冬奥会金牌。他的成功使越来越多的中国人开始对滑雪产生兴趣。我们为韩晓鹏感到骄傲，希望他在下一届冬奥会上再创佳绩。

2.1.6　静态与动态

英语有一种少用(谓语)动词或用其他手段表示动作意义的自然倾向；而汉语则有一种多用动词的固有习惯。英语每个句子中只能使用一个限定式动词(finite verb)，唯一的例外是并列句的动词谓语；而汉语中却存在着连动式和兼语式，以及紧缩句，连动式如"他到了火车站发现火车已经开走了"，紧缩句如"我们下雨也去"，有的句子几乎全句都是动词，如"打得赢就打，打不赢就走，不怕没办法"。

汉语中为数不多的介词，大都是从古代汉语动词演变而来的，有些还具备动词的一般特点，兼属于介词和动词两类。"汉语中的绝大多数的介词，应该划归动词的范畴，只是入句时，表现了相当于英语介词的作用。"

英语名词一般具有信息稳定性、时间稳定性和认知稳定性。英语句子中名词或名词短语的使用可防止将动作主体牵涉进来，使句子更简洁、紧凑，表达更委婉、含蓄。英语还广泛使用由动词等词类派生出来的名词。

由此可见，英语是"静态"的语言，而汉语则是"动态"的语言。英语的静态修辞实质是名词优势和介词优势，而介词优势又是名词优势的必然结果，因为名词与名词之间要借助介词来连接。

因此，在英译汉时常常要变"静"为"动"，摆脱名词化的框架和大量介词的干扰，突出译文的动态色彩。例如：

An inability to build a financially secure foundation is often the main reason to delay plans for starting a family, inadvertently contributing to a further drop in U.S. fertility rates, now at their lowest since records began a century ago.

无法建立有保障的经济基础往往是推迟组建家庭计划的主要原因，这也无意间导致了美国生育率进一步下降。目前美国生育率处于有记录的一个世纪以来的最低水平。

There is a crying need for a new remedy.

现在迫切需要提出新的补救方法。

The rotation of the earth on its own axis causes the change from day to night.

地球绕轴自转，引起昼夜变化。

Television is the transmission and reception of images of moving objects by radio waves.

电视通过无线电波传输和接受运动物体的图像。

综合练习

一、翻译如下句子，看怎样将原文的"静"变为译文的"动"。

1. His very appearance at any affair proclaims it a triumph.

2. What movie will be on this evening?

3. He walked around the house with a gun.

4. A study of that letter leaves us in no doubt as to the motives behind it.

5. The very first sight of her made him fall in love with her.

6. He is a good eater and a good sleeper.

7. You must be a very bad learner, or else you must be going to a very bad teacher.

8. An acquaintance of world history is helpful to the study of translation.

参考译文

1. 无论什么事，只要他一露面，就算成功了。

2. 今晚上映什么电影？

3. 他拿着枪在屋子里走来走去。

4. 研究一下那封信，就使我们对其背后的动机确信无疑了。

5. 他对她一见钟情。

6. 他能吃能睡。

7. 你一定很不善于学习，要不然就是教你的人很不会教。

8. 了解世界史对学习翻译有帮助。

二、翻译以下段落。

Advice to "sleep on it" could be well founded, scientists say. After a good night's sleep, a problem that seemed insurmountable the night before can often appear more manageable, although the evidence until now has been anecdotal. But researchers at the University of Luebek in Germany have designed an experiment that shows a good night's sleep can improve insight and problem-solving ability. "If you have some newly acquired memories in your brain, sleep acts on those memories, restructures them, so that after sleep the insight into a problem which you could not solve before increases," said Dr. Jan Born, a neuroscientist at the university. To test the theory, they taught volunteers two simple rules to help them convert a string of numbers into a new order. There was also a third, hidden rule, which could help them increase their speed in solving the problem.

参考译文

科学家声称"第二天再说"的建议可能颇有几分道理。一夜安眠之后，原本似乎难以克服的问题往往就显得好办一些了，但到目前为止这种说法尚无确凿的根据。不过，德国吕贝克大学的研究人员设计了一个实验，其结果显示，良好的睡眠有助于提高人们的洞察力和解决问题的能力。该大学的神经科学家扬·波恩博士说："如果你脑中有一些新的记忆，在你睡觉的时候，大脑会对它们进行处理和重构。这样一来，到了第二天，你对前一天不能解决的问题就有了更多的认识。"为了检验这种理论，研究人员教给志愿者们两条简单的规则，让他们据此对一串数字进行重新排序。但这个实验中还有另一条潜藏的规则，它能加快志愿者们解决问题的速度。

小结

汉语动词无形态变化，使用方便，且重动态描写，所以汉语中动词用得多。在英语句子中，动词受形态变化的约束，通常只有一个谓语动词。把含有一个以上动词的汉语句子译成英语时，应将主要动词译成谓语，其他次要动词则用目的语的名词、介词和形容词来传达，使译文更加符合目的语的表达习惯。

2.2　英汉语言微观对比与翻译

2.2.1　英汉词汇对比

吕叔湘先生曾经说过："我相信对于中国学生最有用的帮助是让他们认识英语与汉语的差别……让他们通过比较得到更深刻的领会。"英语、汉语分属不同的语言系统，它们的词类有一定的共性，也存在很多的差异。

1 英语词汇若干特点

1) 词源不同

以表示"临危不惧"的词为例。

brave：源自意大利语

bold：古英语

courageous：古法语

valorous、valiant：源自拉丁语

2) 词义轻重不同

以表示"打破、破坏"的英语词语为例。

break：最通用的词语，意思是经打击或施压而破碎

crack：出现了裂缝，但还没有变成碎片

crush：从外面用力往内或从上往下压而致碎

demolish：破坏或铲平(如土堆、建筑物、城堡等)

destroy：完全摧毁，使之无法复原

shatter：突然使一物体粉碎

smash：由于突如其来的一阵暴力带一声响而彻底粉碎

又如表示"闪光"的词。

shine：照耀，指光的稳定发射

glitter：闪光、闪烁，指光的不稳定发射

glare：耀眼，表示光的强度大

sparkle：闪耀，指发出微细的光

3) 词义范围大小和侧重不同

例如，agriculture、farming、cultivation、agronomy都表示"农业"，但4个词语的侧重点不同。

agriculture：指农业科学、农业技术、整个农业生产过程，所包含的范围最广

farming：指农业的实践

cultivation：指农作物的栽培过程

agronomy：农学，指把科学原理运用到农业耕作的实践

又如表示"国家"的英语单词。

country：表示国家的地理范畴

nation：体现在共同的地域和政府下的全民概念

land：给人以国土或家园之感

state：指国家的政治实体

power：表示国家的实力

4) 形容对象和强调的内容不同

empty：用来修饰 house、room、cup、box、stomach、head、words 等词语，表示空的，一无所有

vacant：可用来修饰position、room、house、seat等词语，表示没有人占用的，空缺的

hollow：可与 tree、voice、sound、cheeks 等词连用，表示空洞的，虚的，不实的，下陷的

blank：可以用来修饰look、mind、page、check等，表示空白的，无表情的，无思想的

所以汉译英时，"说"这个词在不同上下文中可分别译成speak、tell、say、express、mention、persuade 等。例如：

他说英语。

He speaks English.

他说谎。

He's telling a lie.

他说他很忙。

He says he is busy.

我说不好。

I'm not sure.

这可说不得。

It must not be mentioned.

别胡说八道！

Don't talk nonsense!

2 英汉词汇差别

英汉词汇之间有着很大的差别，这种差别首先表现在词义上。英国语言学家杰弗里•利奇(Geoffrey Leech)在其《语义学》(*Semantics*)(1987)一书中把最广义的意义划分为以下7 种不同的类型。

概念意义(外延意义)(denotative meaning)：逻辑的、认知的、或外延的内容联想意义

内涵意义(connotative meaning)：通过语言所指传达的意义

风格意义(stylistic meaning)：所传达的关于语言使用的社会环境的意义

情感意义(affective meaning)：所传达的关于说话人或作者感情、态度方面的意义

联想意义(reflective meaning)：通过联想同一表达式的其他意思所传达的意义

搭配意义(collocative meaning)：通过联想词语的常用搭配而传达的意义

主题意义(thematic meaning)：通过组织信息的方式(顺序、重音等)所传达的意义

1) 英汉词语的意义不对应

(1) 外延意义不对应。例如：

红茶 black tea；红糖 brown sugar；

浓汤 thick soup(而不是strong soup)；

白酒 spirits/liquor (不是white wine白葡萄酒)；

眼红/嫉妒 to be green-eyed (红眼病 pink eye，不是red eye)。

(2) 内涵意义不对应。例如：

只要我们坚持改革开放政策，就一定能把我国建设成为强大的社会主义国家。

[译文] So long as we stick to the reform and opening-up policy, we will be able to turn/transform China into a powerful socialist country.

[分析]初学翻译的人很可能把"坚持改革开放政策"译成"insist on the reform and opening-up policy"，这违背了英语惯用法，因为insist on用于表达某人对某事的坚定立场、坚持、坚决要求或强调某事物，这个短语可以表达对某件事情的执着和坚定，也可以表示对某种观点或态度的坚持不变，表示所坚持要求或主张的具体内容。需要注意的是，insist on后面的名词或动名词应该是具体的、明确的，能够清晰地表达出所坚持要求或主张的内容。此外，该短语语气通常比较强烈，表示某人对所坚持的内容有着坚定的信念和决心。

(3) 联想意义不对应。例如：

有一次，译员用英语通知一位外国专家参加一个会议，其中有一句话是"You had better attend the meeting on time."(您最好及时参加这个会。)英语的语法是毫无问题的。但外国专家听后十分不悦，原来"had better do sth."只能用于上级对下级，老师对学生，长辈对晚辈，以及同等地位或年龄的人之间。

(4) 搭配意义不对应。例如：

当前最重要的任务是发展国民经济，提高人民生活水平。

[译文] Our primary task at present is to develop national economy and improve people's living standards.

[分析]将"提高人民生活水平"译为to improve (better) the lives of the people/to improve (uplift) the quality of the lives of the people/to improve the texture of the lives of the people/to improve (raise) standards of living，都是符合英语惯用法的。如译成to raise the level of the lives of the people，译文则成了中式英语。

(5) 情感意义不对应。例如：

过去我们在对外宣传中，一直把"宣传"译为"propaganda"(贬义的成分居多，使人易将它与吹牛、说谎、怀有政治目的等负面含义联系起来)，而现在多使用"publicity"等中性词；"精神文明"被译为"ritual civilization"，该词组在外国人的心目中含有宗教色彩，现在改为"ethical and cultural progress"以及其他译法。

2) 英汉词语的语义错位

英语的上义词和下义词与汉语的不对称，如图2-1所示。

图2-1　英汉词语的语义错位举例

3) 英汉词语语义的宽窄不同

汉语中有些词含义较英语宽，如：

山 hill、 mountain；借 lend、 borrow；拿 take、 bring、 fetch；叫 cry、shout、call；

笑 smile、laugh；鼠 mouse、rat；羊 sheep、goat

英语中有些词含义比汉语宽，如：

wear 穿、戴；river 江、河；marriage 娶、嫁；net 网、帐子；gun 枪、炮

尤以称呼语为典型：

brother 兄弟、同胞、同业、社友、会友

brother-in-law 姻兄、姻弟、内兄、内弟、姐夫、妹夫、大伯、小叔

uncle 伯父、叔父、舅父、姑父、姨父

sister 姐、妹、姑、姨、嫂

aunt 伯母、大妈、婶娘、叔母、姨母、姑母、舅母、姑妈、阿姨

4) 英汉词语的搭配能力不同

将名词用作定语，反映了当代英语简约的总趋势，但在把这类搭配译成汉语时，要进行必要的调整，常常需要增补汉语动词。请看以下例子。

parent ticket 发给家长的入场券

shoe habit 穿鞋的习惯

wheat farmers 种小麦的农民

street sense 在街上辨方向的能力

life work 为之奋斗了一生的工作

smog fighters 清除烟尘的工作人员

community gossips 在邻里间流传的风言风语

age group 按年龄划分的人群

英语和汉语在词的搭配能力方面有所差异。英语中某些动词的搭配能力很强，以动词 "fall" 为例，它在不同的语境之下就有多种搭配方式，在将其译成中文时需要选择不同的词汇，以使译文符合汉语表达习惯，如：

He must have *fallen* from a great height.

他肯定是从很高的地方**摔**下来的。

September had come and the leaves were starting to *fall*.

已到九月了，树叶开始**凋落**。

Falling interest rates may help to bolster up the economy.

利率**下降**可能有助于激活经济。

The houses *fell* away as we left the city.

随着我们离城市越来越远，房屋也逐渐在视线中**消失**了。

They *fell* in love in spite of the language barrier.

尽管有语言障碍，他们还是**相爱**了。

She *fell* back on her usual excuse of having no time.

她以她惯用的办法**推说**没有时间。

Our plans *fell* through because of lack of money.

我们的计划由于缺钱而**落空**了。

2.2.2　英汉句法对比

汉语和英语都经历过漫长的发展，都处于高度完善的状态，词汇分类非常相似，语句结构在表面上也大致相同，从表面上看，许多英语语言学理论应该适用于汉语语法学的学科建设，例如，汉语语句的解析似乎可以套用英语的句法解析模式。但事实上却并非如此，汉语语法化不应受英语语言学理论过多的影响，因为汉语与英语在构词造句方面具有许多本质上的差异。

1 英汉定语位置对比

汉语中一般将定语置于名词之前，即使连用几个定语或使用很长的词组作定语，也要将定语放在名词前面。英语中单词作定语时，通常置于名词之前(特殊情况下置于名词之后)，短语和从句作定语时总是置于名词之后。所以，英语是孔雀型语言，末端开放(right-extending, heavy-tailed like a peacock)。汉语是狮子型语言，首端开放(left-extending, heavy-headed like a lion)。

汉语重前饰，句子的语序一般以思维顺序展开，而中国人的思维方式通常是先考虑事物的环境和外围因素，再考虑具体事物和中心事件。这一点反映到句式上，就是状语总放在谓语或句子主体的前面，定语无论长短，都要置于中心词之前。这样就使得单句的状语部分长，主谓部分短；主语部分长，谓语部分短；修饰成分长，中心词短，整体上形成头大尾小的狮子头形状。

英语重后饰，定语成分除单词外，多数都要置于中心词之后。英语重视末端重量，凡较长的词语及累赘的成分均要后移至句末。有时必须使用形式主语来避免句子的头重脚轻。由此造成句子结构头小尾大，像一只开屏的孔雀。

例如：

Data from online travel agency Ctrip showed the search volumes for outbound hotels have increased significantly compared with the same period of 2019, with Japan, Thailand, South Korea, and Malaysia becoming hot destinations.

在线旅游平台携程的数据显示，相比于2019年同期，出境游酒店的搜索量大幅上升。

日本、泰国、韩国和马来西亚为出境游热门目的地。

Tuniu, another travel portal, said that destinations and museums with a rich cultural atmosphere or those highlighting cultural elements of the Loong were favored by travelers, marking the beginning of the Year of the Loong.

另一家旅游网站——途牛表示，龙年伊始，具有浓郁文化氛围或突出龙文化元素的旅游目的地和博物馆受到了游客的青睐。

Among them, Harbin Ice-Snow World in the northeastern province of Heilongjiang received 329,000 visits from Feb. 10 to Wednesday—the first five days of the holiday—with the traveler number marking a surge of 115 percent from the previous year.

位于中国东北地区黑龙江省的哈尔滨冰雪大世界从2月10日到2月14日(春节假期前五天)共接待32.9万名游客，游客人数比去年同期激增115%。

某些外来语和固定词组中，形容词作定语，常放在所修饰词的后面，例如：

consul general 总领事

secretary general 秘书长

director-general 总干事

president-elect 当选总统

heir apparent 有确定继承权的人

court martial 军事法庭

things foreign 外国事物

2 英汉状语位置对比

如果出现一系列表示时间、地点和方式的状语，汉语的习惯语序是：时间，地点，方式。英语的习惯语序是：方式，地点，时间。此外，多个时间(地点)状语在英语中是由小到大排列的，而在汉语中则正好相反。

Ba Jin was born into a big family in Sichuan Province in China, 1904.

巴金1904年出生在中国四川省的一个大家庭。

The news briefing was held in Room 301 at about nine o'clock yesterday morning.

新闻发布会是昨天上午九点左右在301会议室召开的。

The conference delegates discussed the President's report animatedly in the meeting room yesterday morning.

会议代表昨天上午在会议室热烈地讨论了总统的报告。

3 英汉某些固定短语词序对比

冷热 hot and cold

左右 right and left

水陆 land and water

强弱 weak and strong

沉浮 ups and downs

新旧 old and new

悲欢 joy and sorrow

贫富 rich and poor

好坏 bad and good

迟早 sooner or later

田径 track and field

视听 audio-visual

新郎、新娘 bride and bridegroom

无论晴雨 rain or shine

男女老少 men and women, young and old

钢铁工业 the iron and steel industry

救死扶伤 heal the wounded, rescue the dying

来来回回 back and forth

东南西北 north, south, east, and west

4 英汉句子重心对比

在复合句中，英语的主句为主要部分，一般放在句首，即重心在前。而汉语则一般按照逻辑和时间顺序，将主要部分放在句尾，形成后重心。例如：

Nothing has happened since we parted.

自我们分别后没发生什么事情。

He has to stay at home because he is ill.

他病了，只得待在家里。

He cannot be operated upon as he is very weak.

他身体很弱，不能动手术。

Tragedies can be written in literature since there is tragedy in life.

既然生活中有悲剧，文学作品就可以写悲剧。

The people of a small country can certainly defeat aggression by a big country, if only they dare to rise in struggle, dare to take up arms and grasp in their own hands the destiny of their own country.

小国人民只要敢于起来斗争，敢于拿起武器并掌握自己国家的命运，就一定能打败大国的侵略者。

5 英汉语态对比

在英文文章中被动语态用得较多，而汉语中被动语态用得少。在汉语中，有不少具有被动含义的概念可以用主动形式来表达。

Individualized tuition and assessment are carried on to help the students.

继续实施个性化收费和评估以帮助学生。

The happy man cannot be harried.

吉人自有天相。

A new instant Nespray has been put into the market in HongKong SAR.

新配方雀巢即溶奶粉在港上市。

6 英语多代词，汉语多名词

英语为了避免表达上的重复，多用代词；而汉语结构相对松散，句子相对较短，一般不使用太多的代词。

He hated failure; he had conquered it all his life, risen above it, and despised it on others.

他憎恶失败；他一生曾战胜失败，超越失败，并且藐视别人的失败。

There will be chat shows hosted by robots, and cars with pollution monitors that will disable them when they offend.

届时，将会出现由机器人主持的访谈节目及装有污染监测器的汽车，一旦这些汽车污染物排放超标，监测器就会使其停止行驶。

7 英语多省略，汉语多补充

英语一方面十分注重句子的结构，另一方面又喜欢使用省略。英语中省略的类型有很多：名词的省略，动词的省略，句法方面的省略，情景方面的省略。英译汉时往往需要补充这些省略了的内容。

Ambition is the mother of destruction as well as of evil.

野心不仅是罪恶的根源，也是毁灭的根源。

Reading exercises one's eyes; speaking one's tongue; while writing, one's mind.

阅读训练人的眼睛，说话训练人的口齿，写作训练人的思维。

8 英语多长句、从句，汉语多短句、分句

在英语句子(并列句除外)中，主句只能有一个谓语动词，动词是句子的轴心与核心，然后借用名词来表达。在主干上附加层层修饰成分，句子成葡萄状，多长句、从

句；而汉语多短句、分句。

In the doorway lay at least twelve umbrellas of all sizes and colors.

门口放着一堆雨伞，少说有十二把，五颜六色，大小不一。

Can you answer a question which I want to ask and which is puzzling me?

我有一个问题弄不懂，想请教你，你能回答吗？

由此得出翻译时应注意以下事项：

注意连词，特别是相关的连词，一方面注意逻辑关系，另一方面注意翻译时的灵活性。

注意代词，尤其是关系代词，明确它的先行词是哪一部分，分析代词在定语从句中所起的作用。

注意省略部分，因为省略是长句中常见的现象。译者要把省略部分适当补充出来。

注意使用切分法把英语长句切分成短句。

注意语态的转换。

综合练习

请翻译以下语篇，注意英语句法与汉语句法之间的差异。

The traditional Chinese lunar calendar divides the year into 24 solar terms. White Dew (Chinese: 白露), the 15th solar term of the year, begins this year on Sept. 8 and ends on Sept. 22. White Dew indicates the real beginning of cool autumn. The temperature declines gradually and vapors in the air often condense into white dew on the grass and trees at night.

Varying by geographical location, autumn comes earlier in the west and northeast of China. Right now Kanas in Xinjiang Uygur Autonomous Region, Jiuzhaigou in Sichuan Province, and the Greater Khingan Mountains in Northeastern China are entering the most beautiful season of the year.

From the first day of White Dew and as the season progresses, there is more and more dew. Although sunshine during the day makes it still hot, after sunset, temperatures decrease rapidly. At night, water vapor in the air turns into small drops of water when it encounters cold temperatures. These white water drops adhere to flowers, grass, and trees. When the morning comes, sunshine makes them look crystal clear, spotless, white, and adorable.

Here are some things you should know about White Dew.

Eating grapes

White Dew season comes right when grapes become widely available for sale. Eating grapes in autumn can help dispel one's internal heat and expel toxins.

Eating Longan

Longan fruit around White Dew is big, sweet, and tastes great. There is a tradition in Fuzhou, East China's Fujian Province, that eating Longan on the first day of White Dew can help nourish the human body. It is said that one Longan is as nutritious as an egg. Although this sounds exaggerated, Longan does reinforce the spleen, nourish the blood, calm the nerves, and improve one's looks.

White Dew Tea

Many regular tea drinkers in Nanjing favor White Dew Tea. Tea during White Dew has gone through the hot summer and is in its best state of growth. White Dew Tea is different from spring tea, which is usually too tender and doesn't last long. It is also different from summer tea, which is dry and has a bitter flavor. White Dew Tea instead tastes sweet with a sweet fragrance.

White Dew Wine

For some people in Nanjing, East China's Jiangsu Province, whose hometowns are in Zhejiang Province or the southern part of Jiangsu Province, it is traditional to make White Dew Wine during this season. The wine is made of cereals, such as polished glutinous rice and Gaoliang (a specific type of sorghum), and tastes a little sweet. In the past, country people in those regions all made the wine and served it to guests when entertaining.

Eating sweet potatoes

Many Chinese believe that the best food during White Dew is sweet potatoes. In the old days, peasants had the custom of eating sweet potatoes on the first day of White Dew. Besides being the No. 1 vegetable against cancer, according to Chinese medicine, sweet potato can nourish the spleen. It can prolong life and reduce the risks of disease.

Ten "white" herbal medicines

People in Wenzhou, East China's Zhejiang Province, have a tradition of gathering 10 herbal medicines on the first day of White Dew. The names of these herbal medicines all contain the Chinese word "Bai" which means white, such as Baimujin (white hibiscus). People believe that stewing these herbal medicines with black-bone-white-feather chicken or duck can nourish the human body and cure arthritis.

Offer sacrifices to Da Yu

White Dew is a time for people in the Taihu Lake area of East China to offer sacrifices to Da Yu, a hero who tamed floods by regulating rivers and watercourses. On the first day of White Dew, also on the eighth day of the first lunar month, Tomb-sweeping Day, and the seventh day of the seventh lunar month, people hold sacrificial rites for Da Yu.

参考译文

传统的中国农历将一年分为24个节气。白露是一年中的第15个节气，今年是9月8日开始，9月22日结束。白露预示着秋凉开始，气温逐渐下降。夜间，空气中的水蒸气凝结成白露附着在草木上。

由于地理位置不同，中国西部地区和东北地区的秋天来得更早。现在新疆的喀纳斯、四川的九寨沟和我国东北地区的大兴安岭正进入一年中最美的季节。

从白露时节的第一天开始，随着季节的推移，露水越来越多。虽然白天的光照使得天气仍然很热，但日落后，温度迅速下降。晚上，空气中的水蒸气遇冷变成小水滴。这些白色的水滴附着在花草树木上，清晨，在阳光的照耀下，显得晶莹剔透，洁白可爱。

关于白露你需要知道的几件事。

吃葡萄

白露时节正是葡萄大量上市的季节。秋天吃葡萄可清热排毒。

吃龙眼

白露时节的龙眼非常大，甜美可口。位于华东地区的福建省福州市有个传统：白露第一天吃龙眼可以滋养身体。据说龙眼和鸡蛋一样有营养。虽然听起来有些夸张，但龙眼确实能健脾、补血、安神、美容。

喝白露茶

许多常喝茶的南京人喜欢喝白露茶。因为经过了酷夏，白露茶正处于生长佳期。白露茶不像春茶那样娇嫩、不经泡，也不像夏茶那样干涩、味苦，而是有一股独特的甘醇味道。

酿白露米酒

老家在苏南和浙江的南京人有白露时节酿白露酒的习俗。白露酒用糯米、高粱(一种特殊的蜀黍)等谷物酿成，略带甜味。过去这些地区的乡下人都酿白露酒并用它来待客。

吃红薯

许多中国人认为红薯是白露时节的最佳食物。过去，农家有白露第一天吃红薯的传统。根据中医的说法，红薯不仅是抗癌头号蔬菜，还可以健脾，延年益寿，降低生病的风险。

采十白草药

生活在华东地区的浙江省温州人有白露第一天"采十白"的传统。这些草药的名字都带"白"字，如白木槿。人们认为用这些草药煨乌骨白毛鸡或鸭，食后可滋补身体，治疗关节炎。

祭祀大禹

白露是生活在华东地区的太湖人民祭祀治水英雄大禹的时节。每年的白露时节，以及正月初八、清明节、七月初七，人们举行仪式祭祀大禹。

第3章

英汉文化对比与翻译

有一则趣谈：一所国际公寓发生火灾，里面住有犹太人、法国人、美国人和中国人。犹太人急急忙忙搬出他的保险箱，法国人先拖出他的情人，美国人先抱出他的妻子，而中国人则先背出他的老母亲。

这一趣谈反映了一个事实：不同的民族有着自己区别于其他民族的文化心理素质、思维方式、价值尺度、道德规范和情感取向。

3.1 英汉文化对比

3.1.1 文化的定义

文化(拉丁语cultura；英语culture；德语Kultur)是指人类活动的模式以及给予这些模式重要性的符号化结构。

英国著名人类学家爱德华·伯内特·泰勒(Edward Burnett Tylor，1832—1917)在《原始文化》(*Primitive Culture*，1871)中这样定义文化："所谓文化或文明乃是包括知识、信仰、艺术、道德、法律、习俗，以及包括作为社会成员的个人而获得的其他任何能力、习惯在内的一种综合体。"

20世纪美国文化学家克鲁伯和克拉克洪(Kroeber & Kluckhohn)在《文化：概念和定义的批判性回顾》一书中写道：文化是包括各种外显或内隐的行为模式，通过符号的运用使人们习得并传授，并构成了人类群体的显著成就。文化的基本核心是历史上经过选择的价值体系。文化既是人类活动的产物，又是限制人类进一步活动的因素。

《现代汉语词典》将文化定义为："人类在社会历史发展过程中所创造的物质财富和精神财富的总和，特别指精神财富，如文学、艺术、教育、科学等。"

《中国大百科全书——社会学》中文化的定义如下："广义的文化是指人类创造的一切物质产品和精神产品的总和。狭义的文化专指语言、文学、艺术及一切意识形态在内的精神产品。"

文化是指人类社会历史实践过程中所创造的物质财富、精神财富和相应的创造才能的总和。文化包括物质文化与精神文化，物质文化是指文化中看得见、摸得着的那部分，因此被称为硬文化。相对来说，精神文化就是软文化，而软文化则是文化的深层结构。美国著名翻译理论家奈达(Nida)将语言文化特性分为五类：

ecological culture 生态文化

material culture 物质文化

social culture 社会文化

religious culture 宗教文化

linguistic culture 语言文化

语言是记录人类历史及表达人类生活和思想的工具，每一种语言都有其深远的历史背景和文化内涵。因此，语言是文化的载体，它反映一个民族的特征，语言的发展常常折射文化的变迁。而翻译是在译语中用切近而又最自然的对等语再现原语的信息，它不仅涉及两种语言，而且涉及两种社会文化。翻译是通过语言机制的转换连接自身文化和异国文化的桥梁，翻译是具有不同语言文化背景的人相互交际、达到相互了解的媒介。

3.1.2 中西方文化差异

语言是文化的外在形式，其实质是文化内涵。世界各民族有着不同的文化体系。中西方国家具有各自独特的历史和文化背景，生产活动方式和文化发展水平不同，反映在思维方式、伦理认知等方面就出现了较大的差异。

1 西方的理性思辨与中方的经验直觉

卡尔·普利布兰姆(Karl Pribram)在《思维方式之矛盾》中曾指出："世界各民族之间的相互理解与和睦的关系之所以受到阻碍，不仅是因为语言的复杂多样，还因为思维模式的差异——人们确定知识来源和进行有条理思维方法上的差异。"西方民族思维方式以逻辑分析为主要特征，而以中国为代表的东方民族思维方式则以直观综合为基本特征。西方重理性、思辨，中方重经验、直觉。希腊哲学是西方哲学的源头，古希腊对自然有着浓厚的兴趣，他们关心世界本源、主客体关系、事物如何发展变化等，其文化弥漫着理性思维的色彩，因此抽象思辨是西方思维的特征。与西方向外思维逻辑演绎不同，中国文化通常情况下是从感性的角度出发，重视在经验前提下构建的直觉。中国古代科学和哲学的各种概念是靠向内思维得到的，是对各种经验现象进行总结而提出的。

思维模式的差异是造成跨文化交际出现困难的首要因素。中西方思维模式的差异导致中西方文化交流方式出现明显的不同，具体表现为，中国人在沟通过程中先铺垫、渲染、修饰，通过较为婉转的方式逐渐靠近中心事件，最重要的事情通常留到最后，以压轴的方式出现，起到画龙点睛的作用。而西方国家在这一方面则与我国完全相反，他们一般在沟通中开门见山，直奔主题，先讲最重要的事情，然后按照事件从重到轻的顺序进行交谈。这种思维模式的不同直接导致双方语言表达方式的差异。这就需要翻译人员在翻译中合理调整相关语句的表达顺序，以便适应目标语读者的思维方式。

2 西方的细节分析与中方的整体综合

西方文化结构以细节分析居优，东方文化结构则以整体综合见长。这种差异在中西方语言表达方式上具体体现为：在时间的表达上，中国按照年、月、日的顺序书写，西方国家则按照日、月、年(欧洲国家以及曾经受过欧洲殖民的国家/地区)或月、日、年(美国)的顺序书写。在地址的表达上,中国按国家、省(自治区、直辖市)、地级市、县(自治县、县级市)、区、街道、小区到门牌号的顺序进行表达,突出的是从整体到个体的析出关系,西方国家的表达顺序则与中国的完全相反,突出的是从个体到整体的合成关系。另外,在中国人的姓名结构中,先是宗姓、辈分,其次才是自己的名字,突出的是氏族整体。西方国家的人名则先是自己的名字,再是父名,最后才是族姓,突出的是个体。可见在中华民族的精神文化和意识结构中,从整体出发的综合观占突出地位,而这种整体综合观在考察事物时,常忽略细节和成分分析,提供的往往是关于对象模糊整体的图景。例如,中医治疗疾病时往往从整体上考虑,根据人身体出现的相应症状来进行辨证论治。西医则重视局部而忽视整体之间可能存在的相互依存、相互影响的关系。因此有了"西医看局部,中医看整体"之说。又如,中国传统建筑讲究中轴对称,突出整体、群体,如故宫、阿房宫等;而西方古典建筑则多注重个体,空间上讲究突兀高耸,如典型的科隆大教堂等"哥特式"建筑。

3 中方的伦理与西方的认知

中西方不同的伦理标准和认知方式使各自民族文化沿着不同的道路向前发展。儒家思想是中国非常重要的传统文化之一,关注人道,而非天道,是人生之理,而非自然之性。而西方人对天文地理的浓厚兴趣,使他们形成了探求自然的奥秘、向自然索取的认知传统。儒学重伦理,其具体体现之一是重宗族和宗族关系。中国属于苏丹式亲属社会关系,以大家族为单位,因此,汉语中亲属称谓特别复杂;而西方的亲属系统属于"爱斯基摩型"的亲属称谓系统,强调的是"核心家庭"(nuclear family),越远的亲戚分得越粗,因此父亲的亲戚和相对应的母亲的亲戚是不作区分的。这种区别为中西文化交流带来了障碍。例如:"张明和李丹是表亲。张明的母亲是李丹的姑母,李丹的母亲是张明的舅母。"英文译文为:"Zhang Ming and Li Dan are cousins. Zhang Ming's mother is Li Dan's aunt who is the sister of Li Dan's father, while Li Dan's mother is Zhang Ming's aunt who is the wife of Zhang Ming's mother's brother." 该译文语义是清楚的,反映的关系也清楚,这种关系在中国人看来是直观易懂的,但西方人需要经过一番思考才能弄清楚。按西方人的习惯,父亲的兄弟和母亲的兄弟都是uncle,父亲的姐妹和母亲的姐妹都是aunt。因此,无论是姑母还是舅母,统称aunt,若非要加以区分,只能在"aunt"后冠以名字。例如,张明的母亲叫李维明,李丹的母亲叫王明兰,就称aunt Weiming和aunt Minglan,但这不符合中国人重宗族关系的习惯。

再者,中方重家族本位,而西方重个人本位。中华民族重伦理、讲道德。中国的伦理精神视国家与家庭、社会与个人为密不可分的整体,倡导集体主义(collectivism);而西方更注重个体的人格,认为个人就是原子,不依靠任何人而存在,个人权利任何人不得侵犯，信奉个人本位，自我中心，倡导个人主义。正因为如此，不能简单地将"个人主义"译为"individualism"，这是不准确的。因为"个人主义"在中国文化中意为"一切从个人出发，把个人利益放在集体利益之上，只顾自己，不顾别人的错误思想。个人主义是生产资料私有制的产物，是资产阶级世界观的核心，其表现形式是多方面的，如个人英雄主义、自由主义、本位主义等"(参见《现代汉语词典》)。而"individualism"在《牛津英语词典》中的释义为：①the quality of being different from other people and doing things in your own way(个性、独特的气质)；②the belief that individual people in society should have the right to make their own decisions, etc., rather than be controlled by the government (个人主义，个人至上)。由此可见，汉语中的"个人主义"是贬义词，而英语中的"individualism"是中性词，其确切含义为"个体主义"。

3.2 英汉文化差异对翻译的影响

翻译活动自产生开始，便与各民族之间的文化交流结合在了一起。就其具体操作形式而言，翻译活动被视为不同语言之间的转换活动；而就其实质而言，翻译又被理解为一项跨文化交流活动。王佐良先生曾经说过："翻译的最大困难是两种文化的不同。"因此，解决好翻译中文化差异的问题是保证译作成功的关键。

3.2.1 英汉文化差异导致词汇空缺现象

词汇空缺是指原语词汇所载的文化信息在译语中没有其"对等语"或"对应语"。有些词在一种语言中存在，而在另一种语言中没有与之对等的词。目前存在以下三种词汇空缺的定义：一指各自文化中特有的词汇；二指源语中存在某种为异族文化所不明白、莫名其妙的、易于误解的东西，造成异族文化的空白；三指富有特殊文化色彩的词和表达方式。语言之间的词汇空缺是一种自然现象，存在两种情况：一种是物质生活方面的词汇空缺，另一种是文化方面的词汇空缺。前者指一个民族物质生活中表示特有事物的词语在异族语言中没有与其概念相同的对应语，但进入异族生活后通过音译、意译等手段在异族语言中找到对等语，成为该语言的借词。我们知道语言常常是客观世界的反映，是一种社会现象。人们生活在什么样的环境中，就会产生什么样的语言。如果某一事物在人们所生活的客观环境中不存在，那么语言可能出现空缺。例如，"salad"这种凉拌菜源于法国，英国原先没有这道菜，语言中也不存在这个词，因此只好将它从法语中原封不动地"移植"过来，中国人通过将其音译为"沙拉"把它引入汉语词汇中。

再如，英语从汉语中借去了ginseng、Mahjong、kowtow等词；汉语又从英语中借来了俱乐部、坦克、维他命、咖啡、因特网、模特、沙发等词语。文化方面的词汇空缺主要是指某些具有民族文化色彩的词语或语义无法在另一种民族的语言中找到对应的表达。中国是重视人际关系和亲属关系的国家，表示亲属关系的词大约有33个，比英国、美国多很多。很多词无法在英语中找到对应的表达。

汉族自古以来价值观的核心是天人合一，强调人与自然的和谐，在人与人的关系上重集体主义，轻个人主义。而以英、美为代表的西方强调自由、平等。语言是文化的载体。美国不同阶段的经济文化变化都反映在语言中。随着时代变化，新的词语不断应运而生。继第一次世界大战后的"迷惘的一代"(Lost Generation)和第二次世界大战后的"垮掉的一代"(Beat Generation)，又出现了"Baby Boomers""Yuppies""Dinks""Sandwich Generation""Couch Potato""Mall Rats"等。

英语中"Aunt Jemima""Yuppies""Mall Rats"等文化空缺词汇在汉语中都没有一一对应的词汇。Yuppies(雅皮士)是指都市里处于中上阶层的年轻专业人士(young urban professionals)。在第二次世界大战期间，美国大约有一千三百万人服役，其中许多人都没有结婚。在战后，他们纷纷组建家庭，生儿育女，因此在1946—1964年这18年间，美国人口急剧增长，新生儿的人数共有七千八百万。美国人称这一代为"Baby Boomers"(婴儿潮一代)。这代人一改其父母对战争的"狂热"，对生活采取务实的态度。他们要弥补战争给父母所造成的损失，勤奋工作，少生孩子。他们有抱负，受过高等教育，生活在城市，有专业性的工作，且收入颇丰，生活很富裕。美国将这些成功者称为"Yuppies"，它的前三个字母是"young urban professionals"的缩写。对于"Yuppies"中那些不要孩子的人，美国人将他们称为"Dinks"，它是"Double Income, No Kids"的缩写。其实，"Baby Boomers"并不都是富有的"Yuppies"，有的夫妇不仅有孩子要抚养，还有老人要赡养，这样另一个名字又产生了，那便是"Sandwich Generation"(三明治一代)——同时照顾父母和子女的人，意味着这些人像三明治夹心一样夹在老人和孩子之间，负担很重。美国的电视业发展迅速，几乎所有人都能看到有线电视节目，家庭影剧院的出现更是让许多人沉迷于电视，这种一有时间就坐在沙发上看电视的人被称为"Couch Potato"，也被称为"电视迷"。它不禁使人们想到悠然坐在沙发里一声不吭、一动不动、像土豆似的人。随着商业的发展与繁荣，大型购物中心(shopping mall)不断涌现。逛购物中心成了一种乐趣，尤其是年轻人，他们即使不购物也在中心钻来钻去，像老鼠一样，美国人将他们戏称为"Mall Rats"(购物狂)。

产生于60年代的"Hippie"是美国文化的独特产物，因此在汉语中无法找到与之对等的词语，曾音译为"希比士"或"希比派"，现定译为"嬉皮士"。这个译名虽然比前两个译名要好些，但仍然无法确切表达Hippie的词义内涵，且有可能造成误解。

Hippie 指的是美国社会中一类特殊的人群，他们虽然对当时的社会现实不满，生活方式与众不同，蓄披肩长发，穿奇装异服，沉迷于酗酒、吸毒，但他们并非"嬉皮笑脸"之士，其中不少人对社会问题持有严肃的态度。

还有一些民族文化内涵特别丰富的词语，在翻译时也必须采用释义或注释等方法，说明该词的语用含义，才能使译语读者了解原语独特的文化现象。如：钱先生周岁时"抓周"，抓了一本书，因此得名"钟书"。(舒展文，《钱钟书与杨绛》)其译文为：When Qian was just one year old, he was told by his parents to choose one thing among many others. He picked up a book of all things. Thereupon, his father very gladly gave him the name: Zhongshu(=book lover)。"抓周"是中国古时风俗，在小儿周岁时陈列各种玩物和生活用具，任他抓取，来预测他的志向和兴趣，也近似占卜他的命运。这是中国人独有的风俗，蕴含着"生死在天，富贵由命"的儒家中庸思想观念。在西方根本无此风俗，因此，英语中也无与"抓周"对应的词语。翻译时只能采用释义的方法，用一个长句来解释汉语"抓周"的语用含义，以使英语读者能理解"抓周"的文化内涵。

世界各族虽处于大体相同的生存环境中，却往往有自己独特的社会生活状况，有自己独特的人情风俗，这也导致了巨大的文化空缺。中国人把娶媳妇、贺生日称为"红喜"，把老人过世称为"白喜"。对于没有接触过我国文化的欧美人来说，把娶媳妇说成"红喜"并不费解，英语就把喜庆日称为"red-letter day"。但把上年纪人的去世也当成一大"喜事"，这就令他们感到奇怪了。因此，不同于欧美文化，我国文化把死人称作"白喜"，彰显了一种个性。

对于缔结婚姻，中国人讲究"门当户对""郎才女貌"，英语中则有"marriage of true minds"(真诚的结合)。结婚时，中国人要选择"良辰吉日"，再"拜天地""入洞房"。欧美人则来到教堂，举行"a white wedding"，再去度"honey moon"(蜜月)。文化空缺是一种客观存在的事实，这是由两种文化的特性所决定的。一些文化信息对于本民族语交际的双方来说是不言而喻的，对于另一语言文化的读者来说却是难以理解的，文化空缺的存在为翻译带来了困难，使文化内涵词的翻译更加充满挑战。

汉语中的某些文化内涵词在英语中没有对应词，即属于完全空缺情况的，宜采用音译或音译加注方法。示例如下。

功夫：Kungfu

叩头：kowtow

炕：Kang

太极：Tai Chi

风水：Fengshui

围棋：Weiqi

饺子：Jiaozi

粽子：Zongzi

在中国历史进程和社会发展中(特别是改革开放以来)特有的事物宜通过借译或语义再生译成英语。下面列出了一些例子。

小康社会：a moderately prosperous society

新时代中国特色社会主义：socialism with Chinese characteristics for a new era

"两个一百年"奋斗目标：Two Centenary Goals

中华民族伟大复兴中国梦：the Chinese Dream of national rejuvenation

中国式现代化新道路：a new and uniquely Chinese path to modernization

四个自信：Four-sphere Confidence (confidence in the path, theory, system, and culture of socialism with Chinese characteristics)

"五位一体"总体布局：the Five-sphere Integrated Plan (China's overall plan for building socialism with Chinese characteristics, that is, to promote coordinated progress in the economic, political, cultural, social, and eco-environmental fields)

"四个全面"战略布局：the Four pronged Comprehensive Strategy (China's strategic plan for building a modern socialist country, deepening reform, advancing law-based governance, and strengthening Party self-governance)

源自中国古代文学、哲学思想或佛教文化的特有事物也宜通过借译或语义再生译成英语。示例如下。

儒释道：Confucianism, Buddhism, and Taoism

三纲五常：the three cardinal guides and the five constant virtues as specified in the feudal ethical code

四书五经：the Four Books and the Five Classics

《论语》：*the Analects*

《易经》：*the Book of Changes*

3.2.2　英汉文化差异导致语义联想差异

朱光潜先生(1946)曾在其著作《谈文学》中的《谈翻译》一文中提到：英语中的"fire""sea""Roland""castle""rose"等词语在不同民族中所引起的联想有很大区别。它们对于英国人而言意义较为丰富。同理，中文中"风""月""江""湖""梅""菊""燕""碑""笛""僧""隐逸""礼""阴阳"之类字词，在我们中国人中引起的联想和情趣也绝不是西方人所能完全了解的。

作为人类认识世界的重要途径之一，色彩不但被赋予了物理属性，而且反映出各民族独特的文化特征，因此成为语言文化及翻译领域很重要的研究课题。地理环境、宗教信仰、风俗习惯、民族心理、思维方式等方面的差异导致各民族对各种颜色所产生的联想也不尽相同。比利时人最忌蓝色，认为蓝色是不吉利的凶兆；土耳其人绝对禁止用花色物品布置房间和客厅，他们认为花色是凶兆；日本人忌绿色，而印度人却喜爱绿色。"yellow"在英语中除了是一个表示颜色的词外，在美国俚语中还含有胆小卑怯之意，如a yellow dog(卑鄙的人)、a yellow livered(胆小鬼)。而在汉语中，黄色在封建社会中是法定的尊色，有崇高、尊严、辉煌的意思，如"黄袍""黄屋""黄榜"等。现代汉语中，黄色又被赋予了不同的文化内涵，有"失败"(如"买卖黄了")和"污秽""下流"(如"黄色书刊""扫黄打非")的意思。因此，颜色词语的翻译需要灵活处理。例如，在翻译中国四大名著之一《红楼梦》时，英国翻译家霍克思(Hawkes)认为对汉族而言，红色表示喜庆、吉祥、幸福，但在西方人的心目中，红色意味着流血、暴力或危险，而金黄色和绿色则与汉语中的红色具有类似的联想意义。因此，他在翻译涉及红色的词语时做了一定的变通处理。在英汉、汉英翻译中，有些词可以完全对应，有些词却大相径庭。下面给出了一些例子。

红旗：red flag

红糖：brown sugar

红茶：black tea

红榜：honor roll

红豆：love pea

在英语和汉语中有很多动物名词字面意义一样，但其联想意义有很大差别。如中西方对于"龙"的联想迥然不同。中华民族受图腾文化的影响，对"龙""凤"等非现实动物倍加尊崇，赋予"龙"高贵、尊严的内涵，使其代表皇权、吉祥等积极意义；而"凤"则是美好、才智的象征。古代帝王被尊为"真龙天子"，穿的是"龙袍"，而我们自己是"龙的传人"。人们用"龙凤呈祥""夫龙妻凤"来祝福一对新人。"龙"是中华民族的象征。而在西方文化中"龙"被看作凶恶狠毒的象征，是能喷烟吐火的怪物。《圣经》中把与上帝作对的恶魔撒旦称为"the great dragon"。一些圣徒(如圣麦克尔、圣乔治等)都因杀死"dragon"而被视为英雄。因此"亚洲四小龙"不能简单地译为"Four Asian Dragons"，若译为"Four Asian Tigers"，就不失为一种较好的文化信息的对等，因为"tiger"(老虎)在西方人心中是一种较强悍的动物，至少不会使人联想到某种可怕的动物。另一种情况就是对于同一种概念或理念，中西方用不同的动物作比。例如比喻一个人力气大，汉语的表达为"力大如牛"，英语则是"as strong as a horse"(力大如马)，原因在于中国农业自古以来以牛耕为主，英国古代则主要靠马耕。还有很多联想意义不同的词语，例如：

月亮(团圆)——moon(虚幻)

牧童(悠闲)——cowboy(冒险)

农民(忠厚朴实)——peasant(心胸狭窄)

狗(鄙视)——dog(同情)

3.2.3　英汉文化差异导致语义错位

语义学中词语的上下义关系理论既涉及词汇的同义现象，也涉及词义的多义现象和蕴含性。语义错位是指两种语言的上义词和下义词之间不对称。语义错位有时是和文化密切相关的。如果某一社会对某类事物非常重视，或者某类事物对于该文化社会来说非常重要，在这种文化的语言中往往会产生许多下义词来描述该事物。例如，汉语中的"酒"包括葡萄酒、白酒、啤酒等，那么"酒"就是上义词，葡萄酒、啤酒、白酒就构成了"酒"的下义词。而在英语中存在葡萄酒(wine)、啤酒(beer)、威士忌(whisky)这样的下义词，却没有与"酒"对应的上义词。于是在翻译"酒文化"这样的词语时就会遇到麻烦。同样，英语中有许多与汉语中"杯子"对应的下义词，例如glass(玻璃杯)、cup(茶杯)、goblet(高脚杯)等，但却找不到与汉语中"杯子"对应的上义词。因此，要翻译"去买个杯子！"这样十分简单的句子，必须先弄清句子中的"杯子"到底指哪种杯子，是"glass"还是"cup"，抑或"goblet"。

3.2.4　英汉文化差异导致语用含义差异

在中国，对别人的健康状况表示关心是有教养、有礼貌的表现。但若要对西方人的健康表示关心，就不能按中国的传统方式进行了。一个中国学生得知其美籍教师生病后，关切地说："You should go to see a doctor!"(你应该到医院看看。)不料，这句体贴的话反而使这位教师很不高兴。因为在这位教师看来，有病看医生这种简单的事情连小孩都知道，用不着任何人来指教。如果就某种小事给人以忠告，那显然是对其能力的怀疑，从而大大伤害其自尊心。

中国人在饭桌上的热情好客经常被西方人误解为不文明的行为。因西方人认为：客人吃多吃少完全由自己决定，用不着主人为他加菜添酒；而且饮食过量是极不体面的事情，因此客人吃饭后，主人不必劝他再吃。一位美国客人看到中国主人不断地给他夹菜，很不安，事后他抱怨说："主人把我当猪一样看待。"

中国人路遇熟人时，往往会无所顾忌地说："啊呀，老兄，你近来又发福了！"或者以关切的口吻说："老兄，你又瘦了，要注意身体啊！"而西方人若听你说"You are fat."或"You are so thin."，即使他跟你比较熟悉，也会感到尴尬和难以回答。

西方人崇拜个人奋斗，尤其为个人取得的成就自豪，从来不掩饰自己的自信心、荣誉感以及在获得成就后的狂喜。相反，中国文化不主张炫耀个人荣誉，而是提倡谦虚。

中国人反对王婆卖瓜式的自吹自擂，然而中国式的自我谦虚或自我否定却常常使西方人大为不满。"Your English is very good.""No, no, my English is very poor.";"You've done a very good job.""No, I don't think so. It's the result of joint efforts."这种谦虚在西方人看来，不仅否定了自己，还否定了赞扬者的鉴赏力。这种中国式的谦虚在英语语境下是行不通的。

我国早有"民以食为天"这一思想，因而吃饭问题成了人们经常挂在口头的话题。中国人路遇熟人时总爱寒暄道："吃饭了吗？""吃过了吗？"河南农民在村头田边远远看见路过的陌生人时爱说"吸烟吧？""喝茶吧？"之类的话。在多数情况下人们并不是十分关心别人是不是吃饭了或喝不喝茶，这类话只是一种招呼罢了。中国人听到这些问话时也只是回答说"吃了"或"不啦，不啦"，这实际上是个应酬，表示谢谢问话人的关心或热情。在我们看来这是一种有礼貌的打招呼用语，而若你跟西方人这样打招呼："Have you had your meal?"他们心理上首先的反应是："Yes, I have.""No, I haven't."或"Do you mean to invite me to dinner?"他们会认为你想请他吃饭或者干涉其私事，会引起误解。而汉语中习惯讲的这些打招呼用语亦不能翻译成英语的招呼用语。像汉语中这样的招呼语应视情况译成"Hello!""How do you do!""Nice day, isn't it?"等。

对于"饭桶""吃不开""吃不了兜着走""吃不消""吃不住""吃老本""吃软不吃硬""吃闲饭"和"吃香"等一系列汉语表达，应将它们分别翻译成"good-for-nothing""be unpopular""land oneself in serious trouble""more than one can stand, too much""be unable to bear or support""rest on one's laurels/live off one's past gains""be open to persuasion, but not to coercion""lead an idle life""be very popular"等，才能基本如实传达原文的含义，尽管没有一条译文用"eat"一词。

对于别人的赞扬，中国人通常表示谦虚，并有一套谦虚之词，像"惭愧""哪里""寒舍""拙文"等。而西方人总是高兴地回答"Thank you!"以表接受，或者说"Thanks for saying so. I'm flattered."。

中国人送客时，主人常对客人说"慢走！""小心点！""再见，走好啊！""你们进去吧！""请留步"等。而西方人只说"Bye Bye!""See you later!""See you next time!"，所以我们翻译的时候一般用"Take care!"或"Mind your step!"。

3.2.5　英汉文化差异对品名翻译的影响

西方人习惯以姓氏给公司命名，如爱迪生公司、迪士尼公司、福特公司、威尔逊公司等。但是中国人通常喜欢以喜庆、吉祥的词汇给公司命名，如"百盛""嘉禾""东来顺""全聚德""醉美""九美斋"等，因此，国外品牌进入中国市场时就要仔细考虑这些因素。"家乐福"(carrefour)就是很成功的译例，中国人向往福、禄、喜、寿，追求家庭和睦，希望事业发达，长盛不衰。家乐福这样的名字很符合中国人的喜好，就连美国的语言考试也取名为"托福"来博取中国人的认同。

受文化传统、宗教信仰、语言崇拜、地理环境等因素的影响，中国人和西方人对数字意义的理解也存在着差异。例如，中国的"三枪"名牌内衣，英文译名为"Three Guns"。这一产品若销往日本、哥伦比亚和北非地区，定会倍受欢迎，因为three这个数字在这些地区代表"积极"意义。但若要销往乍得、贝宁、博茨瓦纳等地，则应更换译名。因为在乍得，奇数被视为具有"消极"意义；在贝宁，"3"则有"巫术"的含义。又如，若把我国的商品"十三香"出口到英、美等国，就会遇到麻烦，因为在西方人看来，thirteen是不吉利的数字。因为忌讳，西方人千方百计地避免和"13"接触。在荷兰，人们很难找到13号楼和13号的门牌，他们用"12A"取代了13号。在英国的剧场，找不到13排和13座，剧场的12排和14排之间通常是人行通道。此外，人们还忌讳13日出游，更忌讳13人同席就餐，13道菜更是不能接受了。在日语中，"4"和"死"读音相同，"14"与"重死"同音，"24"与"二重死"同音，因此"4"成为禁忌数字。"7"在欧美国家有积极意义，所以在欧美同样可以看到"7-Up""Mild Seven"(柔和七星牌香烟)和"7-Eleven"(早7点开晚11点关的商店)等品牌。

我国出口一种口红，品名叫"芳芳"，在汉语中这个名字确实很好，我国人一看到"芳芳"二字就不禁在心中生起美的联想：不仅仿佛看到了一位花容月貌的少女，而且好像闻到了她周身传来的香气。可是这品名音译成汉语拼音"Fangfang"，英文读者一看心中不由生起一种恐怖之感，因为fang恰好是一个英文单词，其意是①a long, sharp tooth of a dog(狗的长牙)；②a snake's poison tooth(蛇的毒牙)。于是他们想象的不是一位涂了口红的少女，而是条张牙舞爪的恶狗或毒汁四溅的毒蛇，就像中国人看到了青面獠牙的"鬼怪"一样。由于翻译的这一败笔，口红的销路可想而知。

翻译"轻身减肥片"时，为了迎合大众心理，也需要做出适当的变通。此药是著名的杭州中药二厂的拳头产品，原来的译名为Obesity-reducing Tablets，但美国人看了译名，以为此药是专给肥胖症患者(obese people)吃的，所以许多胖子(并非肥胖症患者)出于面子，不愿问津。其实此药除了能治单纯性肥胖症之外，还能减肥。为了投顾客所好，将原译名改为Slimming Pills，其销售情况大有改善。

综合练习

一、请指出以下汉语品名英文译本存在的问题，并试着给出合适的翻译。

1. "白象"牌电池——"White Elephant" brand battery

2. "芳草"牌牙膏——"Fang Cao" brand toothpaste

3. "金鸡"牌鞋油——"Gold Cock" brand shoe blacking

4. "银耳"汤——"White Fungus" soup

5. "金三角"经济开发区—— a special economic development zone: a "Golden Triangle"

6. "藕粉"——"Lotus Root Starch"

参考译文

1. Silver Elephant或Baixiang("White Elephant"在英语中是固定表达，意思是"昂贵却无用的东西")

2. Fragrant Grass(fang恰好是一个英文单词，其意是①a long, sharp tooth of a dog "狗的长牙"；②a snake's poison tooth "蛇的毒牙")

3. Golden Rooster("cock"一词在英、美等国除有"雄鸡"一意之外，还有"雄性器官之意")

4. Silver Mushroom Soup(fungus一词除了表示"食用菌"外，也指其他不可食用或不可口的物种)

5. Golden Delta(Golden Triangle习惯上用于指东南亚的一个生产和走私毒品的地方)

6. Lotus Root Pudding/Powder(杭州的西湖藕粉是自古出名的滋养品，历史上曾作为"供粉"每年进献给皇帝，许多中国人都知道这一点，但这在西方却鲜为人知。"starch"一词有"淀粉"的意思，因为多吃淀粉容易发胖，而许多西方人都怕发胖，所以该词不宜用作品名)

二、试将下列句子译成英语，注意句子的语用含义。

1. 惭愧！(不敢当；哪里)

2. 欢迎，欢迎！(幸会；久仰)

3. 再会。(保重；有空来玩)

4. 请笑纳。(别嫌弃；一点小意思)

5. 您太客气。(让你破费；不好意思)

6. 多谢！(有劳您了；谢您了)

7. 别客气。(别见外；没什么)

8. 劳驾！(有劳您；请问……)

9. 不见不散啊！

10. 恭喜发财！

11. 一路顺风！

12. 别逼我。

13. 没错。

14. 没门儿!

15. 完全同意。

参考译文

1. I don't deserve it. (I'm pleased to hear that. You flatter me. Thank you for your compliment.)

2. Glad to meet you. (I'm pleased to see you. /It's such a pleasure to see you.)

3. Goodbye. (Take care. See you. /Do come again, please.)

4. I hope you will like it. (Please accept this small gift.)

5. It's so lovely! (Thank you for the gift. /You don't have to do this.)

6. Thanks. (Many thanks. /I'm obliged.)

7. Don't mention it. (It's a pleasure. /My pleasure. /Not at all. /You're welcome.)

8. Excuse me... (Could you be so kind as to... Would you please...? May I trouble you...? Would you mind...?)

9. Be there or be square. (See you there. /Let us meet at the usual place, rain or shine.)

10. Good luck!

11. Plain sailing. (Have a good journey.)

12. Don't push me.

13. You bet. (Quite right. /Sure. /Certainly.)

14. No way. /Over my dead body! /Fat chance! /When pigs fly!

15. I couldn't agree more. /I quite agree.

三、翻译以下段落。

段落一:

Chinese New Year is also known as the Spring Festival. The start of the festival falls on a different day in either January or February, dictated by the lunar calendar. It lasts 15 days and is the most important holiday in the Chinese calendar. The Spring Festival in Chinese eyes is a family reunion. However, in foreigners' eyes, it is not only a kind of homesickness, but a spring migration. Every year sees the largest annual mass migration on the planet as one sixth of the world's population travel home to celebrate with their family members. That is around a billion people making 3.5 billion journeys in a 40-day period. Meanwhile, over 250 million rail journeys are made across China during the festival. Last year, 5.6 million rail tickets were sold in a single day. Every year in the heartland of industrial China thousands upon thousands of motorcyclists brave the weather and hit the road, determined to make it home. In modern

China, to search for work, many people have to move away from home. And they will travel home to be with the loved ones during the Spring Festival.

参考译文

中国新年也称为春节，通常是在一月或者二月的某一天，依农历而定。春节持续15天，是中国最重要的农历节日。在中国人眼里，春节是家人团聚。但在外国人眼里，中国春节是思乡，也是春季大迁移。每一个春节都见证了全世界最大规模的人口迁移，全世界1/6的人回家和家人一起庆祝节日。大约10亿人在40天当中进行了多达35亿次旅行。其中包括超2.5亿次的火车旅行。去年，5600万张火车票一天售完。在中国工业中心地区，每年都有成百上千万人骑上摩托，勇敢地踏上归途，风雨无阻地朝着家的方向前进。在现代中国，很多人为了找工作养家糊口，不得不背井离乡。但在春节期间，他们都会返乡和自己心爱的人团聚。

段落二：

Chinese buzzwords reflect social changes, but it takes time for them to be accepted by British people and become English glossary. Chinese buzzwords often come to the British people's attention through the media. In the case of Chinese words that are gaining publicity in the foreign media, obviously some terms such as "Tuhao" and "Dama" tell us something about trends and phenomena in China that mark interesting shifts in society. "Tuhao" is used to describe uncouth rich. In fact, this word referring to rural landlords who oppressed their tenants and servants in the past is not new at all, but Chinese netizens are using it in a different way, and now it refers to people who spend money like water or those like to show off their wealth. Chinese "Dama", or middle-aged woman, rose to fame after many of them bought gold when the price was low. To date, more than 120 Chinese-linked words have been written into Oxford dictionaries, such as Fengshui, Hutong, Hukou, and Cantonese-based Dim Sum, kowtow. As more Chinese words attract attention among speakers of English, with the Internet as an especially productive channel between languages, this will provide the West with more windows on China, its culture, and concerns. But as to whether or not these words will truly form part of English usage remains to be seen.

参考译文

中国热词反映了中国社会的发展变化，但想要这些词真正被英国人使用尚需时日。中国热词经常因为出现在了英文媒体报道中而引起英国人的关注。显然，在外媒关注的中国热词中，最受关注的是"土豪"和"大妈"，因为这两个词反映了中国社会的发展趋势、现象，表明社会发生了值得关注的变化。"土豪"用来指暴发户。这个词其实并不新，以前指欺压佃户和仆人的乡村地主，现在中国网民用该词表示花钱如流水或喜欢炫富的人。"大妈"一词是指中年妇女，很多中国"大妈"因抄底黄金而一战成名。至今已有120多个中文词条收入牛津词典，如风水、胡同、户口，以及广东话点心、叩头等。随着越来越多的中文词汇引发以英语为母语者的关注，互联网作为不同语言沟通交流的有效渠道，将为西方提供更多了解中国(中国文化和中国热点问题)的途径。至于这些词汇能否真正为英国人所用，还有待观察。

第4章

词义的确定、引申和褒贬

　　词汇是人类语言和生活最紧密的衔接点。正因为有了一个个词汇，人们才能将自己在生产活动、娱乐活动、文化活动及心理情感活动中的经验与感受准确、清楚地表达出来。这一方面说明词汇在人类语言和生活中的重要性，另一方面说明词汇的意义和使用会不可避免地受到地理环境与人文环境的制约。不同地区的人在表达相同或相近的事情时，也许会选择不同的词汇，这样就造成了不同语言在词义上的差异。英国语言学家艾里克·帕特里奇(Eric Partridge)说"词本无义，义随人生"(Words do not have meanings; People have meanings for words.)。约翰逊博士(Dr. Johnson)也说："The idea that for every word in any one language there is another word accurately equivalent to it in every other language, is not in accordance with the facts. In his search for the equivalent of a word the translator meets many difficulties." 他指出，有人认为任何一种语言中的每一个词在其他语言中都有一个与之精确对等的词，这种想法与事实不符。在寻找一个词的对应词时，译者会遇到很多困难。而汉语词义比较严谨，词的含义范围比较窄，比较精确固定，词义的伸缩性和对上下文的依赖性较小，独立性较大。

4.1 词义的确定

英国哲学家维特根斯坦(Wittgenstein)认为词义取决于它在语言中的使用(The meaning of a word is its use in the language.)。

弗思(Firth)则认为每个词用在新的语境中就成为一个新的词(Each word when used in a new context is a new word.)。

4.1.1 根据上下文及习惯搭配确定词义

英语同其他许多语言一样，一词多类、一词多义的现象很普遍。如果只记住某个单词的一两种意思，便不加区别地套译原文，往往会使译文生硬难懂，甚至歪曲原词义。判断一词多义的手段主要是看词的联立关系(the frame of words)，即根据词的组合、搭配判断词义。由于一个词语不是孤立的，而是置身于一篇文章中的，一篇文章是上下密切相关的有机体，因此会受到各方面因素的影响。例如，一个人在父母面前是儿子，在子女面前是父亲，在领导眼里是职员，在下属面前又成为领导，因此他的称呼会在不同的场合发生相应的变化。

看下面几个例子：

(1) He is the *last* man to come. 他是**最后**来的。

(2) He is the *last* man to do it. 他**决不会**干那事。

(3) He is the *last* person for such a job. 他**最不配**干这个工作。

(4) He should be the *last* to blame. 怎么也**不该**怪他。

(5) He is the *last* man to consult. 根本**不宜**找他商量。

(6) This is the *last* place where I expected to meet you. 我怎么也**没想到**会在这个地方见到你。

"last"常被译为"最后的，末尾的"，但除此之外，"last"还有很多其他的含义，如"最近的，上一个的""仅剩下的，最终的""(强调)最不可能的""最不适当的"等，所以要根据上下文进行翻译。

要准确翻译，不能简单地死记单词的各种意义，而应围绕其中心意义(central meaning)，通过上下文来调整它的次要意义(secondary meaning)。另外，要准确地确定词义，还须掌握词项的习惯搭配。对于多义词，不同的词义常有不同的搭配限制。因此，这些词义可以通过它们的典型搭配显示出来。如"fat"一词：

fat pork 多脂肪的猪肉

fat income 优厚的收入

a *fat* pig 肥壮的猪

fat kitchen 贮足食物的厨房

再如"soft"：

soft head 无主见者

soft soaper 奉承者

*soft*ware 软件

"picture"一词原意为"图片"，学生往往反复诵读、记忆，不自觉在心中把这个词义与英文连为一体，而在翻译中形成"条件反射"，认为"picture"的意思就是"图片"。其实"picture"不译为"图片"的例子是不少的：

The park is a *picture* when the flowers are in bloom.

花开时公园里景色如画。

The book gives a good *picture* of everyday life there.

这本书生动地描绘了那里人们的日常生活。

The *picture* is much clearer with the new aerial.

装上新天线后图像清晰多了。

Have you seen her latest *picture*?

你看过她最新拍的电影了吗？

Are you in the *picture* now?

你现在知道是怎么回事了吗？

再如"story"一词的翻译：

This war is becoming the most important *story* of this generation.

这场战争将成为这一代人最重大的事件。

It is quite another *story* now.

现在的情况完全不同了。

Some reporters who were not included in the session broke the *story*.

有些没让参加那次会议的记者把内情捅出去了。

He'll be very happy if that *story* holds up.

如果这一说法当真，那他就太高兴了。

The girl's *story* is one of the saddest.

那个姑娘的遭遇算是最惨的了。

A young man came to Scotti's office with a *story*.

一个年轻人来到斯科特的办公室**报案**。

Officials refused to confirm the *story*.

官员们拒绝证实这条**消息**。

The *story* about him became smaller and by and by faded out from the American TV.

报道中对他的渲染减少了,不久就从美国电视上销声匿迹了。

即使是同一个意思也有不同的表现方法,在翻译时要考虑上下文,选择确切的措辞,如 "He spoke *slowly*." 可译成 "他**慢条斯理地**说"; "He is *slow* of speech." 可译作 "他**口齿不伶俐**"; "The police were *slow* in coming." 可译为 "警察**姗姗来迟**"; "We enjoyed a *slow* Sunday at home." 可译成 "我们在家里**悠闲地**度过了一个星期天"; "He waved his hand *slowly* in contempt." 可译为 "他**懒洋洋地**挥了挥手,一副不屑一顾的样子"。

其实 slow 在不同的上下文里还有其他引申的含义,如:

slow season **淡季**

slow time (与夏季时间相对的) **标准**时间

a tennis court with a *slow* surface **不利于跑动的**网球场

a *slow* starter (拳击中)**开始时采取守势而后猛攻**的选手

Business was rather *slow* last month. 上个月生意**不太景气**。

The book is rather *slow*. 这本书很**乏味**(不精彩)。

What a *slow* party it is! 多么**索然无味**的聚会!

He is *slow* at speech with women yet. 跟女人说话,他还有点**笨嘴拙舌**。

4.1.2 根据冠词的有无确定词义

中文里没有冠词,英文里有冠词。在英语表达中有冠词和无冠词有时意思相差很大,这是我们做翻译时必须注意的。尝试使用前面几个选择词义的方法之后,如果语义还有矛盾或意思不通,则可以考虑一下是否存在冠词。为什么可以根据冠词的有无来确定合适的词义?答案如下。

(1) 冠词原意有 "那" "这" "该" 的意思。没有冠词时,当然就没有这种意思。我们把它的含义考虑进来,就知道它在该处的恰当词义了。例如:

"They are *members of* the Department." 可以译为 "他们是该系的**部分成员**"。而 "They are *the members of* the Department." 则可译为 "他们是该系的**全体成员**"。

(2) 冠词有习惯用法。有些结构有冠词,构成一定的意思。有些结构无冠词,也有一定的意思。按照这些习惯用法,就可以确定合适的词义。例如:

out of question **毫无疑问**

Freedom of navigation is *out of question*.

航行自由完全**没问题**。

Without peace, development is out *of the question*.

没有和平，发展就**无从谈起**。

(3) 表示颜色的词，若词前无冠词，则表示具体的颜色；若有冠词，则表示抽象的颜色或颜色之形象化。例如：

She is dressed *in pink*.

她穿着**粉红色的**衣服。

People sometimes say they are *in the pink* when they are in good health.

人们有时会用"**红光满面**"来表示身体很健康。

(4) 许多词，若前面无冠词，则表示具体的意思；若前面有冠词，则有点转义。例如：

My watch is *behind time*.

我的表**走慢**了。

My watch is *behind the time*.

我的表**过时**了。

Nowadays, short skirts and long boots are very much *in fashion*.

时下短裙和长靴非常**流行**。

He can speak and write English *in a fashion*.

他**勉强**会点英语。

4.1.3 根据文化背景知识确定词义

翻译是将一种文化环境里产生的作品移植到另一种文化环境里，因此是一种跨文化活动。整个翻译过程中，原语文化和译入语文化都在以不同方式起制约作用。而中西文化在风俗习惯、思维方式、宗教信仰等方面有很大差异，只有了解这种文化差异，才能在翻译中确定词义，进行正确表达，使译文既保持原文相关的文化色彩，又符合译入语习惯。

广州别名"五羊城"不宜译为"Five-goat City"，因为"goat"在西方人的观念里是一种淫荡的动物，具有好色、淫秽的联想意义。"You old goat."表示"你这个老色鬼"，而在中国人眼里"羊"则有一种温顺、服从的象征意义。陈小尉教授认为"五羊城"宜译为"Five-Ram City"。

"龙"是中华民族的象征，代表一种气势磅礴的民族精神，成为历代帝王的象征。所以我们是"龙"的子孙、"龙"的传人。而"dragon"一词在西方则是一条拖着长尾、满身长鳞、口中喷火、有双翼的巨大晰蝎(胡文仲，1995)，它是罪恶的象征，因此"望子成龙"应根据文化差异译为"to be ambitious for their children""to have great ambitions for one's children""hope one's children will have a bright future"(参见《汉英词典》)。

下面再看见个具体的示例。

Politicians *shed crocodile tears* over the plight of the unemployed.

面对陷入困境的失业人群，政客们**虚情假意地**表示同情。

crocodile是一种凶残的爬行动物。在西方传说中，鳄鱼一面吞食捕获的动物，一面流着眼泪，以诱使更多的动物上当受骗。crocodile tears喻指"假仁假义、假慈悲"。

It was *Friday* and soon they'd go out and get drunk.

星期五发薪日到了，他们很快就会出去喝个一醉方休。

译文中的"发薪日"并非胡乱翻译。在英国Friday是发薪的日子。我们只有懂得英国文化，才能正确翻译。而在美国有"black Friday"之说，我们要把它译为"黑色星期五"。因为在美国历史上，1869年9月24日爆发了一轮经济危机，四年后的1873年9月19日又发生了另一轮危机，十分凑巧的是这两个日子均是星期五。

That guy's got a *Midas touch*.

在翻译这句话时，先要弄懂"Midas touch"是什么意思，以及这句话要表达的文化内涵是什么。"Midas touch"这个英语表达源于希腊神话中的一个典故。在这个故事中，人物迈达斯(Midas)拥有点石成金的能力。在现代英语中，人们用"Midas touch"(迈达斯的触摸)来形容"某人能把任何事物都转换成金钱"，当我们说一个人"has the Midas touch"的时候，意思是说这个人拥有"做任何事情都能赚钱的能力"。在明白了这一典故之后，我们还要结合社交语境(如商务活动)，最终推断出该句的意思是那人很会做生意，他不必花太多气力，就能像点物成金那样轻松赚钱。所以可以把这句话译为：**那人很会做生意，能轻轻松松赚大钱。**

The United States has now set up a *loneliness industry*.

离开美国社会环境，这句话是很难翻译的。所谓loneliness industry指的是美国社会福利的一部分。由于美国社会的大量孤寡老人无人照顾，成了社会问题，于是，美国政府部门建立了一种名为loneliness industry的社会服务项目。根据这一背景知识，我们可以把它译为：美国政府建立了一种**为孤寡老人服务的社会服务项目**。

语言本身不仅是文化的重要组成部分，也是文化的载体。每一种语言都是一个国家、民族文化发展的产物，都有其久远的历史背景和丰富的文化内涵。

翻译时，要处理好语言和文化的矛盾，要分析和比较两种语言的结构和表达方式的异同，在准确理解原文的基础上，根据原文提供的语境，理解和把握语言所蕴含的深层文化内涵，才能在译文中忠实、准确地表达原文的内容，体现原著的风格与文化背景，再现原文的语言特色和艺术形象，让读者领会异国的风土人情，增长见识。同样，由于中西生产、生活方式不一样，存在不同的政治、历史背景，不同的风俗习惯，只有对此有所了解，才能在翻译中确定词义，选用合适的表达方式，使译文具有可读性。例如，英语中"bridal shower"是指在英、美等国新娘出嫁前家人为她举行的点心茶话会(high tea party)，一般只允许女子参加，新娘的女友常常给她赠送一些小礼品。这个词组如果直译为"新娘淋浴"就是误译，应根据上述风俗习惯，与中国民间风俗结合起来意译为"待嫁酒会"。与之相对应的"bachelor's party"也不宜译为"单身汉聚会"，因为"bachelor's party"是指新郎在娶亲前一两天所举行的茶话会或酒会，一般只允许男子参加，可以译为"告别单身汉酒会"。

4.2 词义的引申和褒贬

有学者认为，翻译中学会抓住精神实质，摆脱原文表层结构的束缚，防止从"实"到"实"的转换，做到"licentious"(破格、自由)，是至关重要的问题。英语和汉语在表达方式上存在着许多差异。有时你在词典上找不到一个单词的合适词义。在这种情况下，就必须采用灵活的手法，从一个词或词组的字面意思加以引申，然后选出比较恰当的汉语来表达。此外，有些词随着时代的发展而被赋予了新的含义，翻译时就必须采用词义引申的办法。

4.2.1 词义的引申

在文章或句子中词义的具体化与抽象化引申是英语中经常使用的修辞手段，采用了这种修辞手段的文章或句子在很多情况下都不能"对号入座"直译成汉语。有时会发现某些词在英汉辞典上找不到适当的词义，如果任意硬套或逐词死译，就会使译文生硬晦涩，不能确切表达原意，甚至会造成误解。这时就应根据上下文和逻辑关系，从该词的根本含义出发，进一步加以引申。引申时，往往可以从以下几个方面来加以考虑。

1 抽象化引申

词义抽象化是指把原文中某些意义比较具体和形象的词在译文中引申为意义比较抽象和一般的词。英语中，特别在现代英语中，常常用一个表示具体形象的词来表示一种属性、一个事物或一种概念。翻译这类词时，一般可将其词义作抽象化引申，译文才能流畅、自然。例如：

After the war, he gave up the *sword* for the *plough*.

战争结束后，他**解甲归田**。

They had their *smiles and tears* but not for the things of this world.

他们有自己的**喜怒哀乐**，但不是由尘世间的事情所引起的。

What is learned *in the cradle* is carried to *the grave*.

儿时所学，**终生**难忘。

He's always a reliable friend, *rain or shine*.

他是一位**在任何情况**下都可以信赖的朋友。

There were times when emigration *bottleneck* was extremely rigid and nobody was allowed to leave the country out of his personal preference.

曾几何时，移民**限制**极为严格，不允许任何人出于个人考虑而移民。

There is a mixture of *the tiger and ape* in the character of the imperialists.

帝国主义既有**残暴的**一面，也有**狡猾的**一面。

I have no *head* for mathematics.

我没有数学方面的**天赋**。

2 具体化引申

具体化引申是指在译文中，用所指意义较窄的词或词组替换原文中所指意义较广的词或词组。英语中有些词在特定的上下文中，其含义是清楚的，但译成汉语时还必须作具体化的引申，否则将不够清楚。

以虚代实的抽象名词能大大简化英语的表达，是一种常见的语言现象。就其特征而言，此类抽象名词可大致分成两类。一类是指形形色色的"人"的抽象名词，例如：

Is Jane a *possibility* as a wife for Richard?

简是做理查德妻子的**合适人选**吗？

His new car made him the *envy* of every boy in the neighborhood.

他有辆新车，这使他成为四邻所有男孩**嫉羡的对象**。

另一类是指各种各样具体事物的抽象名词，例如：

The car in front of me stalled and I missed *the green*.

我前头的那辆车停住了，我错过了**绿灯**。

The Great Wall is a *must* for most foreign visitors to Beijing.

对于大多数来北京的外国游客，长城是**必不可少的参观项目**。

The invention of *printing* was a milestone in human progress.

印刷术的发明是人类进步的一个里程碑。

4.2.2 词义的褒贬

语言本身虽没有阶级性，但在具体使用时不可能不为一定的阶级服务。为了忠实于原文的思想内容，翻译时必须正确理解原作者的基本政治立场和观点，然后选用适当的语言来加以表达。

词汇按照感情色彩可以分为褒义词、贬义词和中性词。英语中有些词本身就带有褒义色彩和贬义色彩，将其译成汉语时应当把原有的褒/贬义相应地译出来。例如：

These *quirks* have helped Pangdonglai become an Internet sensation.

这些**独特的商业模式**使胖东来火爆全网。(褒)

He was a man of high *renown* (fame).

他是位**有名望的**人。(褒)

The tasks carried out by them are *praiseworthy*.

他们进行的事业是**值得赞扬的**。(褒)

Henry keeps *boasting* that he has talked to the President.

亨利总是**吹嘘说**他曾同总统谈过话。(贬)

"He was *polite* and always gave advice *willingly*," she recalled.

她回忆说："他**彬彬有礼**，总是**诲人不倦**。"(褒)

We were shocked by his *coarse* manners.

我们对他的**粗暴**态度感到震惊。(贬)

英语中有些词义是中立的，本身不表示褒义或贬义，但在一定的上下文中可能有褒或贬的意味，译成汉语时就应该使用具有褒/贬意味的相应的词。例如：

The *aggressive* nature of imperialism will never change.

帝国主义**侵略的**本性是绝对不会改变的。(贬)

A good salesperson has to be *aggressive* in today's competitive market.

在当今竞争激烈的市场中，优秀的销售人员应该有**进取精神**。(褒)

He was the kind of person who would *flatter* you to your face, and then slander you behind your back.

他是那种当面**胁肩谄笑**，背地里造谣中伤的人。(贬)

I found it *flattering* that he still recognized me after all these years.

这么多年过去了，他还能认出我来，这让我**受宠若惊**。(褒)

综合练习

一、试将以下词组译成汉语，注意"soft"及"delicate"在不同语境下的含义。

1. soft pillow

2. soft music

3. soft cushion

4. soft wood

5. soft money

6. soft drink

7. soft breeze

8. soft light

9. soft voice

10. soft fire

11. soft hat

12. soft words

13. soft answer

14. soft goods

15. soft heart

16. soft water

17. a soft glance

18. delicate skin

19. delicate porcelain

20. delicate upbringing

21. delicate living

22. delicate health

23. delicate stomach

24. delicate vase

25. delicate diplomatic question

26. delicate difference

27. delicate surgical operation

28. delicate ear for music

29. delicate sense of smell

30. delicate touch

31. delicate food

参考译文

1. 软枕

2. 轻柔的音乐

3. 软垫

4. 软木，软质木材

5. 纸币，支票

6. 不含酒精的饮料

7. 和风，柔和的微风

8. 柔光

9. 低声

10. 文火

11. 呢帽

12. 和蔼的话

13. 委婉的回答

14. 毛织品，纺织品

15. 软心肠

16. 软水

17. 充满深情的一瞥

18. 娇嫩的皮肤

19. 精致的瓷器

20. 娇生惯养

21. 奢侈的生活

22. 虚弱的身体

23. 容易吃坏的胃

24. 易碎的花瓶

25. 微妙的外交问题

26. 细微的差别

27. 难做的外科手术

28. 对音乐有鉴赏力

29. 灵敏的嗅觉

30. 妙笔生花

31. 美味的食物

二、试将以下句子译成汉语，注意词语在不同语境下的含义。

1. He *saw* a man *sawing* trees with a *saw*.

2. Eat what you *can* and *can* what you *cannot*.

3. You *hit the nail on the head*.

4. I'll *report* that official.

5. The boss *gave her the sack*.

6. That girl student is *in the green*.

7. The old lady has *gone to her rest*.

8. That young man has *lost his heart*.

9. That fellow did hard *labor* for 3 years.

10. The woman in *labor* is his wife.

11. I'm *not a little* afraid of snakes.

12. I have *seen* him *through*.

13. Don't *call him names*!

14. The little boy is a *love child*.

15. He is *disinterested* in the affairs.

16. Every life has its *roses* and *thorns*.

17. We have the situation well in *hand*.

18. It is not *right* for children to sit up late.

19. She tried her best to *right* her husband from the charge of robbery.

20. I want you to *account for* every cent you spent.

21. If the stove isn't *made up*, it will go out.

22. Society is *made up* of people with widely differing abilities.

23. They *made up* a bed on the sofa for the unexpected visitor.

24. He saw a dim *figure* moving towards him.

25. The invention of machinery had brought into the world a new era—the Industrial Age. Money had become *King*.

26. John was an *aggressive* salesman who did his job quite well.

27. Hans was too obviously *flattering* the gentleman by saying he was the most courageous man he had ever seen.

28. The boxer was *knocked out* in the second round.

29. The Department of Justice was reluctant to bring *poor cases* into court.

30. Other media closer to the scene dismissed Carter as a *poor loser*.

31. He *bombarded* her with questions.

32. The director's *eyes and ears* are run to everything the actor does.

33. His *hand* is out.

34. Give me a *hand*, please.

35. The office is short of *hands*.

参考译文

1. 他看见一个人正用锯子锯树。

2. 能吃的吃掉，吃不掉的就做成罐头。

3. 你真是一语中的。

4. 我要检举那位官员。

5. 老板解雇了她。

6. 那个女学生正值豆蔻年华。

7. 那个老太太安息了。

8. 那个青年人处于热恋之中。

9. 那个家伙服过三年劳役。

10. 分娩的妇女是他的妻子。

11. 我很怕蛇。

12. 我帮助他渡过难关。

13. 别骂他!

14. 那个小男孩是个私生子。

15. 他在此事上公正无私。

16. 每个人的生活都有苦有甜。

17. 我们能很好地把握局面。

18. 孩子熬夜不好。

19. 她尽力为她丈夫洗脱抢劫的罪名。

20. 我要你把花费的每分钱都交代清楚。

21. 不添柴，炉子就会熄灭。

22. 社会是由具有迥然不同能力的人组成的。

23. 他们把沙发收拾一下，让这位不速之客睡。

24. 他隐约看见一个人影正在向他移动。

25. 机器的发明使世界进入了一个新纪元——工业时代，金钱成了主宰一切的权威。

26. 约翰是个积极肯干的推销员，工作做得相当出色。

27. 汉斯说这位先生是他所见到过的最有胆识的人，这种阿谀奉承未免过于露骨。

28. 该拳击手在第二个回合中被淘汰了。

29. 司法部不愿意将没把握打赢官司的案子拿到法庭上。

30. 对此事比较了解的其他媒体鄙夷地认为，卡特是一个输不起的人。

31. 他向她发出连珠炮似的提问。

32. 导演的注意力完全放在了演员的一举一动上。

33. 他的技能荒废了。

34. 请帮我一下。

35. 这个办公室缺人手。

三、请翻译以下段落

Both WHO's constitution and the Universal Declaration of Human Right assert that health is a human right, not a privilege for those who can afford it. Over time, that right has made its way into both national and international law. But importantly, the right to health is not simply a noble idea on a piece of paper. It has been a platform for major improvements in global health. Since 1948, life expectancy has increased by 25 years. Maternal and childhood mortality have plummeted. Smallpox has been eradicated and polio is on the brink. We have turned the tide on the HIV/AIDS epidemic. Deaths from malaria have dropped dramatically. New vaccines have made once-feared diseases easily preventable. And there are many other causes for celebration. But even as we continue to struggle with old threats, new ones have arisen. Climate change will have profound effects on health. Antimicrobial resistance has the potential to undo the gains of modern medicine. Vaccine hesitancy is putting millions of young lives at risk. Noncommunicable diseases, including heart disease, stroke, cancer, diabetes, hypertension, lung diseases, and mental illnesses have become the major killers of our time. And of course, we continue to face the ever-present threat of outbreaks and other health emergencies.

——2019年6月CATTI英语三级笔译实务真题

参考译文

《世界卫生组织宪章》与《世界人权宣言》均强调健康是一项人权，而不是那些有经济实力者享有的特权。随着时间的推移，健康权已逐渐载入各国法律和国际法律。但重要的是，健康权绝非只是纸上空谈。健康权一直是全球健康状况得以获得重大改善的平台。自1948年以来，预期寿命延长了25岁。产妇和儿童死亡率快速下跌。天花已被消灭，脊髓灰质炎也已处在被消灭的边缘。艾滋病毒/艾滋病的势头得到扭转。疟疾致死的现象急剧减少。得益于新疫苗的出现，曾经让人谈虎色变的疾病也变得易于预防。还有其他进步可喜可贺。但是，就在我们继续对抗既有健康威胁之时，新的健康威胁已经出现。气候变化会对健康产生深远影响。抗微生物药物耐药性有可能让现代医学取得的成果荡然无存。"疫苗犹豫"正危及数百万年轻人的生命。心脏病、中风、癌症、糖尿病、高血压、肺病和精神疾病等非传染性疾病已成为当今时代的头号杀手。当然，我们还无时无刻不面临着疫情和其他突发卫生事件的威胁。

第5章

翻译技巧(一)词类转换

　　在翻译过程中运用词类转换法能使译文流畅，表意确切。为了使译文既忠实于原文又符合汉语习惯，翻译时不能拘泥于某些词汇在原文中的词性，必要时应该采取词类转换的方法，对原词类进行适当的转换。

5.1 翻译中进行词类转换的原因

按照绝大多数语法书的分类，汉英词类的数量大致相等，类别基本对应。汉语的词类大致有十余类，其中实词类有动词、名词、形容词、代词、副词、数词和量词，虚词类有连词、介词、助词、叹词等。英语也有十大类词，其中实词类包括名词(Noun)、动词(Verb)、形容词(Adjective)、副词(Adverb)、数词(Numeral)、代词(Pronoun)，虚词类有介词(Preposition)、连词(Conjunction)、冠词(Article)和感叹词(Interjection)。

英汉两种语言属于不同的语系，英语属于印欧语系(Indo-European Family)，汉语则属于汉藏语系(Sino-Tibetan Family)。这两种语言的词汇构成和使用习惯均存在一定的差异。汉语是分析型(analytic)语言，其典型特征是没有屈折变化(inflection)，也就是说，汉语的名词不会改变自身的形式(form)以变为复数，动词也不用改变自身的形式来表示过去时、现在时或将来时，汉语的词也没有表示阳性和阴性的词缀。汉语词语依靠词序(word order)和虚词(empty word)组合成句子。而英语是分析型和综合型(synthetic)语言，其分析型特征体现在词序和助词(auxiliary)的组句功能上，其综合型特征体现在其丰富的屈折变化形式上。英汉两种语言在词的分类、词的兼类、词类的句法功能以及使用频率等方面都有所不同。英语的词类依据是语法，而汉语的词类是根据词的意义来划分的。有些词类英语中有而汉语中没有，如冠词、引导词、关系代词、名词性物主代词、关系副词、分词、动词不定式、动名词等；同样，有些词类汉语中有而在英语中却难觅其踪，如量词、助词等。汉语词大部分是一词一类，仅有少量兼类词，而一词多类却是英语中的普遍现象。

词类划分的差异必然导致词类转换法的广泛应用。例如，冠词虽然数量微少，却是英语中用法繁多且使用频率很高的功能词之一。因为汉语里没有冠词，也没有与之绝对等同的词语，所以当冠词在句中只起语法作用时往往被省略。然而，对于在句中具有不同程度的词汇意义的冠词，则不能简单地将其忽略。为了恰如其分地表达冠词的意义，必须采取词类转译的方法，如将具有明显数字意味的冠词转译成汉语数词，将具有明显指代意味的冠词转译成汉语代词，等等。

英汉两种语言在词类的句法功能上亦有很大的差异。汉语中一个词类能充当的句子成分比较多，一般不需要转换词类。英语中一个词类能充当的句子成分少，当充当不同的句子成分时，需要进行词类转换。例如，英语中只有动词才能作谓语，而汉语中，除动词外，许多其他词类也能作谓语，如副词、形容词、名词、数量词等。英汉两种语言中各类词的使用频率不同，习惯用法不同，亦会促成翻译中的词类转换。在大多数情况下，英译汉时很难将两种语言的词汇一一对应，所以要"打破语言的外壳，保持实质内容"，有时需要词性变化，否则句子结构欧化，不符合汉语习惯。为了使译文符合汉语习惯，翻译时不必拘泥于原文的表层结构，在忠于原意的前提下，可将原文中某些词的词类转换为汉语的其他词类，从而使译文更加通顺、自然。

5.2　词类转换技巧应用

先来看看什么是词类转换。在翻译中，由于两种语言在语法和习惯表达上存在差异，在保证原文意思不变的情况下，译文必须改变词类，这就叫词类转换(或词类转译)。词类转换分为以下六种。

5.2.1　转译成动词

和英语相比，汉语中动词用得较多，这是一个特点。在一个英语简单句中，往往只有一个谓语动词，而在一个汉语简单句中却可以有几个谓语动词。因此，英语中有不少词类，尤其是名词、介词、形容词和副词，有时会翻译成汉语的动词。

1 英语名词转译成汉语动词

英语中名词占优，尤其在科技英语中，名词化是突出之势。在英汉翻译中，名词转换为动词的现象很普遍，常见的有如下几种。

(1) 英语中动词派生的名词，如liberation、abolition、exploration、application、connection、conclusion、treatment和detection等，以及具有动作意义的名词，如sight、thought、glance、glimpse等，在英译汉中有时会转译成动词。这类名词后面常常跟有一个介词短语(作定语)，转换的结果是名词与介词短语中的名词成了动宾结构，例如：

Until recently Xuchang was mainly known for the *production* of wigs made from human hair. Now it has a better claim to fame.

过去，许昌主要因**生产**真人头发制成的假发而闻名。但如今，它有了更加值得骄傲的新名片。

It makes sense, then, that we need a *combination* of strategies to stay vibrant.

为了保持活力，我们确实需要**综合采用**多种策略。

The circadian rhythm and sleep-wake system are sensitive to light, and even a *glance* can make falling back to sleep more difficult.

昼夜节律和睡眠 - 觉醒周期对光很敏感,哪怕是**瞥一眼**时间都有可能造成入睡困难。

Even those parents who seemed hard and demanding would just melt at the *thought* of their child in tears over a failed test or a broken fingernail.

即使是那些看起来严厉、苛刻的父母,**一想到**自己的孩子因为考试不及格或指甲断裂而流泪,也会心软。

(2) 作为固定词组主体的名词,如make use of、have a look at、have a rest、make no mention of、pay attention to、attach significance to等中的名词,往往可以转译成动词。例如:

An increasing number of teenagers are having problems sleeping due to intense academic pressure or excessive smartphone use, as health experts call for families and schools to attach greater *significance* to the sleep quality among the youth.

由于学业压力大或过度使用手机,越来越多的青少年出现了睡眠问题,健康专家呼吁家庭和学校应更加**重视**青少年的睡眠质量。

More *attention should be paid to* the sleep hygiene of college students and helping them develop a healthy lifestyle.

应更加**关注**大学生的睡眠卫生,帮助他们养成健康的生活方式。

While *having a good command of* the Chinese language, the teachers and students are welcome to visit China more often and have a deeper understanding of China, share a true, multidimensional, and panoramic view of China with more friends, and act as envoys for inheriting and developing the friendship between the two countries.

欢迎师生们在**熟练掌握**汉语的同时,多到中国走走看看,深入了解中国,与更多朋友分享真实、立体、全面的中国,做传承和发展两国友谊的使者。

The attendees *show* great concern about the global problems like resource shortage and environment protection.

与会者对资源短缺、环境保护等全球性问题**高度关注**。

(3) 某些由"动词+er"或"动词+or"构成的名词,有时在句子中并不指某人的身份或职业,而含有较强的动作意味,往往可转译成汉语动词。例如:

That well-known scientist was a great *lover* of literature when he was a child.

那位著名的科学家小时候就**酷爱**文学。

He is a good *eater* and *sleeper*.

他**能吃能睡**。

I am no *drinker*, nor *smoker*.

我既不**喝酒**，也不**抽烟**。

②英语介词转译成汉语动词

英语中含有动作意味的介词，如in、across、through、for、against等，以及作表语的介词短语，作原因、目的状语的介词短语，作方式、陪衬状语的短语等，都可转译为动词。例如：

They seem to do everything in a rush, with an eye *on* the clock, as if they had only a short time to live.

他们办事似乎都很匆忙，眼睛老是**盯着**钟表，好像剩下的日子不多了。

I teach because I enjoy finding ways of getting myself and my students *out of* the ivory tower and *into* the real world.

我教书是因为我喜欢想方设法使自己和学生**走出**象牙塔，**进入**现实世界。

He was out in the field *on* this case for three days.

他在野外待了三天，**处理**这一案件。

③英语形容词转译成汉语动词

英语中表示知觉、情感、愿望等心理状态的形容词在连系动词后作表语时往往转译成汉语动词。如able、afraid、angry、ashamed、aware、anxious、careful、cautious、certain、concerned、confident、content、doubtful、glad、grateful、ignorant(无知的)、sorry、thankful等，这些都是常用作表语的表示心理状态的形容词，可译为动词。有些由动词派生出来的英语形容词也可译成汉语动词。例如：

We are *deeply convinced* of the correctness of the reform and opening up policy and *firmly determined* to pursue it.

我们**深信**改革开放政策是正确的，**决心**继续奉行这一政策。

The manager is *grateful* to the customers for their valuable suggestions.

经理**感谢**顾客们提出的宝贵意见。

He is not *skilled* at dealing with complaints.

他不**擅长**处理投诉案件。

He is *ignorant* of the international situation.

他对国际形势**一无所知**。

If you wake up in the middle of the night, it might be *tempting* to check the time and see how many more hours you have left before morning. But this is a bad idea.

如果你在半夜醒来，你可能很**想**查看时间，看看自己还能睡多久。殊不知，这种行为是错误的。

4 英语副词转译成汉语动词

当具有动作意义的副词作表语或宾语补足语时，可译成汉语动词。例如：

As he ran out, he forgot to have his shoes *on*.

他跑出去时，忘记**穿**鞋了。

No difficulty can hold us *back*.

没有任何困难能**阻止**我们前进。

I must be *off* now. I have other fish to fry.

我得**告辞**了，我还有别的要紧事要做。

She opened the window to let fresh air *in*.

她把窗子打开，让新鲜空气**进来**。

5.2.2 转译成名词

1 英语动词转译为汉语名词

英语中有很多由名词派生或转用的动词，其概念很难用汉语动词来表达。如果找不到相应的动词，可以将其译成名词。例如：

Most U.S. spy satellites are *designed* to burn up in the earth's atmosphere after completing their missions.

美国绝大多数间谍卫星，按其**设计**，将在完成使命后，在地球的大气层中焚毁。

The design *aims* at automatic operation, easy regulation, simple maintenance, and high productivity.

设计的**目的**在于自动操作，调节方便，维护简易，生产率高。

The products of this factory are chiefly *characterized* by their fine workmanship and durability.

该厂产品的主要**特点**是工艺精湛，经久耐用。

The camel is *characterized* by an ability to go for many days without water.

骆驼的**特点**是能在不喝水的情况下行走多日。

On some vital decisions employees were only *informed* after the fact.

对于一些重大决策，员工在事后才得到**通知**。

2 英语形容词、副词转译成汉语名词

英语中有些表示事物特征的形容词用作表语时，往往转译成汉语名词。有时可以在

其后加"性""度""体"等词。例如：

The waste is safely locked away until it is no longer *radioactive*.

废料被安全锁起来，直到其不再有**辐射性**。

Since humanoids are more *flexible* and capable of adapting to complex terrains, Goldman Sachs analysts believe they can expand the market for industrial automation.

由于仿人机器人更具**灵活性**，能够适应复杂的地形，高盛集团分析师认为它们可以扩大工业自动化市场。

Stevenson was *eloquent and elegant* but soft.

史蒂文森**有口才、有风度**，但很软弱。

Fourth, we need to make market infrastructure more *transparent* and *resilient*.

第四，我们需要提高市场基础设施的**透明度**和**弹性**。

另外，在英语中，"the+形容词"可表示某一类人，这样的形容词有sick、wounded、poor、rich、young、old、blind等。

The *rich* will be asked to contribute money; the *strong* to contribute labor.

有钱出钱，**有力**出力。

We must heal *the wounded*, rescue *the dying*, practicing revolutionary humanitarianism.

我们要救**死**扶**伤**，实行革命的人道主义.

英语中有些副词，尤其是以"-ly"结尾的副词，虽然在句子中作次要成分，但其表达的意义和概念却在句子中占有重要地位。这类副词可转译为汉语名词。如：

He is *physically* weak but *mentally* sound.

他**身体**虽弱，但**思想**健康。

5.2.3　转译成形容词

(1) 英语中一些表示特殊身份或性格特征的名词，如fool、gentleman、master、friend、traitor、knave、blunderer，以及由形容词派生出来的名词，如necessity、stupidity、importance等，在英译汉时可翻译为形容词。例如：

They wanted a generation of Americans conditioned to *loyalty* and *duty*.

他们都希望把下一代美国人训练得**忠于祖国**，**尽职尽责**。

He was always such a *gentleman*.

他总是那么**彬彬有礼**。

He was *blunderer* enough to repeat his mistake.

同样的错误他犯两回，可是够**傻**的。

Even in these days, when divorce is so easy and family ties are supposed to be weak, it would probably be a *mistake* to underestimate the influence of families on presidential politics.

即使在家庭纽带十分脆弱、离婚成了常事的今天，低估了家庭在总统政治中的影响力，也是**错误的**。

(2) 表示时间、地点的副词，常可作名词的后置定语，可译为汉语形容词。例如：

The pressure *inside* equals the pressure *outside*.

内部压力等于**外部**压力。

He could hear someone moving around in the room *above*.

他能听到**楼上**屋里有人走动。

(3) 当英语中动词或形容词被译成汉语中的名词时，原来修饰动词或形容词的副词转换成修饰名词的形容词。例如：

The President had *prepared meticulously* for his journey.

总统为这次出访做了**周密的**准备。

Moncada said that Chinese modernization is the modernization of harmony between humanity and nature, and it *impressed* him *deeply*.

蒙卡达表示，中国的现代化是人与自然和谐共生的现代化，这一点给他留下了**深刻印象**。

(4) 有些表数量的名词，以 "a+(形容词)+名词+of" 形式出现时，可译成形容词。例如：

A good number of houses were destroyed by the fire.

许多房子被大火烧毁。

A group of clever criminals are finding ways to break computer codes.

一群聪明的罪犯正在想方设法来破译计算机密码。

5.2.4 转译成副词

(1) 英语形容词有时需要转译为汉语副词。当英语名词翻译为汉语动词时，修饰该名词的形容词通常要转译成汉语的副词。例如：

Warm discussions arose on every corner as to his achievements.

到处都在**热烈地**讨论他的成就。

He had a *careful* study of the map before he started off.

出发前他**仔细地**研究了地图。

We place the *highest* value on our friendly relations with developing countries.

我们**高度**珍视同发展中国家的友好关系。

(2) 英语名词有时须转译成汉语副词。英语中有些意义抽象的名词或名词短语与句子其他成分之间存在一定的逻辑关系，在这种情况下，可以根据其意义将其转译成汉语副词或相应的状语成分。例如：

I have the *honor* to inform you that your request is granted.

我**荣幸地**通知您，您的请求已得到批准。

The new Mayor earned some appreciation by the *courtesy* of coming to visit the city poor.

新市长**有礼貌地**前来访问城市贫民，获得了他们的一些好感。

It would be wise to handle this delicate problem *with calmness and patience*.

冷静而耐心地处理这个微妙的问题是明智的。

Day and night the nurses took care of the sick.

护士**夜以继日地**照顾着病人。

He is so *heart and soul* with us.

他是如此**真心实意地**和我们站在一起。

(3) 英语动词有时须转译为汉语副词。英语中有些动词具有汉语副词的含义，翻译时可转换成汉语副词。例如：

I *succeeded* in persuading him.

我**成功地**劝说了他。

However, misuse of the medication remains rampant among teenagers who *tend to* make purchases through social media platforms or chat groups.

然而，青少年滥用药物的现象仍然频繁出现，他们**往往**通过社交媒体平台或聊天群进行购买。

综合练习

一、试运用词类转换技巧将下列句子译成汉语。

1.Too much *exposure* to mobile phones will do great harm to the eyesight of children.

2. Rockets have found *application* for the exploration of the universe.

3. The *adoption* of this new device greatly cut down the percentage of defective products.

4. When he *catches a glimpse* of a potential antagonist, his instinct is to win him over with charm and humor.

5. Until such time as mankind *has the sense* to lower its population to the points where the planet can provide a comfortable support for all, people will have to accept more "unnatural food".

6. He is no smoker, but his father is a *chain-smoker*.

7. Unfortunately, I was a bit bossy and I was not a good *listener*.

8. My younger brother is a better *teacher* than I.

9. They are *after* fame and position.

10. *Through* the corridor, you will see his garden.

11. This is not John's fault. He was *against* the plan from the very beginning.

12. We marched on *against* the piercing wind.

13. When the switch is *off*, the electricity circuit is *open*.

14. The *cultivation* of a hobby and new forms of interest is therefore a policy of first *importance* to a public man.

15. The medicine is used in the *treatment* of cancer.

16. The thief made a *trembling confession* of his wrongdoing.

17. An *acquaintance* of world history is helpful to the study of current affairs.

18. A *visit* to his grave is scheduled after *conversation*.

19. There is a big *increase* in demand for all kinds of consumer goods in every part of our country.

20. Several of the ladies wept *at the sight of* so much suffering.

21. They are very much *concerned about* the future of their country.

22. My experience ought to be a warning to those who are too *confident* in their own opinions.

23. Are you *sure* that she is innocent?

24. As he is a perfect *stranger* to the city, I hope you will give him the necessary help.

25. I'm a *stranger* to the operation of computer.

26. We found *difficulty* in controlling the air pollution.

27. He acknowledged the *truth* of his statement.

28. Independent thinking is an absolute *necessity* in study.

29. Your financial support is of *great value* to us.

30. Keeping your head clear is of *great importance*.

31. My *conviction* remains that if you want to make poverty history, you have to make corruption and bad leadership history.

32. The products of this factory are chiefly *characterized* by their fine workmanship and durability.

33. As a result, *the rich* became all the richer.

34. Volvo, the Swedish automotive, energy, and food group, increased its profits by ten point nine percent in the first quarter of this year despite a *fall* of five percent in group turnover.

35. He declared that for himself he was still *for* the Charter, details, name, and all.

36. The dominant factor in the growth of the company throughout the years has been its success in maintaining technical superiority in product design and manufacturing techniques.

参考译文

1. 孩子们看手机过多会大大地损坏视力。

2. 火箭已经用来探索宇宙。

3. 采用这种新装置极大地降低了废品率。

4. 发现有人可能反对他，他就本能地用魅力和幽默征服对方。

5. 除非人类有意识地减少人口数量，使地球能够为所有人提供充足的食物，否则将不得不接受更多的"人造食品"。

6. 他不抽烟，但他爸爸却一支又一支不停地抽。

7. 遗憾的是，我这人有点儿专横，不大善于听取别人的意见。

8. 我弟弟比我教得好。

9. 他们在追求荣誉和地位。

10. 穿过走廊，你就可以看到他的花园了。

11. 这不是约翰的过错，他从一开始就反对这项计划。

12. 我们冒着刺骨的寒风前进。

13. 关闭开关，电路断开。

14. 因此，对公众人物而言，培养业余爱好和新兴趣是头等重要的处世之道。

15. 这种药用于治疗癌症。

16. 小偷战战兢兢地坦白了所干的坏事。

17. 读一点世界史，对学习时事是有帮助的。

18. 讨论后，我们将祭扫他的坟墓。

19. 我国各地对各类消费品的需求都在大幅增长。

20. 其中几位女士看到如此惨状后流泪了。

21. 他们非常关心国家的前途。

22. 我的经历应该给那些太坚信自己意见的人敲响警钟。

23. 你敢肯定她是无辜的吗？

24. 他刚到这座城市，希望你能给予他必要的帮助。

25. 我不熟悉计算机操作。

26. 我们发现控制空气污染很难。

27. 他承认自己说的是实话。

28. 在学习中独立思考是必需的。

29. 您的资金支持对我们意义重大。

30. 保持头脑清醒至关重要。

31. 我依然坚信想让贫困成为历史，就必须让腐败和不良领导成为历史。

32. 该厂产品的主要特点是工艺精湛，经久耐用。

33. 结果，富者更富。

34. 沃尔沃是瑞典汽车、能源和食品集团公司。在总营业额下降5%的情况下，今年第一季度利润增长了10.9%。

35. 他声明，就他本人而言，他仍然拥护《宪章》，拥护《宪章》的具体规章制度、《宪章》名称乃至《宪章》的所有内容。

36. 该公司多年来发展壮大的主要因素是一贯成功地保持了产品设计和制造工艺上的技术优势。

二、将下列语篇译成汉语，注意运用词类转换技巧。

Enchantment of the South Sea Islands

The mighty Pacific washes the shores of five continents — North America, South America, Asia, Australia, and Antarctica. Its waters mingle in the southeast with the Atlantic Ocean and in the southwest with the Indian Ocean. It is not on the shores of continents, nor in the coastal islands, however, that the soul of the great Pacific is found. It lies far out where the fabled South Sea Islands are scattered over the huge ocean like stars in the sky.

Here great disturbances at the heart of the earth caused mountains and volcanoes to rise above the water. For hundreds of years tiny coral creatures have worked and died to make thousands of ring-shaped islands called atolls.

The air that sweeps the South Sea Islands is fragrant with flowers and spice. Bright warm days follow clear cool nights, and the rolling swells break in a never-ending roar on the shores. Overhead the slender coconut palms whisper their drowsy song.

When white men first came to the Pacific Islands, they found that the people living there were like happy children. They were tall men and beautiful women who seemed not to have a care in the world. Coconut palms and breadfruit trees grew at the doors of their huts. The ocean was filled with turtles and fish, ready for the net. The islanders had little need for clothing. There was almost no disease.

Cruel and bloody wars sometimes broke out between neighboring tribes, and canoe raids were sometimes made on nearby islands. The strong warriors enjoyed fighting. Many of the islanders were cannibals, who cooked and ate the enemies they killed. This was part of their law and religion. These savages, however, were usually friendly, courteous, and hospitable. Some of the early explorers were so fascinated with the Pacific Islands that they never returned to their own countries/regions.

Notes and Explanations：

1. the South Sea Islands 南太平洋诸岛；South Sea 南半球诸海洋的，南太平洋的

2. wash *v.* 波涛冲洗、拍打

3. mingle with 混合，汇合(注意此句中方位的表达顺序)

4. fabled *adj.* 虚构的，富有神奇色彩的

5. atoll *n.* 环状珊瑚岛，环礁

6. worked and died 繁衍、死亡

7. rolling swells 滚滚巨浪(注意此句译文中所采用的词类转换技巧)

8. drowsy song 催眠曲

9. filled with turtles and fish, ready for the net 鱼鳖成群，张网可得

10. canoe raid 乘独木舟进行攻击(注意此句中将被动语态转为主动语态的翻译方法)

11. cannibal *n.* 吃人的人

参考译文

迷人的南太平洋诸岛

太平洋气势磅礴，滚滚波涛拍打着五洲海岸——北美洲、南美洲、亚洲、大洋洲和南极洲。太平洋在东南方与大西洋汇合，在西南方与印度洋相接。然而，浩瀚的太平洋最精美之处不在其大陆海岸，也不在沿海诸岛，而是在远离陆地的海域。在那里，富有神奇色彩的南太平洋诸岛像天上的繁星一样散布在广阔的海面上。

那里，由于地心引力的剧烈运动，一道道山脉、一座座火山升出水面。千百年来，微小的珊瑚虫在这里繁衍、死亡，形成了数不胜数的称作环礁的环状岛屿。

散发着鲜花和香料芬芳的微风轻轻地吹拂着南太平洋诸岛。在那里，白日明媚温暖，夜晚清澈凉爽。滚滚浪花拍打着海岸，发出永不休止的轰鸣。头顶上空，纤纤椰树沙沙作响，低声吟唱着令人昏昏欲睡的催眠曲。

白人首次登上这些太平洋海岛时，发现生活在那里的人都像孩子一样欢快。男子身材高大，妇女婀娜多姿，似乎对世上的一切都不用操心。他们茅舍门前长着一丛丛椰子树、面包树；海洋里鱼鳖成群，张网可得。岛上的人几乎不需要穿什么衣服，也几乎见不到任何疾病。

邻近部落之间有时会爆发残酷的血战。他们有时乘独木舟去攻击附近的岛屿。这些强悍的勇士乐于战斗。岛民中的许多居民都有吃人的习俗。他们把杀死的敌人煮熟吃掉。这种习俗是他们的法律和宗教的一部分。然而，这些野蛮人通常是友善、谦恭和好客的。一些早期的探险家因为太迷恋这些太平洋岛屿而不再返回自己的国家/地区。

第6章

翻译技巧(二)增词法

英汉两种语言在词法结构、语法结构和修辞方法上存在差异，因此在翻译过程中，往往会出现词的增加和减少的现象。增词(amplification)就是在译文中增加一些原文字面上没有的词、词组，甚至句子，这是由于英汉两种语言在用词、造句以及思维方式上各有特点。增词有时为了补足语气，有时为了连接上下文，有时则是为了避免译文意义含混。增词是有一定规律可循的，主要体现在词汇、语法、逻辑、修辞和谚语等方面。

一般而言，增词法的运用有两种情况：一种情况是把原文句子里"隐含"(implication)或上下文意思清楚而没有写出来的词补进译文里，以便汉语能清楚地(explicitly)表达原文的意思，也就是说这样的增词是出于语义上的需要；另一种情况则是出于句法上的考虑，把原文中省略的句子成分补充进去，使译文的句子表达完整的意思。

6.1 根据意义上或修辞上的需要增词

由于意义上的需要及英汉语言上的差异，英语中重复用词的情况较少，而汉语为了达到一定的修辞效果，经常使用重叠或排比句，将英语翻译成汉语时常需要在名词前增加动词。

6.1.1 增加动词

在一些情况下，增词就是将原文中虽然无其词而有其意的一些词补进译文里。原句为避免用词重复，可能省去再次出现的相同动词，翻译时要把这些词表达出来；当原句的主语或宾语直译成汉语时，译文可能不通顺或不符合译入语习惯，这种情况下可增译动词。例如：

In every Chinese city, we *got into* the streets, shops, parks, theatres, and restaurants.

在中国，我们每到一个城市就**逛**大街、**购**物、**游**公园、**看**演出、**品**名菜。

My part-time job, my English, and *my old classmates* were more than enough to fill my summer vacation.

我要**做**兼职，**学**英语，还要与老同学**聚聚**，这些占去了我暑假的全部时间。

They *build* roads, houses, bridges, ships, pipelines, and canals.

他们**修**路、**盖**房、**架**桥、**造**船、**铺**管道、**挖**运河。

6.1.2 增加形容词、副词

有时根据上下文，需要在一些名词、动词或形容词前增加恰当的形容词或副词，才能使意思明确。例如：

Army will make a *man* of him.

军队会把他锻炼成一个**堂堂正正的男子汉**。

This is grasping at *straws*.

抓住**救命稻草**。

The crowds *melted away*.

人群**渐渐散开**了。

Inflation has now reached *unprecedented* level.

通货膨胀现在已经发展到**空前严重**的地步。

6.1.3 增加名词

1 在不及物动词后增加名词

英语中有些动词有时用作及物动词，有时用作不及物动词；当用作不及物动词时，其宾语实际上隐含在动词后面，译成汉语时应将隐含的宾语翻译出来。例如：

Mary *washes* before meals.

玛丽饭前**洗手**。

Mary *washes* before going to bed.

玛丽睡前**洗脚**。

Mary *washes* for a living.

玛丽靠**洗衣**度日。

Mary *washes* in a restaurant.

玛丽在饭店**洗碗**。

Their host *carved*, *poured*, *served*, cut bread, talked, laughed, and proposed toasts.

热情的主人又是**切肉**，又是**倒茶**，又是**上菜**，又是切面包，有说有笑，还不断敬酒，忙个不停。

Since her earliest walking period she had been as the right hand of her mother. *Scrubbing*, *baking*, errand-running, and *nursing*—what there had been to do she did.

她很小的时候就是母亲的好帮手：擦地板，烤面包，跑差事，照顾弟弟妹妹，样样都是她做的事儿。

2 在形容词前加名词

英语中的形容词表现力很强，隐含的信息也很丰富。某些形容词本身就暗含了名词的意义，在英译汉时常常需要将隐含的名词补译出来。例如：

This camera is easy to operate, *versatile*, *compact*, and has a pleasing modern design.

这种照相机操作简便，**功能**齐全，**结构**紧凑，造型美观。

Compared with those ones, these cameras are *small*, *light*, and *cheap*.

与那些照相机相比，这些照相机**体积小**、**重量轻**而且**价格便宜**。

Keith: A *little*, *yellow*, *ragged* beggar.

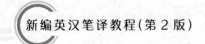

凯斯是个要饭的，**身材矮小，面黄肌瘦，衣衫褴褛**。

3 在抽象名词后增加名词

某些由动词或形容词派生来的抽象名词，翻译时可根据上下文在其后面增添适当的名词，使译文更规范。例如：

to persuade 说服　　persuasion 说服工作

to prepare 准备　　preparation 准备工作

backward 落后的　　backwardness 落后状态

tense 紧张的　　　　tension 紧张局势

arrogant 自满的　　arrogance 自满情绪

mad 疯狂的　　　　madness 疯狂行为

antagonistic 敌对的　antagonism 敌对态度

We were all greatly moved by his *loftiness*.

我们都被他那种**崇高品质**所深深打动。

They wanted to ease the *tension* in the Middle East.

他们试图缓解中东的**紧张局势**。

I was deeply impressed by the *backwardness* of the mountain area.

这一山区的**落后状况**给我留下了深刻印象。

6.1.4　增加表示名词复数的词

汉语名词的复数没有词性变化，很多情况下不必表达出来。但是对于表达多人的名词，可在其后加"们"，如the teachers(教师们)，或者在名词前面加"诸位"或"各位"，如ladies and gentlemen(诸位女士和先生)。此外，翻译英语名词复数时还可以增加重叠词、数词或其他词以表示复数。如：

He stretched his legs which were scattered with *scars*.

他伸出双腿，露出腿上的**道道伤痕**。

Every summer, *tourists* go to the coastal cities.

每到夏季，旅游者**纷纷**涌到海滨城市。

Fortunately "audioblogging" and "GuerillaMedia" did not catch on. But a third did: podcasting, a portmanteau of "iPod" and "broadcasting".

还好，"音频博客"和"游击媒体"**这两个名字**没有流行起来。但是第三个名字火了：播客(podcasting)——一个由"iPod"和"broadcasting"组成的合成词。

Cargo insurance is to protect the trader from *losses* that many dangers may cause.

货物保险旨在使贸易商免受许多风险可能造成的**种种损失**。

Spotify eliminated 200 podcasting jobs; others followed suit.

声破天在播客部门裁员200人，其他公司**纷纷**效仿。

New buildings, massive in span and artful in design, have sprung up everywhere. A plethora of stores and shops have sprouted everywhere.

一幢幢新建的高楼大厦在各处拔地而起，规模宏伟，设计精美。到处冒出了大大小小的数不胜数的商店。

6.1.5　增加表达时态的词

英语动词的时态是靠动词词形变化(如write、wrote)或加助动词(如will write、have written)来表达的。汉语动词没有词形变化，若要表达时态，需要增加汉语特有的时态助词或一些表示时间的词。例如，表达"完成时"往往用"曾""已经""过""了"；表达"进行时"往往用"在""正在""着"；表达"将来时"往往用"将""就""会""便""就要"；等等。除此之外，为了强调时间概念或强调时间上的对比，往往需要增加一些其他表示时间概念的词。例如：

The English language *is* in very good shape. It *is changing* in its own undiscoverable way, but it *is* not *going* rotten like a plum dropping off a tree.

英语**目前**情况很好，**正在**以其不易被察觉的方式发生着变化，而不是像树上掉下来的李子那样**在逐渐**腐烂。

I *had imagined* it to be merely a gesture of affection, but *it seems* it is to smell the lamb and make sure that it is her own.

原来我以为这不过是一种亲热的表示，但是**现在看来**，这是为了闻一闻羊羔的味道来断定它是不是自己生的。

I *knew* it quite well as I *know* it now.

我**当时**和**现在**了解得一样清楚。

The old man *said*, "They *say* his father *was* a fisherman. Maybe he *was* as poor as we *are*."

老头儿说："听人说，**从前**他爸爸是个打鱼的。他**过去**也许跟我们**现在**一样穷。"

6.1.6　增加量词

英语中的数词(包括不定冠词a)与可数名词往往直接连用，它们之间没有量词，而汉语往往借助量词。因此翻译时应根据汉语表达习惯恰当地增加表示其形状、特征或材料等的量词。例如：

first thing 第一件事　　the first oil well 第一口油井　　a carton of cigarette 一条香烟

a bike 一辆自行车　　a computer 一台电脑　　　　a tractor 一台拖拉机

a mouth 一张嘴　　　a full moon 一轮满月　　　　a bad dream 一场噩梦

He was so absorbed in the work that he hasn't had *a bite* since this morning.

他工作得这么专心致志，从早晨到现在连饭都没来得及吃上**一口**。

A red sun rose slowly from the calm lake.

一轮红日从风平浪静的湖面冉冉升起。

Into the dim clouds was swimming *a* crescent moon.

一弯新月渐渐隐入朦胧的云层。

A stream was winding its way through the valley into the river.

一弯溪水蜿蜒流过山谷，汇入江中。

英语中有些动词或动作名词，译成汉语动词时常需要增加一些表示行为、动作量的动量词。例如：have a rest(休息一下)；make a stop(停一下)，等等。

Once, they *have a quarrel*.

有一次，他们争**吵了一番**。

He squeezed his sister too and *gave her a gentle push*.

他也捏了一下他的妹妹并且把她轻轻**推了一下**。

Herb *gave her a sly look*.

赫伯**狡猾**地看了她**一眼**。

I was extremely worried about her, but this was neither the place nor the time for *a lecture* or *an argument*.

我真替她万分担忧，但此时此地，既不宜**教训她一番**，也不宜与她**争论一通**。

6.1.7　增加反映背景信息的词

The *New York Times*, the *Guardian*, *Le Monde*, the *People's Daily*, and the *United Morning Post* all reported the nuclear crises in Korean Peninsula.

美国的《纽约时报》、**英国的**《卫报》、**法国的**《世界报》、**中国的**《人民日报》以及**新加坡的**《联合早报》都对朝鲜半岛的核危机进行了报道。

Duma corresponds to the Senate in America.

俄国杜马相当于美国国会。

The *Pentagon* made no responds to this incident.

五角大楼(指美国国防部)没有对这一事件做出任何反应。

6.1.8　增加概括词

英语和汉语都有概括词。英语中的in short、and so on、etc.等，翻译时可以分别译为"总之""等等""……"。有时候英语句子中没有概括词，而翻译时可增加"两人""双方""等等""凡此种种"等概括词，同时省略英语中的连接词。例如：

We must enable everyone who receives education to develop *morally, intellectually, and physically.*

我们应该使受教育者在德育、智育、体育**三个方面**都得到发展。

They talked about *inflation, unemployment, financial investment, and environmental protection.*

他们谈到了通货膨胀、失业、金融投资以及环境保护**四方面**的问题。

The *Americans and the Japanese* conducted a completely secret exchange of messages.

美日**双方**在完全保密的情况下互相交换了信件。

The thesis summed up the new achievements made in *electronic computers, artificial satellites, and rockets.*

论文总结了电子计算机、人造卫星和火箭**三方面**的新成就。

6.2　根据句法上的需要增词

在了解英语和汉语句法结构的差别，以及准确理解原文的基础上，判断译文在什么地方需要增加词句，才能将原文含义准确表达出来。在翻译中，有时需要增加适当的词，才能准确、通顺地表达原文的思想内容。

6.2.1　增补原文回答句中的省略部分

由于英汉两种语言的表达方式不尽相同，在英语中，有些句子成分可以省略而不会影响全句意思的完整表达，但是翻译成汉语后就可能出现语义不够明确或者句子不够通顺的现象；还有一些词，虽然在英语原文中意义明确而完整，但是翻译成汉语后却不通顺。在这种情况下，就需要使用增词法。

Few children can eat when excited with the thoughts of a journey; *nor* could I.

孩子们一想到要去旅行，心情激动，很少能吃下东西，我同样吃不下去。

Is this your book? Yes, *it is.* 这是你的书吗？**是我的**。(Yes, it is. = Yes, it is mine.)

Rebecca: "What! Don't you love him (Amelia's brother)?" Amelia: "Yes, of course, *I do*."

里贝卡："怎么？你不爱他(爱米丽的哥哥)？"爱米丽："我当然爱他。"

(Yes, of course, I do. = Yes, of course I love him.)

6.2.2　增补原文句子中所省略的动词

Reading *makes* a full man; conference (...) a ready man; writing (...) an exact man.

读书**使人**充实，讨论**使人**机智，写作**使人**准确。

An eagle and a fox had long *lived* together as good neighbors: the eagle (...) at the summit of a high tree; the fox (...) in a hole at the foot of it.

一只鹰和一只狐狸长期友好地**住**在一起，鹰**住**在高高的树顶上，狐狸**住**在树下的洞里。

We don't *retreat*; we never have (...) and never will (...).

我们不**后退**，我们从没有**后退**过，将来也决不**后退**。

6.2.3　增补原文比较句中的省略部分

Better be wise by the defeat of others than *by your own*.

从别人的**失败中**吸取教训比从**自己的失败**中吸取教训更好。

He is more *concerned* about others than about himself.

他**关心**别人胜于**关心**自己。

The footmen were as ready to *serve* her as they were their own mistress.

仆人们愿意**服侍**她，就像愿意**服侍**自己的女主人一样。

$$综合练习$$

一、将下列句子译成汉语。

1. Not to educate him (the child) is to condemn him to repetitious *ignorance*.

2. *Oxidation* will make iron and steel rusty.

3. This *lack of resistance* in very cold metals may become useful in electronic computers.

4. You have to overcome your *complacency*.

5. What a *leader* he is!

6. What a *sight*!

7. He was always looking for a shortcut to *fame and fortune*.

8. Miss Havisham sent her out to *attract* and *torment* and do mischief, with the malicious assurance that she was beyond the reach of all admirers.

9. Aunt Harriet used to *entertain* lavishly.

10. This computer is indeed *cheap and fine*.

11. He is a *complicated* man—*moody*, *mercurial*, with a *melancholy streak*.

12. He allowed the *father* to be overruled by the *judge*, and declared his own son guilty.

13. In general, the metals are good conductors, with silver *the best* and copper *the second*.

14. Courage in excess becomes foolhardiness, affection *weakness*, thrift *avarice*.

15. The molecules of hydrogen get closer and closer with the *pressure*.

16. Mary *washes* after getting up.

17. Sept. 11 delivered both a shock and a surprise—*the attack*, and *our response to it*—and we can argue forever over which mattered more.

18. He was *wrinkled* and *black*, with scant gray hair.

19. Man, *was*, *is*, and always *will be* trying to improve his living conditions.

20. When I turned around, John was grinning, *expectant*, studying my face intently to see if he had pleased me. He *had*.

21. Fortune knocks at every man's door once in a life, but in a good many cases, the man is in a neighboring saloon and does not hear *her*.

22. They *had always been* able to control things. *Now* control *was getting away* from all of them.

23. We *don't regret*, we *never have had*, and we *never will*.

24. I *was*, and *remain*, grateful for the part he played in my release.

25. I *had* never thought I'd be happy to find myself considered unimportant. But this time I *was*.

26. Can you manage *without* help?

27. *Past retirement age*, Dr. Masefield is as vigorous as ever.

28. Hydrogen burns in air or oxygen, *forming* water.

参考译文

1. 如果我们不对儿童进行教育，那么他们将会陷入世世代代的愚昧状态。

2. 氧化作用会使钢铁生锈。

3. 这种在超低温中金属电阻降为零的现象，可能会在电子计算机中发挥作用。

4. 你必须克服自满情绪。

5. 他真是一个出类拔萃的领袖！

6. 多么美的景色啊！

7. 他一直在寻觅成名、致富的捷径。

8. 郝薇香小姐把她放出去招蜂引蝶，去折磨男人，去害男人，其恶毒用心就是让追求她的男人对她永远望尘莫及。

9. 哈丽特阿姨过去时常慷慨地款待客人。

10. 这台电脑真是物美价廉。

11. 他是一个性格复杂的人——喜怒无常，反复多变，有些忧郁寡欢。

12. 法官的责任感战胜了父子私情，他最终宣判自己的儿子有罪。

13. 一般来说，金属都是良好的导体，其中以银为最好，铜次之。

14. 勇敢过度，即成蛮勇；感情过度，即成溺爱；俭约过度，即成贪婪。

15. 随着压力的增加，氢分子间距逐渐减小。

16. 玛丽起床后洗脸。

17. 9·11事件带给我们的是震惊和意外——令人震惊的是这场袭击，令人意外的是我们对这一事件的反应，至于哪一个更要紧，我们可能会永远争论不休。

18. 他满脸皱纹，皮肤黝黑，头发灰白稀疏。

19. 人类过去、现在和将来一直在努力改善自己的生活条件。

20. 我转过身，只见约翰正咧着嘴笑，满脸期待的神情；他热切的目光想从我的脸上探明他是否博得了我的欢心。他确实博得了我的欢心。

21. 每个人的一生中，幸运女神都只来敲一次门，可是许多情况下，那个受到眷顾的人竟在隔壁的酒馆里，听不见她敲门。

22. 他们从前一向是能够控制局面的，现在局势失控了。

23. 我们不后悔，我们从来就没后悔过，我们将来也不会后悔。

24. 我的获释是他成全的，对此我过去很感激，现在仍然很感激。

25. 以往我从未想过，当我发觉人们认为我无足轻重时，我会感到高兴。但这次情况确实如此。

26. 如果没有人帮忙，你能应付得了吗？

27. 虽然已经过了退休年龄，可梅斯费乐德博士仍然和以前一样精力充沛。

28. 氢气在空气或氧气中燃烧，就会形成水。

二、将下列语篇翻译成汉语。

China launched an unmanned module on Thursday containing what will become living quarters for three crew on a permanent space station that it plans to complete by the end of 2022, state media reported. The module, named "Tianhe", or "Harmony of the Heavens", was launched on the Long March 5B, China's largest carrier rocket, at 11:23 a.m. (03:23 GMT) from the Wenchang Space Launch Centre on the southern island of Hainan.

Tianhe is one of three main components of what would be China's first self-developed space station, rivalling the only other station in service—the International Space Station (ISS). The ISS is backed by the United States, Russia, Europe, Japan, and Canada. In contrast, the fate of the ageing ISS — in orbit for more than two decades—remains uncertain. The project is set to expire in 2024, barring funding from its partners. Russia said this month that it would quit the project from 2025.

The Tianhe launch was the first of 11 missions which it will take to construct and outfit the space station with everything it needs in order to host its initial crew. Unlike the International Space Station which can hold six comfortably and up to eight if needed, China's space station will initially be capable of supporting up to three astronauts at once. That number could change dramatically in the future if China decides to further build out the station and add new modules and new living areas. In the later missions, China will launch two other core modules, four manned spacecraft, and four cargo spacecraft. At least 12 astronauts of both genders are training to fly to and live in the station, including veterans of precious flights and newcomers. When completed by late 2022, China's space station is expected to weigh about 66 tons.

After years of successful rocket and commercial satellite launches, China put its first astronaut into space in October 2003. It was only the third country/region to independently do so.

Since that ShenZhou-5 mission, China has sent other astronauts into orbit, placed crew on the original Tiangong Station, and conducted a space walk. The launch of a space lab Tiangong-1 in 2011 and Tiangong-2 in 2016 helped China test the program's space rendezvous and docking capabilities. China plans another mission in 2024 to bring back lunar samples and to land people on the moon, and possibly build a scientific base there. No timeline has been proposed for such projects. China aims to become a major space power by 2030. It has ramped its space program with visits to the moon, the launch of an uncrewed probe to Mars, and the construction of its own space station. The Chinese space agency has been moving fast in its aim to catch up to the U.S. and Russia in the new space race.

——2022年6月CATTI英语三级笔译实务真题

参考译文1

官方媒体报道称，中国于本周四成功发射无人太空舱，这将成为永久空间站三名机组人员的生活区，计划于2022年底前完成整体拼装。该核心舱名为"天和"，于本周四上午11:23(格林尼治标准时间03:23)搭乘中国规模最大的运载火箭——长征五号B运载火箭，在海南岛南部的文昌航天发射中心成功发射。

天和核心舱是中国首个自主研发空间站的三大主要模块之一。中国空间站堪与目前唯一在役的另一空间站——国际空间站(ISS)媲美。国际空间站目前由美国、俄罗斯、欧盟、日本、加拿大共同运营。虽然国际空间站在轨运行了二十多年,但目前状况尚不明确。如果合作伙伴不再提供项目资金,国际空间站项目将于2024年宣告到期失效。本月,俄罗斯表示将在2025年退出该项目。

建成空间站并为其配备所需的一切,以便正式接纳第一批宇航员入驻,整个过程共需要完成11次发射任务,发射天和核心舱是11次任务中的首次。国际空间站比较宽敞,可以轻松容纳6到8名宇航员,而中国空间站最初一次至多只能容纳3名宇航员。若中国日后决定扩建空间站,新增模块,开拓生活区,则容纳人数还可显著增加。中国还会在后续发射任务中发射另外两个核心模块、四艘载人飞船和四艘货运飞船。目前中国共有至少12名宇航员正在接受培训,其中有男性,也有女性,既有经验丰富的航天老将,也有资历尚浅的航天新人,他们将会飞向太空,入驻空间站生活。2022年末中国空间站将完全建成,总重预计为66吨。

经过多年努力,中国成功发射火箭与商用飞船,并在2003年10月将第一名宇航员送上太空,一跃成为世界上第三个独立成功发射载人航天飞船的国家/地区。

神舟五号发射任务圆满完成之后,中国将其他多名宇航员送入太空,在原有的天宫空间站完成太空行走。2011年,空间实验室天宫一号发射成功,2016年,天宫二号发射成功,帮助中国测试了空间站的空间交会对接能力。中国计划在2024年启动另外一项太空任务,带回月球样品,实现宇航员登月,极可能在月球上设立科研基地,但是具体时间安排尚未发布。中国有志在2030年前发展成为世界航天强国,现已加大发展航天项目的力度,包括探月工程、发射火星探测器、建造自己的空间站等。中国航天局正在努力加快步伐,力求在新的一轮航空竞赛中,赶超美国和俄罗斯。

第7章
翻译技巧(三)重复法

  翻译作为语际交流，不仅是语言的转换过程，而且是文化移植的过程。王佐良先生曾经说过："翻译的最大困难是两种文化的不同。"因此，解决好翻译中文化差异的问题是保证译作成功的关键。

  英语中的反复(repetition)也是一种极常用的修辞格，用于强调某种事物的意义，以形成优美的节奏。但从总体上说，英语是一种忌重复(redundancy)的语言，主张"言以简洁为贵"(Brevity is the soul of wit.)；为了强调，英语有时也使用重复手段，但一般不重复原词，多用代词复指以使行文简练。

  英语回避重复的主要方法：指代法——代词；换词法——范畴词、同义词或准同义词；替代法——替代词语和替代句型；省略法——省略相同的词语；保留介词法；紧缩法。

7.1 重复的意义

"汉语的重复作为一种修辞手段有两种作用。一是为了强调，重复表达一个意思，或增添修饰语，加强语义。二是为了便于词语搭配，或平衡节奏，增加可读性。"前者称为语义性重复，后者称为修辞性重复。这些具有重复语义的词语或句子，可有效地增强语势、强化语义、增强表达效果。

汉语喜欢重复，英语崇尚简洁，这是中西方审美心理差异所形成的不同的审美标准，汉译英时对于汉语的重复词语或重复结构必须有所删减，以使译文适应读者的审美心理，符合英语的表达习惯。

汉语中的某些成语为了音韵整齐、语义对称而使用两组同义词，译成英语时往往只需要译出其中一组词义，以避免重复。例如：

花言巧语 ——fine words

油嘴滑舌 ——glib-tongued/a smooth tongue

捕风捉影 ——to catch at shadows

铜墙铁壁 ——bastion of iron/Guards and Wards

精疲力竭 ——exhausted/be worn out/be run down/be tired out

随波逐流 ——to swim with the stream

水深火热 ——in deep waters

咬牙切齿 ——to gnash one's teeth

土崩瓦解 ——to fall apart

自吹自擂 ——to blow one's own trumpet

汉语讲究句子的平衡、气势或音韵节奏，为此，常连续使用两组结构相似、语义相同的平行结构，译成英语时往往只需要译出其中一组词义。如：

此时鲁小姐卸了浓妆，换几件雅淡衣服，公子举目细看，**真有沉鱼落雁之容，闭月羞花之貌**。(吴敬梓：《儒林外史》)

By this time Miss Lu had changed out of her ceremonial dress into an ordinary gown, and then Zhu looked at her closely. *He saw that her beauty would put the flowers to shame.*

句中"沉鱼落雁之容"和"闭月羞花之貌"都是形容女性之娇美，这种对仗的修辞形式有结构对称、增强语势之效，读起来还具有音韵之美，翻译时译出主要语义即可。

英语中代词的使用频率大大高于汉语，对于汉语中重复出现的名词，翻译时可用相应的代词指称汉语名词，这是避免重复、简化译文语句的有效方法。

此外，汉语和英语中的排比句是一种常见的、富有表现力的修辞手法，通常采用三个或三个以上结构相同、语义相关、语气连贯的词组或句子排列成串，以达到"壮文势，广文义"的目的；但英语的排比强调结构上的整齐匀称，汉语的排比不仅强调齐整美，还强调反复美。相同词语反复出现是形式整齐的汉语排比修辞的重要标志。对于汉语排比句的翻译，有时可照原文结构直译，但有时为适应英美读者"言贵简洁"的审美心理，对其中反复出现的共同词语或结构必须予以简化，以使译文符合英语的表达习惯。

英语重替代，汉语重重复。在英语中，除非有修辞需要，否则很少在句子中重复使用同一个词或结构，而在汉语中重复现象比比皆是。英语为避免重复多按语法形式进行省略，如省略所有格、形容词和介词后面的名词，省略助动词、不定式后面的动词以及系动词后面的表语。主谓一致时，往往使用代词、同义词、近义词及代替句型等来替代前文出现过的词语和结构。汉语则倾向于使用相同的词语或结构呼应前文出现过的词语或结构。我们来看下面的例子：

We must *adhere* to the socialist road, the people's democratic dictatorship(i.e. the dictatorship of the proletariat), the Communist Party's leadership, and Marxism-Leninism and Mao Zedong Thought.

我们必须**坚持**社会主义道路，**坚持**人民民主专政(即无产阶级专政)，**坚持**共产党的领导，**坚持**马列主义、毛泽东思想。

Let us stretch out our arms to embrace *spring*, which is *one* of the revolutions, of the people, and of science.

这是革命的**春天**，这是人民的**春天**，这是科学的**春天**！让我们张开双臂，热烈拥抱这个**春天**吧！

汉族历来有求偶对称的审美心理，崇尚对称工整所造就的形式美。中国古代四方形的城郭，北京的四合院民居，故宫、庙宇中的四方形大殿等，无不流露着"对称工整"的审美构思。《周易·系辞》记述："易有太极，是生两仪，两仪生四象，四象生八卦。"这也许是汉族求偶对称的心理渊源。

汉语成语大多采用四字结构，古诗赋和骈文也常采用四字句的行文格式，此外还有大量的按固定格式形成的"四字格"，由于它们读起来铿锵悦耳，结合排比修辞手法，颇有行云流水或势如破竹之感，对人们的日常表达和文学语言有着广泛而深远的影响，故四字结构在汉语中是非常常见的语言现象。例如：

Sunset dances; nightlife sings under a star-filled sky; moonlight drips soft silver to tuck you in. This is the Sheraton Bal Harbour Resort where the days hesitate to end and the memories linger forever.

在繁星密缀的天宇之下，夕阳翩翩起舞，夜之生灵尽情歌唱；月华轻柔，流银泻玉，把你俩舒适地裹在其中。这就是喜来登港湾旅游胜地。这里幸福时光恋恋不舍，美好记忆长萦脑际。

——肖新英(译)

上文摘自喜来登酒店广告。原文文字清新优雅，流畅自然，充分显示了英语广告的语言魅力。对应的汉语译文保留了原文的修辞手段、形象和意境，同时遵循汉语的表达习惯，灵活运用四字词语和叠韵短语。排比结构朗朗上口，大大增强了节奏感，汉语的可吟唱性跃然纸上，一幅引人入胜、令人陶醉的海滨度假美景呼之欲出。

江岸上彩楼林立，彩灯高悬，旌旗飘摇，呈现出一派喜气洋洋的节日场面。千姿百态的各式彩龙在江面上游弋，舒展着优美的身姿，有的摇头摆尾，风采奕奕；有的喷火吐水，威风八面。

High-rise buildings ornamented with colored lanterns and bright banners stand out along the river banks. On the river itself, gaily decorated dragon-shaped boats await their challenge, displaying their individual charms to their hearts' content. One boat wags its head and tail; another spits fire and sprays water.

原文辞藻华丽，文采斐然，描述生动，场面壮观；但若照原文直译，则原文的结构和过多的修饰语会使译文累赘冗余，令人厌读，很可能产生适得其反的效果。译者充分考虑了西方读者的审美情趣，灵活处理了中英文在行文习惯上的差异，调整句子长度并删去了"呈现出一派喜气洋洋的节日场面""风采奕奕""威风八面"等词句，通过"gaily decorated"和"displaying their individual charms to their hearts' content"，以简洁明快的语句，表达原文中龙舟赛场壮观热烈的气氛和千姿百态的龙舟风采。

7.2 重复法的应用

重复法是指在译文中适当地重复原文中出现过的词语，以使意思表达得更加清楚；或者进一步加强语气，突出某些内容，以收到更好的修辞效果。一般而言，英语往往为了行文简洁而尽量避免重复。所以，英语经常借助替代、省略或变换等其他表达方法。相反，重复却是汉语表达的一个显著特点。在许多场合不仅需要重复某些词语，而且只有重复这些词语，才能使语义明确，表达生动。为了使汉语译文达到准确、通顺和完整的标准，在翻译中，常常需要对一些关键性的词加以重复。

7.2.1　重复名词

重复英语中作宾语或表语的名词。例如：

Marketing economy is itself the *product* of long course of development, of a series of revolutions in the modes of production and of exchange.

市场经济本身是一个长期发展过程的**产物**，是生产方式和交换方式一系列变革的**产物**。

The three most important *effects* of electric current are heating, magnetic, and chemical effects.

电流最重要的三种**效应**就是热**效应**、磁**效应**和化学**效应**。

7.2.2　重复动词

英语句子中"动词+介词"结构在第二次或者第三次出现时往往省略动词，在汉语译文中则要重复动词。例如：

He encouraged this bumptious young man to *write* of his own region—of its bleak poverty and of its women old before their time.

他鼓励这个狂妄的年轻人**写**自己的故乡——**写**故乡的荒凉和贫困，**写**故乡未老先衰的女人。

Then he *spoke of* the rise of charity and popular education, and in particular of the spread of wealth and work.

接着他**谈到**了慈善事业的兴起和教育的普及，特别**谈到**了财富和工作面的扩大。

But his wife kept *dinning* in his ears *about* his idleness, his carelessness, and the ruin he was bringing on his family.

可他老婆总在他耳边**唠叨**个没完。**说**他懒惰，**说**他粗心，还**说**一家人都要毁在他身上。

7.2.3　重复代词

(1) 英语代词的使用非常频繁，而汉语中除非必要，一般不宜多用代词。因此，在翻译中，除了适当地将原文中的一些代词直译外，还经常将某些代词所替代的名词重复译出，以使译文意思清楚明了。例如：

Even as the doctor was recommending *rest*, he knew that *this* in itself was not enough, that one could never get real rest without a peaceful mind.

尽管医生建议**休息**，但他知道**休息**本身是不够的，如果心情不平静，是休息不好的。

Jesse opened his *eyes*. *They* were filled with tears.

杰西睁开**眼睛**，眼里充满了泪水。

He hated *failure*; he had conquered *it* all his life, risen above *it*, and despised *it* in others.

他讨厌**失败**，他一生中曾战胜**失败**，超越**失败**，并且藐视别人的**失败**。

(2) 当英语用物主代词its、his、their等代替句中作主语的名词(有时附有修饰语)时，译文往往可以不用代词而重复其作主语的名词(有时附有修饰语)，以使其指代明确清晰。

Big powers have *their* strategies while *small countries* also have *their* own lines.

强国有**强国**的策略，**小国**有**小国**的路线。

Happy families also had *their own* troubles.

幸福的家庭也有**幸福家庭**的苦恼。

Each country has *its own* customs.

各国有**各国**的风俗。

(3) 在翻译英语中的关系代词which、that或关系副词whoever、whenever、wherever等时，有时使用重复法处理。

As each currency's *value* is stated in terms of other currencies, French francs, then, have a value in U.S. dollars, *which* have a value in British pounds, *which* have a value in Japanese yen.

由于每一种货币的价值都需要通过其他货币体现出来，因此，法国法郎的价值可以通过美元体现，**美元价值**可通过英镑体现，而**英镑价值**可通过日元体现。

Needs are the basic, often instinctive, human *forces that* motivate a person to do something.

需要是一种本能，也是人类最基本的驱动力，这些**驱动力**激励人们去行动。

Wherever there is oppression, there is resistance.

哪里有压迫，**哪里**就有反抗。

7.2.4　其他情况下的重复

(1) 在重复法中，有时采用两字重叠、四字重叠或四字对偶等修辞手段，使译文更生动。

There has been too much *publicity* about that case.

这件事已经闹得**满城风雨**，**沸沸扬扬**。

Easy *come*, easy *go*.

来得容易**去得**快。

No pains, *no* gains.

一分耕耘，一分收获。

Nothing venture, *nothing* gain.

不入虎穴，焉得虎子。

(2) 为了强调，英语中往往重复关键词，以加深读者/听者的印象。英译汉时可以采用同样的手段。英文中有重复的词，译文也重复同样的词。

And that government of *the people*, by *the people*, for *the people*, shall not perish from the earth.

并且使这个民有、民治、民享的政府永世长存。

Gentlemen may cry *peace*, but there is no *peace*.

先生们尽管高喊和平，和平，但是依然没有和平。

Kids are *kids*.

孩子终究是孩子。

综合练习

一、将下列句子译成汉语。

1. You can *do* that work very well if you care to.

2. Light *travels* more quickly than sound does.

3. People use natural science to understand and change *nature*.

4. A good play serves to educate and inspire *the people*.

5. Students must be cultivated to have the ability to analyze and solve *problems*.

6. For the purpose of attaining freedom in the world of nature, man must use natural science to understand, conquer, and change *nature*.

7. We *talked* of ourselves, of our prospects, of the journey, of the weather, of each other—of everything.

8. Ignorance is *the mother* of fear as well as of admiration.

9. *Whoever* violates the disciplines should be criticized.

10. *Wherever* there is matter, there is motion.

11. The use of poison gas is a clear *violation* of international law—in particular of the *Geneva Convention*.

12. For China, the first thing is to *throw off* poverty. To do that, we have to find a way to develop fairly rapidly.

13. "Stop thief! Stop thief!" There is a magic in the sound. The tradesman *leaves* his

counter, and the carman his wagon; the butcher *throws down* his tray, the baker his basket, the milkman his pail, the errand-boy his parcels, the schoolboy his marbles, the pavior his pickaxe, and the child his battledore.

14. "Oh," thought she, "I have been very wicked and *selfish*—selfish in forgetting their sorrows—selfish in forcing George to marry me. I *know* I am not worthy of his—I know he would have been happy without me—and yet—I *tried*, I tried to give him up."

参考译文

1. 如果你肯做那项工作，你就能做得很好。

2. 光传播的速度要比声音传播的速度快得多。

3. 人们利用自然科学来理解自然，改变自然。

4. 一部好的电视剧可以教育人，启发人。

5. 必须培养学生分析问题和解决问题的能力。

6. 人为了在自然界里得到自由，必须用自然科学来了解自然、征服自然和改造自然。

7. 我们谈到自己，谈到前途，谈到旅程，谈到天气，谈到彼此的情况——谈到一切事情。

8. 无知是羡慕的根源，也是恐惧的根源。

9. 谁违反了纪律，谁就应该受到批评。

10. 哪里有物质，哪里就有运动。

11. 毒气的使用明显违背了国际法，尤其违背了《日内瓦公约》。

12. 对于中国，首要的事情就是摆脱贫穷，而为了摆脱贫穷，我们必须找到一条快速发展的道路。

13. "捉贼！捉贼！"这个声音里有一种魔力。商人离开了柜台，赶车的离开了车子，屠夫放下了盆子，面包师放下了篮子，挤牛奶的放下了提桶，杂役放下了包裹，小学生丢下弹子，铺路工人丢下尖锄，小孩子丢下球拍。

14. 她暗暗想到："唉，我真恶劣，真自私。爸爸妈妈那么可怜，我不把他们放在心上，又硬要嫁给乔治，可见我只顾自己。我明知自己配不上他，明知他不娶我也很快乐，可是——我努力叫自己松了手让他去吧，可是总狠不下心。"

二、将以下语篇译成汉语。

Today we have higher buildings and wider highways, but shorter temperaments and narrower points of view;

We spend more, but enjoy less;

We have bigger houses, but smaller families;

We have more compromises, but less time;

We have more knowledge, but less judgment;

We have more medicines, but less health;

We have multiplied our possessions, but reduced our values;

We talk much, we love only a little, and we hate too much;

We reached the moon and came back, but we find it troublesome to cross our own street and meet our neighbors;

We have conquered the outer space, but not our inner space;

We have higher income, but less morals;

These are times with more liberty, but less joy;

We have much more food, but less nutrition;

These are the days in which it takes two salaries for each home, but divorces increase;

These are times of finer houses, but more broken homes;

That's why I propose that as of today;

You do not keep anything for a special occasion, because every day that you live is a SPECIAL OCCASION.

Search for knowledge, read more, sit on your porch, and admire the view without paying attention to your needs;

Spend more time with your family and friends, eat your favorite food, and visit the places you love;

Life is a chain of moments of enjoyment; not only about survival;

Use your crystal goblets.

Do not save your best perfume, and use it every time you feel you want it.

Remove from your vocabulary phrases like "one of these days" or "someday";

Let's write that letter we thought of writing "one of these days"!

Let's tell our family and friends how much we love them;

Do not delay anything that adds laughter and joy to your life;

Every day, every hour, and every minute is special;

And you don't know if it will be your last.

参考译文

今天我们拥有了更高的楼宇以及更宽阔的公路，但是我们的性情却更为急躁，眼光也更加狭隘；

我们消耗的更多，享受到的却更少；

我们的住房变大了,但我们的家庭却变小了;

我们妥协更多,时间更少;

我们拥有了更多的知识,可判断力却变差了;

我们有了更多的药品,但健康状况却更不如意了;

我们拥有的财富倍增,但其价值却减少了;

我们说的多了,爱的却少了,我们的仇恨也变多了;

我们可以抵达月球并返回地球,但却难以迈出一步去亲近我们的左邻右舍;

我们可以征服外太空,却征服不了我们的内心;

我们的收入增加了,但道德却少了;

我们的时代更加自由了,但我们拥有的快乐时光却越来越少;

我们有了更多的食物,但所能得到的营养却越来越少了;

现在每个家庭都可以有双份收入,但离婚的现象却越来越多了;

现在的住房越来越精致了,但却出现了更多破碎的家庭;

这就是我为什么要说,让我们从今天开始;

不要将你的东西留给某一个特别的时刻,因为你生活的每一天都是那么特别。

探求知识,多读一些书,坐在你家的门廊里,欣赏眼前的风景,不要带上任何功利的想法;

多花点时间和亲朋好友在一起,吃你爱吃的食物,去你想去的地方;

生活是一串串的快乐时光;我们并不是仅为了生存而生存;

举起你的水晶酒杯吧。

不要舍不得洒上你最好的香水,想用的时候就享用吧。

从你的词汇库中移去所谓的"有朝一日"或者"某一天";

曾打算"有朝一日"写的信,就在今天写吧!

告诉家人和朋友,我们有多爱他们;

不要延迟任何可以给你的生活带来欢笑与快乐的事情;

每一天、每一小时、每一分钟都是那么特别;

你无从知道这是不是最后一刻。

第8章

翻译技巧(四)省略法

英语和汉语在语法上差异较大，例如：英语有冠词，而汉语却没有；英语重形合，连接词较多，而汉语重意合，连接词较少；英语中介词丰富，至少有280个，汉语中介词则较少，只有三十几个；英语中经常使用代词，尤其是人称代词、关系代词等，而汉语中代词用得较少。因此，英译汉时可根据具体情况将冠词、连接词、介词、代词等略去，使译文简练、通畅。

省略法(omission)，也称为减省译法，是指在翻译中，原文中有些词在译文中可以省略，不必翻译出来，因为译文中虽然没有这个词，但是已经具有了原文这个词所表达的意思，或者这个词在译文中的意义是不言而喻的。

一般来说，汉语比英语简练。在英汉翻译中，许多在原文中必不可少的词语若要原原本本地译成汉语，就会成为不必要的冗词，译文会显得十分累赘，因此省略法在英译汉中使用得非常广泛，其主要目的是删去一些可有可无、不符合译入语习惯表达法的词语，如实词中代词、动词的省略，虚词中冠词、介词和连词的省略等，使译文更加通顺流畅，更符合译入语表达习惯。使用省略法时要遵循如下原则：不能把原文的某些思想内容删去，且不能改变原文的意思。

汉语意合句多，不强调形式上的完整，只要不妨碍意义的表达，即可省去形式上的东西；英语形合句多，注重把各种关系用语言形式表达出来。因此，在汉译英时往往需要增补必要的关联词(连词、介词等)；在英译汉时则往往可以省去这些关联词。

8.1 按句法需要省略

有些词语在英语中使用得比较广泛(如关联词、代词)，或不能随便省略(如冠词、介词、连系动词等)，而在汉语中却使用得较少或可以省略；有些词语在汉语中使用得比较广泛(如范畴词、量词、语气助词等)，而在英语中却可以省略或较少使用。

8.1.1 省略代词

滥译代词，与滥译冠词一样，是造成生硬牵强的"翻译腔"的重要原因。相对于英语，汉语中经常省略主语。这种人称代词的省略实际上是采用零前指(zero anaphora)的照应形式进行语篇的衔接。请看下面的例子：

贾母一面说，一面来看宝玉，只见今日这顿打，不比往日，又是心疼，又是生气，也抱着哭个不了。(曹雪芹《红楼梦》)

From the sight that met *her* eyes *she* could tell that this has been no ordinary beating. *It* filled *her* with anguish for *the* sufferer and fresh anger for *the* man *who* had inflicted it, and for a long time *she* clung to the inert form and wept... (D. Hawkes, Trans. *The Story of the Stone*)

上文是摘自《红楼梦》中的一段话。原文中主语"贾母"只在段首出现一次，之后就全部省略了。而在大卫·霍克斯(David Hawkes)的英译本中，所有的句子都有主语，而且为了避免重复，前文中出现的具体名词在后文中用代词替代，这体现了汉英两种语言在句法表达上的差异。

李讷和汤普森指出，汉语中零式指称的使用远多于英语，并且由于汉语是意合语言，零式指称不受句法限制。他们通过实验，得出"零式指称才是汉语的常规"这一结论。鉴于李讷和汤普森的语料取自中国古典白话小说，胡壮麟(1994)又从现代汉语的角度加以说明。许余龙(1992)对三部现代汉语小说中的零前指照应和人称照应进行了分析，发现零前指的运用受以下因素的影响。

(1) 篇章的信息结构和结构特征。例如，当段落中相连句子的话题涉及同一个人或事物，构成一个话题链时；或者当段落中相连的句子都比较短且结构简单时，就倾向于采用零前指。

(2) 篇章的整体语义因素和局部语义因素。例如，如果某一人或事物是整个篇章语义结构的组织核心；各句中动词、名词等成分表达的施事、动作、受事等关系能表达哪类人干哪类事，且前后句子间联系明显，就容易出现零前指。

(3) 语用因素。作者一般都遵守合作原则，如果他认为读者能确定零前指的照应项，则会倾向于使用零前指。

(4) 语体风格因素。在法律文件、科技文体等正规、严谨的文体中，零前指的使用频率会大大降低。

(5) 主题显著。只有在主题显著的语言里才能采用零前指的形式。汉语是主题显著的语言，零前指的使用符合汉语重意合、具有开放性、竹节式结构的特点。

在语篇行文与表达习惯上，英语与汉语的重要差异之一就是代词的使用频率不同。英语中每个句子(包括从句)都有主语，但汉语却习惯于：前一部分已有主语，后一部分的主语如果与前一部分的相同，则要求省去，以免重复。在中国古典文学之精华的唐诗宋词元曲中，代词使用频率极低。通读《宋词三百首》，很难找出50个代词来。例如：

昨夜西风凋碧树，

( )独上高楼，

( )望尽天涯路。

( ) 欲寄[ ]彩笺兼尺素，

山长水阔( )知[ ]何处。

——晏殊《蝶恋花》

原文中实际上一个代词都没有，若用形式化句法进行分析，可以认为原文省略了括号中的六个代词——四个(我) 两个[你]。

而对于英语，代词的使用极为频繁，原因多样。从语法上讲，英语作为印欧形态语言的一支，句子主谓二分，主语不可省略；及物动词必有宾语，介词必有宾语。而为了避免不断地重复名词词组，这些主语、宾语之类就常常使用代词。另外，物主代词的使用也常为英语的语法要求。如"He put a book on his head"中"his"就是语法上必须有的。

英语和汉语在代词使用频率上的差异，有诗为证：

松下问童子，

言师采药去。

只在此山中，

云深不知处。

——贾岛《寻隐者不遇》

其英语译文为：

A Note Left for an Absent Recluse

I ask your lad neath a pine-tree.

"My master's gone for herbs," says he.

125

"Amid the hills I know not where,

For clouds have veiled them here and there."

——许渊冲(译)

原诗中任何形式的代词都没有，而许渊冲的译文使用了6个人称代词。

中国语言学家申小龙研究汉语特点时，打破了"主谓二分"的印欧语言句子观对汉语的束缚，提出全新的汉语句型系统：主题句、施事句、关系句三分天下。其中，施事句成分包括时空坐标、施事者、事件，但只有事件是必不可少的核心，这个核心是动词组的铺排，而不是带主语的小句。

《人民日报》上有一例语篇是一位14岁英国男孩写的汉语短文，对英汉翻译很有启示意义。短文内容如下：

今年我在英国上学，**我的**学校是一个寄宿学校。第一个月时，我人生地不熟，但**我的**朋友很友好，所以那学期过得很快。**我的**学校里有很多同学，**他们**分别来自日本、英国、中国、法国和德国。在**我们的**学校里你能做不少的事情。

——安(英国)

英国男孩写此短文时，学汉语已有五年。从这篇短文来看，他的汉语水平还是很不错的，然而很明显，他受母语的影响，用了过多的代词。实际上六个黑体代词统统可以省略，而且六个代词的省略不仅不会导致意义含混，还会使短文更地道，更接近中国人的自然表达。

从这篇短文的遣词造句可以猜测，这很可能是男孩先用英语思考，后用汉语翻译的产物，像最后一句话有可能译自"In our school you can do a lot of things."。六个代词若回译过去，正好都是英文必须使用代词之处。这篇短文的"外国味"主要反映在代词的过多使用上，若省略六个代词，短文就更有"中国味"了。这个活生生的例子对英汉翻译不乏启示作用。

在英语中，完整的句子(祈使句除外)都有主语。当谓语动词是及物动词时，宾语往往必不可少，因此代词会反复出现；而汉语句子中，前后主语若指的是同一人或事物，后面的主语就不再重复，宾语也经常会因为前面已提到过而省略。所以在汉语的译文中，重复出现的代词大多可以省略。因此，在进行英汉翻译时要省略多次出现的主语人称代词、泛指人称代词、部分宾语代词和物主代词。

1 省略作主语的人称代词

根据汉语习惯，前句出现一个主语，后句的主语如果相同，就不必重复出现。英语中通常每句都有主语，因此人称代词往往多次出现，翻译时这种人称代词常常可以省略。英语中，泛指人称代词作主语时，即使是作第一个主语，在汉语译文中往往也可以省略。请看下面的例子：

The products should be sampled to check *their* quality before *they* leave the factory.

产品出厂前应该进行抽样检查。

I had many wonderful ideas, but *I* only put a few into practice.

我有很多美妙的想法，但是只有少数付诸实践了。

The significance of a man is not in what he attained but rather in what *he* longs to attain.

人生的意义不在于所得，而在于追求。

We live and learn.

活到老，学到老。

Your face used to be red and now *it's* pale. You were thin and now *you're* fat. I can't believe that it's you, Mr. White.

你的脸过去是红红的，现在变苍白了。你过去瘦瘦的，现在胖乎乎的。我简直不敢相信，这就是你呀，怀特先生。

2 省略作宾语的代词

英语中有些作宾语的代词，不管前面是否提到过，翻译时往往可以省略。

The more he tried to hide his mistakes, the more he revealed *them*.

他越是想要掩盖他的错误，就越是容易暴露。

She duly apologized on Thursday through her WeChat account. "Many criticisms are very insightful. I deeply reflect on them and humbly accept *them*."

她于周四通过其微信账号正式道歉："许多批评都很有见地。我深刻反思，虚心接受。"

3 省略物主代词

英语句子中的物主代词出现的频率相当高。一个句子中往往会出现好几个物主代词，如果每个物主代词都被翻译出来，那么汉语译文将显得非常啰嗦。所以在没有其他物主代词出现的情况下，在翻译时物主代词大多被省略。试比较：

Jeff was about to head into the freezing air when *his* mother stopped *him* and, *she* carefully put *his* gloves on *his* hands.

译文(1)：天气极为寒冷，Jeff 正要出门，被母亲叫住了，细心地给他戴上手套。

译文(2)：天气极为寒冷，Jeff 正要出门，他的母亲叫住了他，她细心地把他的手套戴在他的手上。

英语原文中有五个代词，译文(1)省略了四个，译得比较自然，而译文(2)不注意代词的适当省略，比较生硬。再看下面的例子：

The mother and the eldest daughter weeded the ridges, passing before the others...A younger son, of twelve years old, brought sea sand in a donkey's creels from a far corner of the field. They mixed the sand with the black clay. The fourth child, still almost an infant, staggered about near *his* mother, plucking weeds slowly and offering them to *his* mother as gifts.

母亲和大女儿在除垄上的草，把旁人甩在后面……二儿子十二岁，从老远的地头把海滩上的沙子装进鱼篮，赶着毛驴驮了回来。他们把黑土掺上了沙子。老四还是个小不点儿，在母亲身边摇摇晃晃转悠着，慢吞吞地拔起杂草，当礼物送给母亲。

He shrugged *his* shoulders, shook *his* head, cast up *his* eyes, but said nothing.

他耸了耸肩，摇了摇头，两眼看着天，一句话也没说。

4 非人称代词"it"的省略

"it"起着代词的作用，在原文中，当它被用作非人称代词或在文中没有任何实质性意义的时候，翻译过程中往往可以省略。

(1) 非人称代词"it"常用来表示天气、季节、时间、距离等概念，多在句中作主语，根据汉语表达习惯，常不译出。例如：

It was midnight. There were few people in the street.

时值午夜，街上行人稀少。

The report suggests that 2023 marks a significant turning point in the power sector, as *it* is likely the year when peak emissions were reached, signaling the beginning of a decline in fossil fuel generation on a global scale.

该报告表明，2023年标志着电力行业的一个重大转折点，因为这一年电力行业碳排放量很可能达到峰值，标志着全球化石燃料发电量开始下降。

(2) 强调句中"it"的省略。英语中的"It is that..."强调句型用来增强句子中某些成分的语气，在此情况下"it"只是强调句的标志，在句中起到填补主语位置的作用，没有任何实质性意义，因此，在翻译过程中"it"必须省略，否则读者会不知所云。例如：

It is the water that is the basis of life and drawn up by the clouds from the deep sea.

水才是生命的基础。云彩把水分从深邃的大海带到了天空。

It is the rise of brands like Xiaomi and Transsion that has helped people, even those living in the remote African tribes, embrace the smart era.

正是小米和传音等品牌的崛起，帮助人们(甚至包括那些生活在非洲偏远部落的人们)拥抱智能时代。

(3) 先行词"it"的省略。英语中常用先行词"it"作形式主语或形式宾语，而将真实主语(或真实宾语) 放置在其后。翻译时"it"不必译出。例如：

It hasn't been clear when the new flyover is open to traffic.

新立交桥何时通车尚不清楚。

It is only shallow people who judge by appearances.

只有浅薄的人才会以貌取人。

It is fair to say that Chinese people stay decent and confident in the trade war.

可以说，中国人在贸易战中保持了体面和自信。

Only when it is raised to the height of national strategy can *it* be possible to coordinate the "wisdom" of biodiversity conservation and economic development, and harmony with land resource planning under the background of "a big chess game".

只有提升到国家战略高度，才可能在"一盘大棋"的背景下，将生物多样性保护与经济发展"智慧"相协调，并与土地资源规划相协调。

8.1.2 省略冠词

英语有冠词，汉语没有冠词；因此，英语中用来表示一类或独一无二的事物的冠词在英译汉时应该省略。例如：

With the world ever changing so fast, the cease from learning for just a few days will make *a* person lag behind.

世界瞬息万变，几天不学习就会落后。

Why do some of us make great achievements known forever and why are they remembered forever even though they leave *the* world?

为什么有的人功业千秋，永垂不朽？

Let's not be *a* man full of promises but without any deeds, like Rudin, one of the characters by Turgenev.

千万不要像屠格涅夫笔下的罗亭那样，成为语言的巨人、行动的矮子！

但是，当不定冠词用来表示数量时，不可省略。例如：

He left without saying *a* word.

他**一句话**都没说就离开了。

8.1.3 省略介词

一般来说表示时间或地点的英语介词短语译成汉语时若放在句首常可省略介词，例如：

Rumors had already spread *along the streets and lanes*.

大街小巷流言四起。

Now complains are heard *in all parts* of that country.

该国**各地**怨声载道。

On Xiaohongshu, a 33-year-old user, who goes by the handle Momo and didn't give her real name for privacy reasons, frequently gives tips on how to style Chinese clothing.

小红书上一位自称 Momo 的 33 岁的用户(出于隐私原因没有透露真实姓名),经常就如何设计中式服装给出建议。

The Shenzhou XVIII manned spaceship was launched on *April 25* by a Long March 2F carrier rocket from the Jiuquan Satellite Launch Center in northwestern China.

4月25日,搭载神舟十八号载人飞船的长征二号F运载火箭在位于中国西北部的酒泉卫星发射中心点火发射。

需要注意的是:若时间或地点状语不放在汉语译文句首,与之搭配的介词通常不省略。例如:

The tides he believes have turned *in* the last decade or so with young Chinese becoming more aware and confident of their place *in* the world, and embracing China's culture and history.

他认为,**在**过去十年左右的时间里,随着中国年轻人越来越意识到自己**在**世界上的地位,并对中国的文化和历史越来越有信心,潮流已经发生了变化。

On Chinese social media platforms Weibo and Xiaohongshu, searches for "new Chinese style" and "new Chinese style outfits" hashtags exceeded 100 million in early April, according to state news agency Xinhua.

据新华社报道,4 月初,**在**中国社交媒体平台微博和小红书上,"新国风"和"新中式服装"标签的搜索量超 1 亿次。

The "Mamianqun" or "horse face skirt" is being worn *in* cities like Shanghai, Beijing, and Chengdu as young people in China are giving the attire a modern twist, with unconventional pairings and choice of fabrics.

这种马面裙**在**上海、北京和成都等城市流行起来,中国的年轻人用非传统的搭配和面料为这种服装注入现代气息。

8.1.4　省略连词

汉语词语之间连接词用得不多,其上下逻辑关系常常是暗含的,由词语的次序来表示。汉语可通过语序的排列把各句子成分和句与句之间的关系理顺,也可通过上下句的搭配,把原因、结果、条件、时间等逻辑关系隐含地表达出来。英语则不然,连接词用得比较多。因此,英译汉时,可以省略某些连词。例如:

What they found *was that* walking at least 2,300 steps a day was really good for the heart and blood vessels, and the more people walked, the more they reduced the risk of dying from cardiovascular disease.

他们发现，每天走路不少于 2300 步对心脏和血管都有很大的好处。走得越多，死于心血管疾病的风险就越低。

We can all take action on climate: eating a bit less meat, *and* walking *and* cycling a bit more will cut our emissions and make us healthier.

我们每个人都可以采取行动应对气候问题。比如，少吃一点肉、多走路、骑自行车可以减少温室气体的排放，并且有益健康。

Chang'e 6 was originally envisioned as a backup mission for Chang'e 5, *if* things went awry.

嫦娥六号探测器原本是嫦娥五号探测器的备份，以防万一。

8.1.5　省略动词

英语句子中一般要有谓语动词，但在汉语中谓语不一定由动词充当，形容词或名词都可以，因此在将英语翻译成汉语的时候，我们可能要省略谓语动词。主要有以下两种情况。

(1) 省略一些连系动词。例如：

They *are* to be very cheap and good.

它们物美价廉。

When the pressure *gets* low, the boiling point *becomes* low.

气压低，沸点就低。

(2) 省略一些与有动作含义的名词搭配用的动词。例如：

Solids expand and contract as liquids and gases *do*.

如同液体和气体一样，固体也能膨胀和收缩。

For this reason television signals *have* a short range.

因此，电视信号的传播距离很短。

8.2　因修辞需要省略

在英译汉过程中，从汉语的修辞需要和汉语的表达习惯出发，在不影响原句的完整性和不违背原文意思的前提下，为了修辞的需要，我们常将某些词语、句子成分甚至是从句省略不译或从简译出，以使译文干净利落，流畅精练。例如：

Part-time work applicants who had worked at a job would receive preference *over those who had not.*

应聘兼职工作，有经验者优先。

如果按照原文进行直译，译文为"应聘兼职工作者，有经验者要比那些没有经验的人优先。"译文虽然忠实于原文，但却显得比较啰嗦，因为"有经验者优先"已经暗含了"比较对象为没有经验的人"，所以译文中可以省去原文中的此类表达。

A small island has played a *disproportionately* large role in the thinking of evolutionary biologists.

岛屿虽小，但在影响进化论生物学家思维的过程中起到的作用却非常大。

本句中的disproportionately一词主要是说small与large之间比例失调，说得直接些，就是一个这么小，而另一个居然那么大。所以翻译时可以将disproportionately省掉，而用其他表达法将该词的意思融入整句之中，如"却非常大"。再如：

I felt a trifle shy at the thought of presenting myself to a total stranger with the announcement that I was going to *sleep under his roof*, eat *his food*, and drink *his whisky*, till another boat came in to take me to the port for which I was bound.

我要去见一个素不相识的人，向他宣布我得**住在他家、吃他的、喝他的**，直到下一班船到来，把我带到我要去的港口为止——想到这儿，我真有点不好意思了。

此处，若把"sleep under his roof, eat his food, and drink his whisky"直译为"睡在他的屋顶下、吃他的食物、喝他的威士忌"，则会使语言极为繁冗，不够精练。采用减省译法处理原文，既准确地传达了原意，又使行文简洁，气韵十足，一气呵成。

Her dark eyes made little reflected stars. She was looking at him as *she was always looking at him* when he awakened.

她那双乌黑的眼睛就像亮晶晶的星星在闪烁，他平素醒来的时候，她也是这样望着他。

此句中有两个"she was looking at him"，如不作省略而将其译为"她像平常望他时那样望着他"，汉语就显得啰嗦、拗口。

综合练习

一、将下列句子译成汉语。

1. If *I* had known *it*, I would not have joined in *it*.

2. When will he arrive? *You* can never tell.

3. But *it's* the way I am; try as I might, I haven't been able to change *it*.

4. *If* you give him an inch, he will take a yard.

5. After getting up, I wash *my* face, brush *my* teeth, and comb *my* hair.

6. He put *his* hands into *his* pockets and then shrugged *his* shoulders.

7. They held *their* position.

8. I put on *my* zip suit and went out.

9. *He* who idles away the time is nothing but a living death.

10. Any excuse will serve, if *one* has not a mind to do it.

11. *A* wise man will not marry *a* woman who has attainments but no virtue.

12. Her dark hair waved untidy across *her* broad forehead, *her* face was short, *her* upper lip short, showing a glint of teeth, *her* brows were straight and dark, *her* lashes long and dark, and *her* nose straight.

13. As I know more of mankind *I* expect less of *them*, and I'm now ready to call a man a good man more easily than formerly.

14. *It* will be a waste of time going to the railway station too early.

15. Smoking is prohibited *in* public places.

16. *In* 1405, the great Chinese navigator Zheng He sailed from China to Sumatra and that was 90 years before Columbus.

17. The soft can overcome the hard, *and* the weak can defeat the strong.

18. He looked gloomy *and* troubled.

19. Like charges repel each other *while* opposite charges attract.

20. Early to rise *and* early to bed makes a man healthy.

21. *As* it is late, you had better go home.

22. *If* winter comes, can spring be far behind?

23. He was so tired *that* he could hardly keep his eyes open.

24. *Before* the night was far advanced, the soldiers began to move against the enemy.

25. *In the course of* the same year, war broke out in that area.

26. In *actual* fact, the United States is pursuing a policy of encouraging the aggressor...

27. Take the whole into consideration, *but* do the job bit by bit.

28. One's mind works fast *when* it is in great danger.

29. *While* the prospects are bright, the road has twists *and* turns.

30. *If* you confer a benefit, never remember it. *If* you receive on, remember it always.

参考译文

1.早知如此，我就不参加了。

2.他什么时候到？说不准。

3. 我就是这个脾气，虽几经努力，却未能改变。

4. 他这个人得寸进尺。

5. 起床后，我洗脸，刷牙，梳头。

6. 他双手插兜，耸了耸肩。

7. 他们守住了阵地。

8. 我穿上拉链服，走了出去。

9. 虚度年华者，虽生犹死。

10. 如果不想做，总会找到借口。

11. 聪明的人是不会娶有才无德的女子为妻的。

12. 她的黑发蓬蓬松松地飘拂在宽阔的前额上，脸是短短的，上唇也是短短的，露出一排闪亮的牙齿，眉毛又直又黑，睫毛又长又黑，鼻子笔直。

13. 随着我对人类了解越多，我的期望就越低，相比于过去，我现在更容易说人家是好人了。

14. 过早去火车站是浪费时间。

15. 公共场所禁止吸烟。

16. 1405年，中国伟大的航海家郑和从中国航行到了苏门答腊岛，这比哥伦布早了90年。

17. 柔能克刚，弱能制强。

18. 他看上去有些忧愁不安。

19. 同性电荷相斥，异性电荷相吸。

20. 早睡早起身体好。

21. 不早了，你得回家了。

22. 冬天来了，春天还会远吗？

23. 他很疲倦，连眼睛都睁不开了。

24. 入夜不久，士兵们开始向敌人进攻。

25. 同年，该地区爆发了战争。

26. 实际上，美国在推行一种鼓励侵略者的政策……

27. 大处着眼，小处着手。

28. 急中生智。(省译了引出时间状语从句的连词when)

29. 前途是光明的，道路是曲折的。

30. 施恩勿记；受恩勿忘。

二、将以下语篇译成汉语。

Thoughts for a New Year

Most of us look away when we pass strangers. It is the exceptional person who stops to help the woman maneuvering her kids and groceries up the staircase. We rarely give up in line or on the subway or bus. Locked into our automobiles, we prefer gridlock to giving way.

These daily encounters, when they are angry or alien, diminish our lives. When they are pleasant, we feel buoyed. Yet when we sit at home and make resolutions, we think about what we can accomplish in private spaces: home, work. Too many have given up the belief that they control the shared, the public world.

As individuals we can change the contour of a day, the mood of a moment, and the way people feel. The demolition and reconstruction of public life is the result of personal decisions made every day: the decision to give up a seat on the bus; the decision to be patient or pleasant against all odds; the decision to let that jerk take a left-hand turn from a right-hand lane without rolling down the window and calling him a jerk.

It's the resolution to be a civil, social creature. This may be a peak period for the battle against the spread of a waistline and creeping cholesterol. But it is also within our will power to fight the spread of urban rudeness and creeping hostility. Civility doesn't stop nuclear holocaust and doesn't put a roof over the head of the homeless. But it makes a difference in the shape of a community, as surely as lifting weights can make a difference in the shape of a human torso.

参考译文

新年随想

当我们与陌生人擦肩而过时，多数人往往把目光移开。要是有人停下来帮妇女把孩子抱上楼，把食品杂货搬上楼，反而会被人看成另类。无论是排队还是乘地铁或公共汽车，我们很少让位于他人。坐在自己的汽车里，我们宁愿堵塞交通也不愿给人让路。

如果我们每天经历的都是令人生气或反感的事，那么生活会变得索然无味；但如果每天遇到的都是开心的事，便会使我们精神振奋。然而，当我们坐在家里做出各种决定的时候，我们考虑的仅是在个人天地——家庭和工作里可以实现的目标。太多人已经忘了实际上自己也管理着这个共同的世界。

作为个体，我们可以改变一天的状态、一时的情绪，以及人们的心情。公共生活的毁坏和重建是个人每日所做种种决定的综合结果。这些决定包括：公共汽车上让座；逆境中保持耐心或乐观；让那个笨蛋从右车道往左拐而不摇下车窗骂他蠢。

这是做文明人和社会人的决定。今天也许是人们为减小腰围、降低胆固醇而斗争的高峰期。然而，反对城市野蛮行为和人际敌对态度的蔓延，也是我们想做就能做到的事。文明不能阻止核战争，也不能为无家可归者提供栖身之所，但却能改变一个社会群体的面貌，犹如举重能改变一个人的体形一样。

第9章

翻译技巧(五)正反转换法

　　众所周知，语言是文化的载体，中西文化都经历了长时间的积淀，人们有着各自的语言表达习惯，有时对于相同的自然陈述客体，人们会从不同的角度加以考察，因而出现了截然相反的表达。例如，在公共场所刚刚刷过油漆的座椅边，可以看见"油漆未干"这样的警示语，汉语通过"未"这个否定词来直接提醒人们不可以坐那个椅子。而英语不用"The paint is not dry."，而用"Wet paint."，含蓄地把客观事实告诉人们。又如，在中国许多地方都会遇到"游客止步""闲人莫入"之类的告示，对应的英语表达是"Crew only"或 "Private"，并不含有否定的形式。其否定意思(员工之外的人不许进入)是隐含的，是一种汉语少有而英语中大量存在的"暗否定"。接电话时对方说"Hold the line, please?"对应的汉语却是"请别挂断电话"。英文中说"Be generous with your praise!"，汉语却是"不要吝惜对他人的赞扬!"，这样的例子不在少数。

9.1 正反转换法的文化基础

英语和汉语有相同之处，那就是在表达同一事物或同一概念时，往往可以从正面叙述，也可从反面叙述。比如我们可以说"很困难"(quite difficult)，也可以说"很不容易"(far from easy)；说做某事"竭尽全力"(do one's best)，也可以说"不遗余力"(spare no effort)；可以说某个学生成绩"还好"(good)，也可以说"不错"(not bad)。但由于思维方式的不同，英语中有些从正面表达的内容在汉语中习惯从反面表达；而有些英语从反面来表达的内容在汉语中则习惯从正面来表达。因此，英译汉时常常有必要进行转换。这就是通常所说的"正说反译与反说正译"法。如英语中的"Keep off the grass."，汉语中常说成"请勿践踏草坪"；英语中说"I won't keep you waiting long."，汉语中却说"我一会儿就回来"。不论是正说反译还是反说正译，归纳起来主要有以下要求：保证语义明确，加强修饰效果，尊重译入语习惯，保证译文通畅易懂。

9.2 正反转换法的应用

所谓反面表达，是指英语中含有"not""never""no""none""nobody""nothing""nowhere""neither""nor""seldom""hardly""scarcely""rarely""barely""little""few""un-""im-""ir-""in-""dis-""less-"等否定词、半否定词或否定前/后缀的表达，以及汉语中含有"不""没""无""未""甭""别""休""莫""毋""勿""非"等否定成分的表达，反之，不含这些成分的则视为正面表达。

翻译方法很多，要根据具体语境来选择最佳的翻译方法。以下情况常常采用反译法。具体说来，用"反面表达"翻译英语"正面表达"的句子的情况有以下5种。

9.2.1 正说反译的应用

1 本身表示否定意义的谓语动词或动词词组

常见的本身表示否定意义的谓语动词或动词词组有fail、fall short、be frustrated、

fizzle out、escape、slip away、elude、stop、cease、overlook、ignore、neg1ect、refuse、grudge、disdain、reject、turn down、forbid、prohibit、exclude from、bar、ban、expire、be blind to、deny、avoid、omit、forget、prevent from、live up to、resist、miss、lack等，译成汉语时为了使译文通顺有时要从反面来表达。例如：

When asked whether or not they know anything about the Nanjing Massacre recently, many ordinary Japanese *avoided* answering the question and the majority of respondents said they simply just didn't know.

最近，当被问及是否了解南京大屠杀时，日本许多普通民众都**避而不答**，大多数受访者表示根本不知道南京大屠杀的事。

Passengers who *fail* to buy train tickets can join a waiting list on the 12306 system, with more temporary trains to be added based on the waiting lists.

没有买到火车票的乘客可以加入 12306 系统的候补名单，铁路部门将根据候补名单增加临时列车。

AI will begin to *live up to* the hype by starting to generate real economic value through its application across industries.

人工智能将**不负**之前天花乱坠的宣传，开始通过在各个行业的应用产生真正的经济价值。

They *refused* to release their hostages unless certain conditions were met.

除非某些条件得到满足，否则他们**不会**释放人质。

2 含否定之意的介词或介词短语

有些介词或介词短语是正面表达，翻译成汉语时为了使译文通顺有时要从反面表达，如above、against、below、beneath、beyond、instead of、out of、without、but for。请看以下例子：

All international disputes must be settled through negotiations *instead of* any armed conflicts.

一切国际争端都应通过谈判**而不是**武装冲突来解决。

Out of sight, *out of* mind.

眼**不**见，心**不**烦。

But for the storm, we should have arrived earlier.

要是没有遇上暴风雨，我们早到了。

3 形式肯定但意思否定的固定搭配

某些固定结构也是形式肯定、意思否定，例如：absent (from)、free from、safe

from、different(from)、far from、few、little、alien to、anything but、know better than、too...to...、rather than、awkward(不熟练，不灵活，使用起来不方便)、bad(令人不愉快的，不受欢迎的，不舒服的)、blind to(看不到、不注意)、dead(无生命的、无感觉的、不毛的)、difficult(不容易的)、foreign to(对……来说是陌生的，与……无关)、short of(不足，不够)、poor(不好的，不幸的)、ignorant of(不知道)等。这些固定结构翻译成汉语时为了使译文通顺有时要从反面来表达。例如：

Far from being separate, the mind and body form an indivisible whole.

心智与身体**绝不是**分离的，它们形成了一个不可分割的整体。

The problem is *anything but* easy.

这个问题**绝不**简单。

Some of the excuses were *more than* could be believed.

有些借口**令人难以置信**。

He is *more* brave *than* wise.

他**有勇无谋**。

4 含有if、before、unless、until、would rather 的句子或使用虚拟语气的句子

有些含有if、before、unless、until、would rather 的句子或使用虚拟语气的句子，形式上是正面表达，却要从反面翻译。例如：

She will die of hunger *before* she steals.

她**宁愿饿死也不愿**去偷。

The cultural life of the country will sink into atrophy *unless* more writers and artists emerge.

如果没有更多的作家和艺术家出现，这个国家的文化生活将衰退。

He himself believed in freedom, so much so that he *would rather* die than live *without* it.

他非常崇尚自由，**不自由，毋宁死**。

5 某些正面表达的英语习语

有些英语习语从正面表达，对应的汉语却习惯上从反面表达。例如：

As the saying goes, "Men only weep when deeply hurt."

俗话说，"**男儿有泪不轻弹，皆因未到伤心处**"嘛。

Bite off more than one can chew.

贪多嚼不烂。

Let sleeping dogs lie.

莫惹是生非。

A bird in the hand is worth two in the bush.

双鸟在林不如一鸟在手。

9.2.2　反说正译的应用

有些从反面表达的句子，在直译的情况下要么词不达意，要么译入语读者无法理解。因此要从正面加以表达，以恰当地再现原文的意思。不妨从以下4个方面加以分析。

1 双重否定

双重否定相当于肯定。这里所说的包括否定词与含有否定意义的词连用的情况。例如：

There is *no* rule that has *no* exception.

任何规则都有例外。

Nothing is *impossible* to a willing mind.

有志者事竟成。

There is *no* evil *without* compensation.

恶有恶报。

He can *hardly* open his mouth *without* talking shop.

他一开口总是三句话不离本行。

2 形式否定，意思肯定

有些否定的形式表示肯定的意思。例如：

She *couldn't* have come *at a better time.*

她来得**正是时候**。

Your article will be published *in no time.*

你的文章**很快**就会刊发的。

I *couldn't agree* with you *more.*

我**太赞成**你的看法了。/完全同意。

Don't lose time in posting this letter.

赶快把这封信寄出去。

综合练习

一、将下列短语译成汉语。

1. ice-free harbour

2. nuclear-weapon-free zone

3. free from anxiety

4. take French leave

5. beyond dispute

6. frost-free refrigerator

7. crew only

8. free from arrogance and rashness

9. Keep Upright

10. Keep Top Side Up

11. Keep off the grass.

12. agreeable sweetness

参考译文

1. 不冻港

2. 无核武器区

3. 无忧无虑

4. 不辞而别

5. 无可争论

6. 无霜冰箱

7. 闲人莫入

8. 不骄不躁

9. 保持直立/竖放

10. 请勿倒置

11. 请勿践踏草坪

12. 甜而不腻

二、将下列句子译成汉语。

(一) 运用正说反译翻译技巧将下列句子译成汉语。

1. Children were *excluded* from getting in the building.

2. To our disappointment, he *failed* to take the overall situation into account.

3. Such a chance was *denied* to me.

4. His parents *forbade* him to marry Mary.

5. Her child was in a terrible state of *neglect*.

6. Learn how to be *instead of* do.

7. I gave him advice *instead of* money.

8. I have read your article. I *expected* to meet an older man.

9. He *sits out* the other guests.

10. He is *the last* man to accept a bribe.

11. He has a *short memory*.

12. I would rather die *before* I would betray my country.

13. The troops *would rather* take a roundabout way than tread on the crops.

14. He was utterly *in the dark* about what had happened in the department yesterday.

15. *Leave me alone*!

16. *Call a spade a spade*.

17. He *knows better than* to do such a thing.

18. It's *too* dark here for us *to* read the words on this slip of paper.

19. He yelled "*freeze*!"

20. The sea food *goes against* my stomach.

21. That's *all Greek* to me.

22. When you called on me this morning, I was still *in bed*.

23. His *lack of* consideration for the feelings of others angered everyone present.

24. Travelling alone, she was sitting *still* in the corner of the carriage.

25. It is gravity that *keeps* us *from* falling off the earth.

26. He raised his hand to scratch his head with *embarrassment*.

27. This book contained *too much* gossip and *too many* distortions and falsehoods *to* warrant comment.

28. A person who does a *regrettable* action is often regretful afterwards.

29. You are quite a *stranger* here.

30. The guerrillas would rather fight to death *before* they surrendered.

31. *Before* he could stop me, I had rushed out of the classroom.

32. *Opportunity knocks but once*.

33. *Fully clothed*, he fell across his bunk and was instantly a sleep.

34. As a human being, we should demonstrate our intellectual and moral superiority by respecting others for who they are—*instead of* rejecting them for who/what they are not.

35. Work does *much more than* most of us realize to provide happiness and contentment.

36. She was *deaf to* all advice.

37. I *stayed awake* almost the whole night.

38. *Seats shall be reserved for warm body only*.

39. The explanation is pretty *thin*.

参考译文

1. 儿童不许进入这栋楼。

2. 令我们失望的是，他不顾大局。

3. 我没有得到这样一个机会。

4. 他的父母不许他与玛丽结婚。

5. 她的孩子简直没人管。

6. 要学习如何做人，而不是做事。

7. 我给了他忠告，而不是钱。

8. 拜读了你的大作，没想到你这样年轻。

9. 别的客人都走了，他还不走。

10. 他决不会接受贿赂。

11. 他的记性不好。

12. 我宁可死，也不背叛我的祖国。

12. 部队宁可绕道走，也不踩庄稼。

14. 他对昨天系里发生的事全然不知。

15. 别管我!

16. 直言不讳。

17. 他不至于干这样的事。

18. 这里光线太暗了，看不清这个便条上写的字。

19. 他喊道："别动!"

20. 海鲜不合我口味。

21. 我对此一窍不通。

22. 你早晨来看我的时候，我还没有起床。

23. 他只顾自己，不顾别人，使在场的每个人都很生气。

24. 她没有同伴，一动不动地坐在车厢一角。

25. 是重力使我们不至于从地球上抛出去。

26. 他不好意思地抬起手挠了挠头。

27. 这本书里无聊的话太多，歪曲和弄虚作假之处太多，不值一评。

28. 一个人如果做了不该做的事，日后往往会懊悔。

29. 这儿的人都不认识你。

30. 游击队员们宁愿战斗到死也决不投降。

31. 他还没来得及阻拦，我就已经跑出了教室。

32. 机不可失。

33. 他衣服也没脱往床上横着一躺，很快就睡着了。

34. 作为德才兼备的人，我们应该不分高低贵贱地尊重他人，不要因为他人没有某种身份或地位而去鄙视他们。

35. 工作能使人感到幸福与满足，它在这方面所起的作用比我们大多数人意识到的要多得多。

36. 她什么劝告都不听。

37. 我昨晚几乎一夜没睡。

38. 请勿用物品占位。

39. 这个解释站不住脚。

(二) 运用反说正译翻译技巧将下列句子译成汉语。

1. We must *never stop* taking an optimistic view of life.

2. You *cannot* make omelets *without* breaking eggs.

3. If that *isn't* what I want!

4. He *can't* see you quickly enough.

5. He is *no more than* a puppet.

6. A poor man is *no less* a citizen *than* a rich man.

7. *Nothing* is *more* precious than life.

8. He *can't* be more careless.

9. His speech leaves *no room* to improvement.

10. The music is like *nothing* on the earth.

11. I *couldn't* feel *better*.

12. I *can't* agree with you *more*.

13. All the articles are *untouchable* in the museum.

14. Some people can eat what they like and get *no fatter*.

15. It is *no less than* blackmail to ask such a high price.

16. It is the same old story of not being grateful for what we have *until* we lose it, of not being conscious of health until we are ill.

17. No deposit will be refunded *unless* the ticket is produced.

参考译文

1. 我们对生活要永远抱乐观态度。

2. 有失才有得。(正面表达)/不破不立。(反面表达)

3. 我所要的就是这个呀!

4. 他想尽快和你见面。

5. 他只是一个傀儡。

6. 穷人、富人都是公民。

7. 生命最可贵。

8. 他太粗心了。

9. 他的演讲完美之至。

10. 此曲只应天上有。

11. 我觉得身体好极了。

12. 我太赞成你的看法了。

13. 博物馆内一切展品禁止触摸。

14. 有些人爱吃什么就吃什么,照样瘦。

15. 要价这么高,简直是敲诈。

16. 物失方知可贵,病时倍思健康。

17. 凭票退回押金。

三、将以下语篇译成汉语。

Thinness and Vainglory

"No woman can be too rich or too thin." This saying often attributed to the late Duchess of Windsor embodies much of the odd spirit of our times. Being thin is deemed as such a virtue.

The problem with such a view is that some people actually attempt to live by it. I myself have fantasies of slipping into narrow designer clothes. Consequently I have been on a diet for the better—or worse—part of my life. Being rich wouldn't be bad either, but that won't happen unless an unknown relative dies suddenly in some distant land, leaving me millions of dollars.

Where did we go off the track? When did eating butter become a sin and a little bit of extra flesh unappealing if not repellent? Many religions have certain days when people refrain from eating and excessive eating is one of Christianity's seven deadly sins. However, until quite recently, some people still had a problem getting enough to eat. In some religious groups, wealth was symbol of probable salvation and high morals, and fatness a sign of wealth and well-being.

Today the opposite is true. We have shifted to thinness as our new mark of virtue. The result is that being fat—or even only somewhat overweight—is bad because it implies a lack of moral strength.

Our obsession(迷恋) with thinness is also fuelled by health concerns. It is true that in this country we have more overweight people than ever before and that in many cases being overweight correlates with an increased risk of heart and blood vessel diseases. These diseases, however, may have as much to do with our way of life and our high-fat diets as with excess weight. And the associated risk of cancer in the digestive system may be more of a dietary problem—too much fat and a lack of fiber than a weight problem.

The real concern, then, is not that we weigh too much, but that we neither exercise enough nor eat well. Exercise is necessary for strong bones and both heart and lung health. A balanced diet without a lot of fat can also help the body avoid many diseases. We should surely stop paying so much attention to weight. Simply being thin is not enough? It is actually hazardous if those who get or already are thin think they are automatically healthy, and thus free from paying attention to their overall life-style. Thinness can be pure vainglory(虚荣).

翻译要点注解：

1. No woman can be too rich or too thin. 注意 cannot...too...的译法，不可照字面直译，注意双重否定的翻译。

2. attribute...to... 认为……属于……

3. Duchess of Windsor 温莎公爵夫人(1896—1986)，英王爱德华八世之妻

4. live by 以……为生

5. slip into 匆忙穿上

6. designer clothes 时髦的服装

7. for better or worse 不管是福是祸，不管是好是歹，不管结果怎样

8. go off the track 背离常规

9. extra flesh 赘肉

10. unappealing adj. 无吸引力的，相貌平庸的

11. repellent adj. 令人厌恶的，讨人嫌的

12. refrain v. 抑制，自制，避免；to refrain from smoking 戒烟

13. salvation n. 赎罪，得救(从罪恶的力量或惩罚中解救出来)

14. obsession n. 迷恋，着迷

15. fuel v. 激起

16. have as much to do with... as with... 既与……紧密相关，也与……有很大关系

17. be more of a dietary problem than... 更像是饮食问题而不是……

18. but that we neither exercise enough nor eat well 而是我们锻炼不够，吃得也不科学

(注意，well不宜译作"好")

    19. balanced diet 均衡的饮食

    20. those who get or already are thin 那些瘦了或本身就瘦的人

    21. free from paying attention 不注意(正说反译)；be free from 没有……的，摆脱了……的

参考译文

瘦身与虚荣

    "女人的钱再多也不多，女人再瘦也不瘦。"这句话常被认为是已故的温莎公爵夫人说的，很大程度上体现了当代的奇怪精神——瘦被视为难得的优点。

    此观点的问题在于有些人实际上想以此为生活准则。我自己就幻想能轻松套上瘦小的时装。因此，不管生活是好是坏，我一直都在节食。再说，有钱也不是什么坏事，但这种情况不会发生在我身上——除非一个不知名的亲戚突然死在某个遥远的国度，给我留下了千百万美元的遗产。

    我们在何处背离了生活常规？什么时候吃黄油成了一种罪过？稍稍多一点赘肉就毫无魅力，甚至令人厌恶？许多宗教都有特定的禁食日，暴食是基督教不可饶恕的七宗罪之一。然而，直至前不久，一些人还有吃不饱的问题。过去，在有些宗教团体中，财富是可能得到救赎和道德高尚的象征，而肥胖则是财富和康乐的象征。

    今天恰恰相反。瘦已转变为优秀的新标志，其结果便是肥胖成了坏事——哪怕稍稍超重也不行，因为这意味着缺乏意志。

    对健康的关心也助长了人们对瘦身的痴狂。的确，目前美国体重超标的人比以往任何时候都多，而且在许多情况下，肥胖与心血管疾病风险的上升息息相关。不过除了与超重密切相关，这些疾病与我们的生活方式及高脂肪饮食习惯也有很大关系。患消化系统癌症的相关风险更像是饮食问题而非体重问题——食物高脂肪低纤维。

    这么看来，问题的关键不是体重超标，而是我们既锻炼不充分，又吃得不科学。锻炼对强健骨骼、心肺健康都很必要。低脂肪均衡饮食也有助于身体远离多种疾病。我们显然不应再过分关注体重了。仅仅瘦是不够的。如果那些瘦了或本来就瘦的人认为他们自然而然就可保持健康，因而不注意总体生活方式，实际上会很危险。瘦可谓纯属虚荣。

第10章

翻译技巧(六)定语从句译法

　　傅雷先生曾经说过："东方人与西方人的思维方式有基本分歧，我人重综合，重归纳，重暗示，重含蓄；西方人则重分析，细微曲折，挖掘唯恐不尽，描写唯恐不周。"汉语学家王力先生指出："西洋语法是硬的，没有弹性；中国语法是软的，富有弹性。……所以中国语法以达意为主。英国人写文章往往化零为整，而中国人写文章却往往化整为零。"

定语从句(attributive clause) 也叫形容词从句(adjective clause)，此类从句由关系词(relative) 引导，在主从复合句(complex sentence) 中起形容词作用，修饰主句中的名词、代词或用作名词的其他类词，被定语从句修饰的词称为先行词(antecedent)。一般情况下，定语从句总是跟在它所修饰的先行词的后面。引导定语从句的有关系代词(relative pronoun: who, whose, that, which, as, but, than)和关系副词(relative adverbial: when, where, why)。关系代词和关系副词通常位于从句之首，它们除了用于连接主句和从句外，还在从句中充当句子成分，在从句中，关系代词通常作主语、表语、宾语，关系副词则通常作状语。

一般来说，英语句子常用各种形式的连接手段，如连接词、分句或从句，注重显性衔接(overt cohesion)，句子形式完整，结构紧凑而严谨，注重以形显义。汉语造句则少用或不用形式连接手段，注重逻辑事理顺序和句子的功能、意义，通过隐性连贯(covert cohesion) 以神通形，结构简练、明快。谈到这种句子结构差异时，庄绎传教授曾形象地说道："我感觉汉语句子结构好比一根竹子，一节一节地连下去；而英语的句子结构好比一串葡萄，主干可能很短，累累果实附着在上面。"虽然英汉两种语言的句子结构存在本质上的差别，但按照杨莉藜的观点，可以粗线条地划分为主谓结构、支配结构、限定结构和并列结构。在翻译的过程中，这4种结构在语内和语际可以相互转换。英语中的定语从句属于限定结构，下面我们通过具体例子来看在翻译过程中这种结构是如何转换成汉语的不同结构的。

定语从句的修饰对象一直是翻译中经常遇到而难以把握的问题。要作出正确的判断，必须具备多方面的知识。定语从句可以按照它与先行词在逻辑含义上的紧密程度分为限制性定语从句和非限制性定语从句两大类，而具体翻译方法也因其紧密程度的差别有所不同。值得注意的是，有些定语从句和主句之间还存在着状语关系，这就要求译者根据具体的上下文加以辨别。在翻译定语从句时我们可以采用前置法、后置法、结构转换法、融合法、断句拆译法等把定语从句译成汉语中的偏正结构、介词结构、独立分句等，或将其融入主句中。

语言学家指出，英语的定语从句可以向右无限扩展；而汉语中没有定语从句之说，作为修饰成分的定语习惯上放在被修饰词之前，呈封闭状。英汉定语结构的差异如下所示。

This is the cat.

这就是那只猫。

This is the cat that killed the rat.

这就是那只捕杀了老鼠的猫。

This is the cat that killed the rat that ate the cake.

这就是那只捕杀了偷吃了蛋糕的老鼠的猫。

This is the cat that killed the rat that ate the cake that lay in the room.

这就是那只捕杀了偷吃了放在房间里的蛋糕的老鼠的猫。

This is the cat that killed the rat that ate the cake that lay in the room that Jack lived in.

这就是那只捕杀了偷吃了放在杰克居住的房间里的蛋糕的老鼠的猫。

不难发现，汉语译文从第三句起便读不通了。要使译文通顺，就得将其切分开来处理：这就是那只捕杀了老鼠的猫。那只老鼠偷吃了放在房间里的蛋糕。而杰克就住在这间房里。

再请看下面的例子。

Nearly everyone knows the story of "the dog that worried the cat that caught the rat that ate the grain that lay in the house that Mr. Bubble built."

几乎人人都知道这个故事："冒泡先生盖了房，房里堆了粮，耗子把粮食吃光，猫把耗子抓伤，狗又把猫逼上房。"

因此，英语的定语从句不一定都翻译成所修饰先行词的定语。根据具体的语境，翻译定语从句时经常采用的方法与技巧一般有以下几种。

10.1　前置法

前置法，顾名思义，就是在翻译时将定语从句提到它所修饰的先行词之前。定语从句可以大体上分成限制性定语从句(restrictive attributive clause)和非限制性定语从句(non-restrictive attributive clause)。限制性定语从句和先行词(antecedent)的关系很密切，是对先行词的修饰和限定，如果去掉，整个句子就显得不完整了。采用前置法翻译的定语从句一般是限制性定语从句，而且句子不太长，否则容易出现中间过于臃肿的现象。这时候，只要将其译成带 "的" 字的定语词组并将其放在被修饰词前，即可将英语复合句译成汉语的简单句。例如：

I propose to offer a theory which, as far as I am aware, has not previously been set forth, that only those animals capable of speech are capable of laughter and that therefore man, being the only animal *that* speaks, is the only animal *that* laughs.

我试图提出一种理论，据我所知，这种理论还未有人提出过，那就是只有能说话的动物才会笑，人是唯一能说话的动物，所以也是唯一会笑的动物。

He *who* has never tasted what is bitter does not know what is sweet.

没有吃过苦的人不知道什么是甜。

Chances favor the minds *that* are prepared.

机会青睐有准备的人。

The survey suggests the proportion of adolescents who reported being cyber bullied has increased since 2018, from 12% to 15% for boys and 13% to 16% for girls.

调查显示，自2018年以来，遭受过网络暴力的青少年比例有所增长，其中男生的比例从12%上升至15%，女生的比例则从13%增长至16%。

10.2 后置法

所谓后置法就是保持原句的顺序，将原句的定语从句(尤其是定语较长、较复杂的限制性定语从句和起补充说明作用的非限制性定语从句)译成和主句并列的一个分句，并将其放在主句之后。采用此种译法时可以使用句号分开主句和从句，重复先行词，例如：

Our aim is to establish in Ghana a strong and progressive society... where poverty and illiteracy no longer exist and disease is brought under control; and where our educational facilities provide all the children of Ghana with the best possible opportunities for the development of their potentialities.

我们的目的是在加纳建立一个强大、进步的社会……在这里，贫困和文盲不再存在，疾病得到控制；在这里，我们的教育机构为加纳所有的孩子提供发展他们潜力的最好机会。(两个并列句，表示并列关系)

What should doctors say, for example, to a 50-year-old man coming in for a routine physical check up just before going on vacation with his family who, though he feels in perfect health, is found to have a form of cancer that will cause him to die within 5 months?

比如说，有位50岁的男士在与家人外出度假之前进行常规身体检查。虽然他自己感觉身体很好，却查出患有某种癌症，5个月之内就会死亡。这时候医生该说什么呢？

Days and nights are very long on the moon, where one day is as long as two weeks on the earth.

在月亮上，白天和黑夜都相当长，月亮上的一天等于地球上的两周。

Both picnics and BBQ are friendly, informal social events that offer an opportunity to enjoy a meal outside in pleasant surroundings.

野餐和烧烤都是友情洋溢、不拘礼节的社交活动，让人们有机会在舒适的环境中享受户外用餐。

The ability to tap into a trend known as "special forces" tourism—where young people travel long distances to briefly visit a cheap attraction before heading home—is increasingly important in China.

所谓的"特种兵式"旅游，正是现在年轻人热衷的一种旅行方式——他们选择长途跋涉，并在归途之前匆忙探访某处物美价廉的景点。在当前的中国市场，能够敏锐捕捉并成功变现这一旅游趋势，是一种重要的商业智慧。

There are now tools being released which claim to be able to differentiate human text from that written by artificial intelligence.

现在正陆续推出一些工具，据称可以区分人类自创文本和人工智能生成文本。

10.3　融合法（定语从句谓语化）

融合法是指用从句的关系代词与主句某成分的代替关系，根据意思将定语从句重新组织成汉语单句。此种译法主要适用于限制性定语从句，此法把原句中的先行词译成主语，定语从句译成谓语结构。英语中的there be结构就可以采用这种译法来处理。例如：

There are more and more foreign investors *who* have the intention to do business and live in Dalian.

越来越多的外国投资者有意在大连经商和生活。

There is a man downstairs *who* wants to see you.

楼下有人要见你。

There are some metals *that* are lighter than water.

有些金属密度比水小。

There have been many great men *who* have emerged from slums.

有很多伟人出身于贫民窟。

There were men in that crowd *who* had stood there every day for a month.

在那群人中，有些人每天站在那里，站了一个月。

10.4　译成状语从句

定语从句和主句之间还存在着状语关系。从语义的角度看，这类定语从句一般相当于状语，表达原因、结果、条件、时间、目的、让步等含义，其功能与状语从句的功能大致相同。在翻译时我们一般将状语性定语从句译为状语从句，使译文简练明了。此种译法在限制性定语从句和非限制性定语从句中均适用。下面从功能上来分析英语的状语性定语从句的译法。

10.4.1　译成原因状语从句

从语境来分析，这类定语从句在意义上与原因状语从句大致相当。此类定语从句所表示的原因逻辑关系均可用表示原因的从属连词because、since、as 等来改写。限制性定语从句和非限制性定语从句均可表示原因，但后者更为常见。例如：

The strike would prevent the docking of ocean steamships, *which* require assistance of tugboats.

罢工将使远洋货轮无法靠岸，**因为**它们需要拖船的帮助。

Rushing throngs, *who* was blinded by the darkness and the smoke, rushed up on a street and down the next, trampling the fallen in a crazy fruitless dash toward safety.

由于黑暗和浓烟蒙蔽了视线，狂奔的人群沿着大街小巷奔跑，践踏着倒下的躯体，慌乱而徒劳地向着安全地方冲闯。

Vegetarianism is definitely unsatisfactory for growing children, *who* need more protein than they can get from vegetable sources.

对生长发育中的儿童来说，素食主义肯定是不可取的。**因为**他们需要的蛋白质不可能全部从植物类食品中获得。

We know that a cat, *whose* eyes can take in many more rays of light than our eyes, can see clearly in the night.

我们知道**由于**猫的眼睛比我们人的眼睛能吸收更多的光线，因此猫在夜里也能看得很清楚。

10.4.2　译成结果状语从句

当定语从句所表示的是主句中某一动作或状态所产生的结果时，其意义相当于so that引导的结果状语从句，修饰主句的谓语动词。在翻译时，根据其意义及汉语的表达习惯，可加上适当的连词。例如：

Copper, *which* is used so widely for carrying electricity, offers very little resistance.

铜的电阻很小，**所以**广泛用于传输电力。

It is fortunate that men have worked out new plane shapes *which* enable the plane to go through sound barrier with little difficulty.

幸运的是，人们已设计出新的机型，**使**飞机能毫不费力地通过音障。

Scientists have developed a second generation of the blood substitute *that* solves the problem of blood storage.

科学家们已经研究出第二代血液代用品，**从而**解决了血液的贮存问题。

10.4.3　译成条件状语从句

表示条件的状语性定语从句既可表示真实条件又可表示非真实条件。表示真实条件含义时，这类从句通常表达一种先决条件，可以翻译成"如果……""只要……"等。表示非真实条件含义的时候，此类定语从句往往用虚拟语气来表达一种假设的情况，可译为"假如……""要是……"等。例如：

Men become desperate for work, any work, *which* will help them to support their family. (=...as long as it will help them to support their family.)

人们极其迫切地要求工作，不管什么工作，**只要**它能够维持家人的生活就行。

It may seem somewhat odd to get water from fire, but we shall find that water is a common by-product of any fire in *which* hydrogen takes part.

火中取水，似乎有点离奇？但我们不难发现：水是火燃烧后所产生的一种常见的副产品；**只要**燃烧过程中有氢气的存在，便会产生水。

Nowadays it is understood that a diet *which* contains nothing harmful may result in serious disease if certain important elements are missing.

现在人们已经懂得，**如果**饮食中缺少某些重要成分，那么即使其中不含任何有害物质，也会导致严重疾病。

No one *who* is dependent on anything outside himself, upon money, power, fame, or whatnot, is or ever can be secure.

若想通过身外之物(如金钱、权力、名誉之类的东西)获得安全感，就永远不会有安全感。

Food *which* is kept too long decays because it is attacked by yeasts, mould, and bacteria.

食物**如果**存放过久，就会腐烂，因为会受到酵母、霉菌和细菌的侵蚀。

10.4.4　译成时间状语从句

当定语从句所表示的动作与主句所表示的动作几乎同时发生时，其含义相当于由连词when、while或as等引导的时间状语从句，修饰主句中的谓语动词。这类定语从句可以当作时间状语从句来处理，在翻译时，往往需要加上相应的连词"当……的时候"。例如：

It was a keen disappointment when I had to postpone the visit *which* I had intended to pay to China in May.

原计划5月来华，后不得不推迟，深表遗憾。

An electrical current begins to flow through coil, *which* is connected across a charged condenser.

当线圈同充电的电容器相连接时，电流就开始流经线圈。

I came across our English teacher, Miss Howe, *who* was taking a walk in the park yesterday afternoon.

昨天下午，我们英语老师豪小姐在公园里散步时，我碰巧遇见了她。

10.4.5　译成目的状语从句

当定语从句所表示的是主句中某一动作或状态发生的目的或动机时，其含义相当于由连词so that、in order that等引导的目的状语从句，修饰主句的谓语动词。这类定语从句可以转换成目的状语从句。例如：

Private schools in the United States have a wide range of programs *that*(=so that they) are offered to meet the needs of certain students.

美国私立学校设课繁多，**以**满足某些学生的需求。

In the late 1960s, a type of filter was introduced in Britain and elsewhere *that* would have made cigarettes safer.

20世纪60年代后期，英国和其他一些国家/地区曾采用一种过滤嘴**来**减少香烟的危害。

I'll try to get an illustrated dictionary dealing with technical glossary, *which* will enable me to translate scientific literature more exactly.

我要设法弄一本有插图的科技词典，**以便**把科学文献译得更准确。

The Wall Street multi-millionaires are looking for new markets overseas *where* they can dump their surplus goods.

华尔街的亿万富翁在海外寻找新的市场，**以便**倾销他们的剩余货物。

10.4.6　译成让步状语从句

当定语从句中某一动作或状态与主句中的某一动作或状态在逻辑上有一定矛盾，但并不影响主句的事实或语气的突然转折时，该从句的含义相当于由连词though、although

引导的让步状语从句。在翻译时，需要加上"但是""然而""却"等连词以使行文流畅，语气连贯。例如：

Although we have suffered heavy losses by assisting the French and during the Dunkirk evacuation, we have managed to husband our air fighter strength in spite of poignant appeals from France to throw it improvidently into the great land battle, *which* it could not have turned decisively.

尽管我们因为援助法国和敦刻尔克大撤退而损失惨重，但还是设法保存了空战实力，我们没有因为法国的强烈呼吁而草率地将其投入地面战斗。**即使**当时我们这样做，也是回天乏术，败局已定。

Glass, *which* breaks at a blow, is capable of withstanding great pressure.

尽管玻璃一打就碎，仍然能承受很大压力。

A gas occupies all of any container in *which* it is placed.

气体**不论**装在什么容器里，都会把容器装满。

Electronic computers, *which* have many advantages, cannot do creative work or replace human beings.

尽管电子计算机有许多优点，但是它们不能进行创造性的工作，也不能代替人类。

Immigrants are quickly fitting into this common culture, *which* may not be altogether elevating but is hardly poisonous.

移民很快适应了这种共同的文化，这**虽然**总体上算不上振奋人心，却也没什么害处。

本句由两个层次组成，一个是主句"Immigrants are quickly fitting into this common culture,"从句是"which may not be altogether elevating but is hardly poisonous."这句话中有明显的连接词"but"，故将which译为"虽然"。

综上所述，不难看出，理解和翻译定语从句的时候不仅要重视语句形式的研究，还要从实际意义着手进一步探讨其语义功能。只有这样，才能正确地理解和翻译状语性定语从句，并忠实传达原文所表达的含义。无论是普通意义的定语从句还是状语性定语从句，都体现了英语里一个貌似形合、实则意合的现象，翻译时译者需要仔细领会原句所蕴含的深层逻辑意义，然后准确无误地译出其内涵意义。

综合练习

一、将下列句子译成汉语。

(一) 用前置法翻译下列句子。

1. If marriage exists only as an intimate relationship that can be terminated at will, and family exists only by virtue of bonds of affection, both marriage and family are relegated to the

marketplace of trading places, with individuals maximizing their psychological capital by moving through a series of more or less satisfying intimate relationships.

2. Someone with a history of doing more rather than less will go into old age more cognitively sound than someone who has not had an active mind.

3. The root is that part of the vegetable which least impresses the eyes.

4. People tend to be more impressed by evidence that seems to confirm some relationship.

5. A person who is a sack of all trades has many skills.

6. The time of day when you feel most energetic is when your cycle of body temperature is at its peak.

7. An electric field is a space where an electric force exists.

8. Pollution is a pressing problem which we must deal with.

9. A man, who bites others, gets bitten himself.

10. Even a skilled writer probably could not describe all the features that make one face different from another.

11. Have you set the day when you will move?

12. Creating a "European identity" that respects the different cultures and traditions which go to make up the connecting fabric of the Old Continent is no easy task and demands a strategic choice.

13. Furthermore, humans have the ability to modify the environment in which they live, thus subjecting all other life forms to their own peculiar ideas and fancies.

14. My brother-in-law's laugh, which was very infectious, broke the silence.

15. A youngster, who has no playmates of his age living nearby, may benefit greatly from attending nursery school.

参考译文

1. 如果婚姻只是一种可以任意终结的亲密关系，而家庭只靠爱情的纽带来维持，那么婚姻和家庭将沦为可以自由买卖的市场，每个人都可以穿梭于一系列或多或少让自己满意的亲密关系，从而使自己的心理资本得到最大的增值。

2. 习惯于多动脑的人进入老年后在认知能力上要比一个从来不积极动脑的人更健全。

3. 根是植物中最不引人注目的部分。

4. 人们往往对看上去能证实某种关系的迹象有更深刻的印象。

5. 一个全才的人是一个掌握许多技能的人。

6. 一天中人们精力最充沛的时刻是体温循环处于巅峰的时刻。

7. 电场就是电力存在的空间。

8. 污染是我们必须解决的一个紧迫的问题。

9. 害人者，反害己。

10. 即使是高明的作家，也可能无法描写出将一个面孔与另一个面孔区别开来的全部特征。

11. 你搬迁的日子定了吗？

12. 不同的文化和传统把欧洲大陆编织成一体，要创造出一种尊重这些不同文化和传统的"欧洲特征"绝非易事，需要作出战略选择。

13. 而且，人类还有能力改变自己的生存环境，从而让所有其他形态的生命服从人类的独特想法和想象。

14. 我姐夫那富有感染力的笑声打破了沉默。

15. 对于周围没有同龄伙伴和自己玩的儿童，上托儿所大有益处。

(二) 用后置法翻译下列句子。

1. In Europe, as elsewhere, multi-media groups have been increasingly successful groups which bring together television, radio, newspapers, magazines, and publishing houses that work in relation to one another.

2. When that happens, it is not a mistake: it is mankind's instinct for moral reasoning in action, an instinct that should be encouraged rather than laughed at.

3. Although there are some men who like children and may have considerable experience with them, others do not particularly care for children and spend little time with them.

4. Behaviorists suggest that the child who is raised in an environment where there are many stimuli which develop his or her capacity for appropriate responses will experience greater intellectual development.

5. They are striving for the ideal which is close to the heart of every Chinese and for which, in the past, many Chinese have laid down their lives.

6. In conclusion, I wish to acknowledge my deep obligation to Dr. X and to Prof. Y, both of whom have read the manuscript and offered the most helpful criticism.

7. We are not conscious of the extent to which work provide the psychological satisfaction that can make the difference between a full and an empty life.

参考译文

1. 在欧洲，像在其他地方一样，多媒体集团越来越成功；这些集团将相关的电视、广播、报纸、杂志和出版社组合在一起。

2. 产生这种反应并没有错，这是人类用道德观念进行推理的本能在起作用。这种本能应得到鼓励，而不应遭到嘲笑。

3. 尽管有些男人喜欢孩子而且对抚养孩子有相当多的经验，其他男人却不是特别关心孩子，几乎不和孩子待在一起。

4. 行为主义者认为，如果孩子在一个有许多刺激物的环境中长大，而这些刺激物又能培养他作出适当反应的能力，这个孩子就会有更大的智力发展。

5. 他们正在为实现理想而努力，这个理想是每个中国人所心心念念的，在过去，许多中国人为了这个理想而牺牲了生命。

6. 最后，我要对X博士和Y教授表示深切的谢意。他们两位都曾审阅了原稿并提出了极为有益的评价。

7. 我们还没有意识到工作能给人带来多大的心理满足感，这种满足感能够决定你过的是充实的生活还是空虚的生活。

(三) 用融合法翻译下列句子。

1. There are some countries/regions in the world where there is little rain at any time.

2. I don't know any parent who would choose the word fun to describe raising children.

3. There were some Americans some years ago who said that the United States should play the so-called "China card". That is absurd. China is not a card that the United States can play.

4. I saw a cow that was grazing under a tree.

5. In recent years an interesting fact has been brought to public attention: As educational levels, salaries, and the cost of living have increased, more and more people are now having fewer and fewer children to the point where schools in many cities have to close down.

6. The promotional campaign that emphasized Cheer as an effective "all temperature" detergent was lost on the Japanese who usually wash clothes in cold water.

参考译文

1. 世界上有些国家/地区终年少雨。

2. 我认识的为人父母的人中，没有谁认为抚养小孩好玩。

3. 几年前曾有一些美国人说美国应打所谓"中国牌"，这是荒谬可笑的。中国不是一张可以任美国打的牌。

4. 我看见一头牛在树下吃草。

5. 最近几年一个有趣的情况引起了人们的注意：随着教育水平、工资和生活成本的提高，越来越多的人不想多生孩子，以至于许多城市的学校不得不关门。

6. 这个促销活动重点强调该洗涤剂适用于任何温度，在日本却反应平平，那是因为日本人习惯于用冷水洗衣服。

(四) 翻译下列句子，注意将其中的定语从句译为相应的状语从句。

1. In learning a foreign language, say English, one should first pay attention to speaking, which is the groundwork of reading and writing.

2. Again he adjusted his tie after loosening the knot which seemed to make his breathing hard and heavy.

3. You must grasp the concept of "work" which is very important in physics.

4. The coffee, which had been boiling for a long time, tasted rancid.

5. He turned a deaf ear to our demands, which enraged all of us.

6. The ambassador was giving a dinner for a few people whom he wished especially to talk to or hear from.

7. Scientists say this could lead to design changes in airplanes that would save hundreds of millions of dollars in fuel costs.

8. The first computers used the same types of components which made equipment very large and bulky.

9. For any machine whose input and output forces are known, its mechanical advantage can be calculated.

10. Anyone who should do such a thing would be a great fool.

11. He who laughs last laughs best.

12. Nothing is difficult in the world for anyone who dares to scale the height.

13. Anybody who commits the land power of the United States on the continent of Asia ought to have his head examined.

14. They amounted to near twenty thousand pounds, which to pay would have ruined me.

15. "No man is fit to be a naturalist, "said he, "who does not know how to take care of specimens".

16. The thief, who was about to escape, was caught by the policemen.

17. Samuel Bruh was just an ordinary-looking citizen like you and me, except for a curious, shoe-shaped scar on his left cheek, which he got when he fell against a wagon- tongue in his youth.

18. Chinese trade delegations have been sent to African countries, who will negotiate trade agreements with the respective governments.

19. They are trying to provide better controls, which may eliminate these troubles.

20. They have built up a new college here, where students will be trained to be engineers and scientists.

21. He insisted on building another house, which he had no use for.

22. Tom, who had been prevented by illness from studying, passed the examination.

23. The books, some of which had already been damaged, were sold out.

参考译文

1. 学习一门外语，比如英语，首先要注意说，因为说是读和写的基础。

2. 他松了一下领结，又整了整领带，好像是领带使他感到呼吸困难和急促。

3. 你必须掌握"功"这个概念，因为它在物理学中很重要。

4. 这咖啡因为煮的时间长了，所以尝起来味道不新鲜。

5. 他对我们的要求充耳不闻，使得我们大家都很生气。

6. 大使打算设宴招待一些人，因为他希望专门与他们交谈或听取他们的意见。

7. 科学家们说，这项成就将引起飞机设计上的变化，从而可以在飞机燃料费用方面节约数亿美元。

8. 首批计算机采用同类元件，致使设备既庞大又笨重。

9. 对任何机器，如果知其输入力和输出力，就能求出其机械效益。

10. 无论是谁，只要做出这样的事，就是个大傻瓜。

11. 谁笑到最后，谁笑得最好。

12. 世上无难事，只要肯登攀。

13. 如果谁要把美国的陆军派遣到亚洲大陆，那他就应该检查一下他的脑子是否正常。

14. 金钱总额将近两万英镑，如果要我个人赔，非要了我的命不可。

15. "假如一个人不知道如何保管好标本，"他说，"那他绝不适合做博物学家。"

16. 小偷正要逃跑时，被警察抓住了。

17. 萨缪尔·布鲁这位老兄相貌平平，犹如你我，只不过年少时有一回摔倒，撞在大车辕杆上，从此，左颊上留下了一道疤痕；那疤痕倒也别致，形状像只小小的鞋印，令人感到好奇。

18. 中国贸易代表团前往非洲各国，届时将与非洲各国政府进行贸易协定谈判。

19. 他们正在设法提供较好的控制方法，去消除这些故障。

20. 他们已在这里建了一所新的学院，以培养工程师和科学家。

21. 他坚持要再建一幢房子，尽管他并无此需要。

22. 尽管汤姆生病耽误了学习，他考试还是及格了。

23. 那些书虽然有些已损坏，但都卖出去了。

二、翻译以下语篇，注意定语从句的处理。

Three Days to See(Excerpts)

All of us have read thrilling stories in which the hero had only a limited and specified time to live. Sometimes it was as long as a year, sometimes as short as 24 hours. But always we were interested in discovering just how the doomed hero chose to spend his last days or his last hours. I speak, of course, of free men who have a choice, not condemned criminals whose sphere of activities is strictly delimited.

Such stories set us thinking, wondering what we should do under similar circumstances. What events, what experiences, and what associations should we crowd into those last hours as mortal beings, what regrets?

Sometimes I have thought it would be an excellent rule to live each day as if we should die tomorrow. Such an attitude would emphasize sharply the values of life. We should live each day with gentleness, vigor, and a keenness of appreciation which are often lost when time stretches before us in the constant panorama of more days and months and years to come. There are those, of course, who would adopt the Epicurean motto of "Eat, drink, and be merry". But most people would be chastened by the certainty of impending death.

In stories the doomed hero is usually saved at the last minute by some stroke of fortune, but almost always his sense of values is changed. He becomes more appreciative of the meaning of life and its permanent spiritual values. It has often been noted that those who live, or have lived, in the shadow of death bring a mellow sweetness to everything they do.

Most of us, however, take life for granted. We know that one day we must die, but usually we picture that day as far in the future. When we are in buoyant health, death is all but unimaginable. We seldom think of it. The days stretch out in an endless vista. So we go about our petty tasks, hardly aware of our listless attitude toward life.

The same lethargy, I am afraid, characterizes the use of all our faculties and senses. Only the deaf appreciate hearing, and only the blind realize the manifold blessings that lie in sight. Particularly does this observation apply to those who have lost sight and hearing in adult life. But those who have never suffered impairment of sight or hearing seldom make the fullest use of these blessed faculties. Their eyes and ears take in all sights and sounds hazily, without concentration and with little appreciation. It is the same old story of not being grateful for what we have until we lose it, and of not being conscious of health until we are ill.

I have often thought it would be a blessing if each human being were stricken blind and deaf for a few days at some time during their early adult life. Darkness would make them more appreciative of sight and silence would teach them the joys of sound.

假如给我三天光明(节选)

我们都读过震撼人心的故事，故事中的主人公只能再活一段很有限的时光，有时长达一年，有时却短至一日。但我们总是想要知道，注定要离世的人会选择如何度过自己最后的时光。当然，我说的是那些有选择权利的自由人，而不是那些活动范围受到严格限定的死囚。

这样的故事让我们思考，在类似的处境下，我们该做些什么？作为终有一死的人，在临终前的几个小时内我们应该做什么事，经历些什么或与谁联系？回忆往昔，什么使我们开心快乐？什么又使我们悔恨不已？

有时我想，把每天都当作生命中的最后一天来过，也不失为一个极好的生活法则。这种态度会使人格外重视生命的价值。我们每天都应该以优雅的姿态、充沛的精力、抱着感恩之心来生活。但当时间以无休止的日、月和年在我们面前流逝时，我们却常常不知道珍惜。当然，也有人奉行"吃、喝、享受"的享乐主义信条，但绝大多数人还是会因为即将到来的死亡而悔恨不已。

在故事中，将死的主人公通常都在最后一刻因突降的幸运而获救，但他的价值观通常都会改变，他变得更加理解生命的意义及其永恒的精神价值。我们常常注意到，那些生活在或曾经生活在死亡阴影下的人无论做什么都会感到幸福。

然而，我们中的大多数人都认为生命是理所当然的。我们知道有一天我们必将面对死亡，但总认为那一天还在遥远的将来。当我们身强体健之时，死亡简直不可想象，我们很少考虑到它。日子多得好像没有尽头。因此我们一味忙于琐事，几乎意识不到我们对待生活的冷漠态度。

我担心同样的冷漠也存在于我们对自己官能和意识的运用上。只有聋子才理解听力的重要，只有盲人才明白视觉的可贵，尤其是那些成年后才失去视力或听力的人，最能理解耳聪目明的可贵，而那些视力或听力从未受损的人很少充分利用这些宝贵的能力。他们的眼睛和耳朵模糊地感受着周围的景物与声音，心不在焉，也无所感激。正像我们只有在失去后才懂得珍惜一样，我们只有在生病后才意识到健康的可贵。

我经常想，如果每个人在年轻的时候都失明失聪几天，也不失为一件幸事。黑暗将使人们更加感激光明，而寂静将告诉人们声音的美妙。

第11章

翻译技巧(七)名词性从句译法

　　名词性从句包括主语从句、表语从句、宾语从句和同位语从句。在翻译时，此类从句的语序通常可以不变，即可按原文的顺序译成相应的汉语。但有时也需要一些其他处理方法。

11.1 主语从句的译法

主语从句是指在复合句中充当主语的从句，通常放在主句谓语动词之前。主语从句可以使用不同的引导词，这些引导词根据主语从句所缺句子成分的情况进行选择。主语从句的使用保持了句子的平衡，尤其是当主语从句较长时，常会用形式主语it代替，而把主语从句放到句末。构成主语从句的方式有下列两种。

11.1.1 关联词或从属连词位于句首的主语从句

关联词引导的主语从句是指连接副词或连接代词引导的主语从句。此类从句一般放在句首，充当主从复合句的主语。这样的关联词有how、why、when、where、whenever、wherever、what、which、who、whatever、whoever等，从属连词有that、whether、if等。例如：

Whether the Government should increase the financing of pure science at the expense of technology or vice versa often depends on the issue of which is seen as the driving force.

结构分析：句子的框架是Whether...or...often depends on...。Whether...or引导的主语从句作整个句子的主语，financing应根据上下文译成"经费投入"；介词结构of which is seen as the driving force是宾语the issue的后置定语，of介词结构中又包含了which引导的介词宾语从句。

参考译文：政府究竟是减少对技术的经费投入来增加对纯理论科学的经费投入还是相反，往往取决于把哪一方看作驱动力。

How well the predictions will be validated by later performance depends on the amount, reliability, and appropriateness of the information used and on the skill and wisdom with which it is interpreted.

结构分析：句子的框架是How...depends on...and on...。整个句子的主语由how引导的主语从句担任；谓语动词depends后面跟了两个由and连接的并列宾语(即on...and on...)，在第二个宾语中，介词with+which引导的定语从句修饰先行词the skill and wisdom。

参考译文：这些预测在多大程度上为后来的表现所证实，取决于所采用信息的数量、可靠性和适宜性，以及以什么样的技能和才智来解释这些信息。

What could be a key to jetlag and winter blues is the hormone melatonin, which is known to regulate body rhythms.

结构分析：句子的框架是What...is the hormone melatonin, which is...。what引导了一个主语从句，而由which引导的非限制性定语从句修饰hormone melatonin。句中的jetlag是"时差综合征"，blues不能译成"蓝色"，而是"忧郁"之意。

参考译文：解除时差综合征和冬季忧郁症的关键是褪黑激素，众所周知，这种激素能够调节人体节奏。

11.1.2　it+谓语+that(whether)引导的主语从句

对于it+谓语+that(whether)引导的主语从句，如果先译主句，可以将其顺译为无人称句。有时也可先译从句，再译主句。如果先译从句，便可以在主句前加"这"。例如：

And it is imagined by many that the operations of the common mind can by no means be compared with these processes of scientists, and that they have to be acquired by a sort of special training.

结构分析：句子的框架是And it is imagined...that..., and that...。这是典型的句型：It+is+p.p.(过去分词)+that clause。其中，It是形式主语，句子真正的主语是两个并列的that引导的主语从句，由连词and连接。operations此处不能译成"操作"，根据上下文应译成"活动"，这里的processes要译成"思维过程"，而不能简单地理解成"过程"。

参考译文：许多人认为，普通人的思维活动根本无法与科学家的思维过程相比，并且这些思维过程必须经过某种专门训练才能掌握。

Furthermore, it is obvious that the strength of a country's economy is directly bound up with the efficiency of its agriculture and industry, and that this in turn rests upon the efforts of scientists and technologists of all kinds.

结构分析：句子的框架是Furthermore, it is obvious that..., and that...。这是典型的句型：It+is+*adj.*+that clause。其中，It是形式主语，真正的主语是由连词and连接的两个并列的主语从句：that the strength of...bound up with...和that this...rests upon the efforts...。第一个主语从句中的词组be bound up with是"与……有关联"之意；在第二个主语从句中，代词this指代前文中的the efficiency of its agriculture and industry，译为"效率的提高"。

参考译文：再者，显而易见的是，一个国家的经济实力与其工农业生产效率密切相关，而效率的提高又有赖于各类科技人员的努力。

It is a matter of common experience that bodies are lighter in water than they are in air.

结构分析：有时为了使译文成分完整，可以补充上泛指的主语(如人们、大家……)。

参考译文：物体在水中比在空气中轻，对此，大家已达成共识。

类似的结构还有：

it is (universally) known that... 大家都知道……

it is believed that... 人们都相信……

It is strange that she should have failed to see her own shortcomings.

真奇怪，她竟然没有看出自己的缺点。

11.2 表语从句的译法

表语从句是位于主句的连系动词后面、充当主句表语的从句，它通常由that、what、why、how、when、where、whether等连词和关联词引导。一般来讲，可以先译主句，后译从句。例如：

Nutritional experiments have made it evident that vitamins are indispensable for one's growth and health.

营养实验证明：维生素对人们的健康和生长是不可缺少的。

Galieo's greatest glory was that in 1609 he was the first person to turn the newly invented telescope on the heavens to prove that the planets revolve around the sun rather than around the earth.

伽利略的最光辉的业绩在于，他在1609年最先把新发明的望远镜对准天空，以证明行星是围绕太阳旋转的，而不是围绕地球旋转。

Things are not always as they seem to be.

事物并不总是如其表象。

对于that(this) is why...句型，如果选择先译主句，后译从句，可以将其译成"这就是为什么……""这就是……的原因""这就是……的缘故"等。如果选择先译从句，再译主句，一般可以将其译为"……原因就在这里""……理由就在这里"等。例如：

That is why heat can melt ice, vaporize water, and cause bodies to expand.

这就是热能使冰融化，使水蒸发，使物体膨胀的原因。

对于this(it) is because...句型，一般先译主句，再译从句，可将其译成"是因为……""这是……的缘故""这是由于……"。例如：

This is because the direct current in a wire always flows in one direction.

这是由于直流电在导线中总沿着一个方向流动。

对于this is what...句型，如果先译主句，后译从句，通常将其译为"这就是……的内容""这就是……的含义"等。如果先译从句，后译主句，通常将其译为"……就是这个道理""……就是这个意思"等。例如：

This is what we have discussed in this article.

这就是我们在本文中所讨论的内容。

If I have seen farther than other men, it is because I have stood on the shoulders of giants.

—Newton

假如我比别人望得远，这是因为我站在了巨人的肩上。

——牛顿

11.3　宾语从句的译法

宾语从句可以分为两种：一种是跟在动词后的宾语从句；另一种是跟在介词后的宾语从句。翻译宾语从句时，语序一般不变。例如：

There are now 31 million kids in the 12-to-19 age group, and demographers(人口学家) predict that there will be 35 million teens by 2010, a population bigger than even the baby boom at its peak.

结构分析：句子的框架是There are...kids..., and demographers predict that...。这是一个并列复合句，在第二个并列分句中，谓语动词predict后面跟了一个that引导的宾语从句；在该宾语从句中，a population bigger than even the baby boom at its peak是35 million teens的同位语。

参考译文：12至19岁年龄组的孩子目前有3100万，人口学家预测，到2010年，青少年人数将达到3500万，比二战后生育高峰期出生的孩子还多。

If parents were prepared for this adolescent reaction, and realized that it was a sign that the child was growing up and developing valuable powers of observation and independent judgment, they would not be so hurt, and therefore would not drive the child into opposition by resenting and resisting it.

结构分析：句子的框架是If parents were..., and realized that..., they would not..., and...。主句是they would not be so hurt, and therefore would not...，里面有两个并列的谓语(would not be和would not drive)，在第二个谓语词组中，有介词词组by resenting and resisting it，其中it指代前文中的this adolescent reaction；在if引导的状语从句中，也有两个并列的谓语部分(were prepared for..., and realized that...)，在第二个谓语部分中，that

引导的宾语从句作realized的宾语，该宾语从句中又包含了that引导的同位语从句that the child was growing up... and independent judgment，该从句作a sign的同位语。

参考译文：如果做父母的对这种青春期的反应有所准备，而且认为这是一个显示孩子正在成长、正在发展可贵的观察力和独立的判断力的标志，他们就不会感到如此伤心，也就不会因对此有愤恨和反对的情绪而把孩子推到对立面去。

However, some are questioning whether the compulsory "face scanning" constitutes violations of people's privacy, as it involves the collection of tremendous sensitive personal biometric information.

结构分析：句子的框架是 some are questioning whether...as it involves... 句子开头是表示转折关系的副词 However，译为"但是""可是""不过"等；主句是现在进行时，现在分词 questioning 后面是由 whether 引导的宾语从句 whether the compulsory "face scanning" constitutes violations of people's privacy。该句的逻辑关系并不复杂，采取顺译法即可，即按照原文的顺序进行翻译。

参考译文：不过，也有人质疑强制实行"人脸识别"是否侵犯了人们的隐私，因为这涉及极其敏感的个人生物识别信息的收集。

11.4　同位语从句的译法

英语中的同位语从句用于解释前面某一名词的内容，也就是将这一名词的含义具体化，其地位和此名词是同等的。此类从句常用that或whether来引导。同位语从句常用来说明fact、theory、sense、question、conclusion、news、experience、evidence、proof、condition、law、conjecture、doubt等词的具体含义。翻译此类从句时，一般有两种处理方法：一种是把从句译成一个独立的句子，并在其前加"即……""这……"等词，或在从句所修饰的名词之后加冒号或破折号；二是用"的"字把从句放在它所修饰的词之前。例如：

Even though wealth has grown greatly in the United States, there is much concern that its distribution has become increasingly uneven, with the rich getting a great deal richer, while others are being left behind—if true, it is an unhealthy situation breeding social unrest.

结构分析：句子的主干是Even though wealth has grown..., there is much concern that...distribution has become uneven, with...。主句是there is much concern that...，that引导的同位语从句作concern的同位语，在此同位语从句中，介词结构with..., while...中包含while连接的并列分句，while表示对比，相当于whereas，译成"而"；破折号之后是总

结句，这里的if true是省略句，完整的句子为if it is true。

参考译文：虽然美国的财富大大增长，但是有许多人担心美国的财富分配已变得越来越不均衡，富人变得更富，而其他人则落在后面——这种情况如果属实，这将是一种不健康的局面，孕育着社会动乱。

This is a universally accepted principle of international law that the territory sovereignty doesn't admit of infringement.

结构分析：句子的主干是This is a...principle that...。主句是This is a universally accepted principle of international law，而that引导的同位语从句作principle的同位语。翻译时，可以先译从句(即从句前置)，再译主句。

参考译文：一个国家的领土主权不容侵犯，这是国际法中尽人皆知的准则。

It is scarcely surprising, then, that education systems have for several decades past been severely criticized, partly on the ground that education prepares people to live in an already outdated society.

结构分析：句子的主干是It is...surprising...that education systems have...been...criticized, ...on the ground that...。这是典型的It+is+*adj.*+that clause句型。其中，It是形式主语，真正的主语是that引导的主语从句，而主语从句又包含了that引导的同位语从句that education prepares people to live in an already outdated society，该从句作介词词组on the ground中ground的同位语，ground在这里的意思是"根据"。

参考译文：那么教育体制在过去几十年中受到严厉的批评，就不那么令人感到惊讶了，批评者的部分根据是，这种教育教人们如何在一种已过时的社会中生存。

综合练习

一、将下列含有名词性从句的句子译成汉语。

1. How and when human language developed and whether animals such as chimpanzees and gorillas can develop a more elaborate system of communication are issues at present being researched, but as yet little understood.

2. From the end of the Second World War until very recently, it was generally accepted in Britain that the State should provide a full range of free educational facilities from nursery schools to universities.

3. From handmade workshops to industrialized production, what remains unchanged is Chinese people's love for traditional food.

4. What we require is a theory which is based on various experiments and which enables us to explain more complicated phenomena.

5. That the world's first compass was invented by the Chinese people is a well-known historical fact.

6. It seemed inconceivable that the pilot could have survived the crash.

7. That substances expand when heated and contract when cooled is a common physical phenomenon.

8. Whatever I saw and heard on my trip gave me a very deep impression.

9. A simple experiment will show whether or not air does have weight.

10. He believes that the highly mobile American society leaves individuals with feelings of rootlessness, isolation, indifference to community welfare, and shallow personal relationships.

11. It is necessary for young people to understand how our society depends upon scientific and technological advancement and to realize that science is a basic part of modern living.

12. We fail to learn that pain is the body's way of informing the mind that we are doing something wrong, not necessarily that something is wrong.

13. The result of invention of steam engine was that human power was replaced by mechanical power.

14. This is where the shoe pinches.

15. Men differ from brutes in that they can think and speak.

16. Our practice proves that what is perceived cannot at once be comprehended and that only what is comprehended can be more deeply perceived.

17. The law of conservation and transformation of energy states that energy is indestructible and the total amount of energy in the universe is constant.

18. He expressed the hope that he would come over to visit China again.

19. She had no idea why she thought of him suddenly.

20. The fact that the gravity of the earth pulls everything towards the center of the earth explains many things.

21. Not long ago the scientists made an exciting discovery that this "waste" material could be turned into plastics.

22. While China has a clear-cut answer to the question "whether China and the United States can properly deal with their relations," the ball is now in the U.S. court.

23. The least we can get from what is mentioned above is the conclusion that the world is in constant change and motion.

24. Is this definition quite satisfactory that "a thermometer is an instrument for measuring heat and cold"?

25. There is only a remote possibility that many other elements will be found.

26. An order has been given that the researchers who are now in the sky-lab should be sent back.

27. But considering realistically, we had to face the fact that our prospects were less than good.

参考译文

1. 人类的语言是如何发展起来的，是什么时候形成的，诸如黑猩猩和大猩猩一类的动物中是否会形成一种更加复杂的交流系统，都是现阶段人们研究的课题，但对此人们还知之甚少。

2. 从第二次世界大战结束直到最近，英国人普遍接受这样一个观点：国家应该提供从幼儿园到大学的全方位的免费教育设施。

3. 从手工作坊到工业化生产，不变的是中国人对传统美食的热爱。

4. 我们需要的是建立在各种实验基础上的一种理论，它使我们能够解释更复杂的现象。

5. 世界上第一枚指南针是中国人发明的，这是众所周知的史实。

6. 驾驶员在飞机坠毁之后，竟然还能活着，这看来是不可想象的事。

7. 物质热胀冷缩是一个常见的物理现象。

8. 旅行中的所见所闻都给我留下了深刻的印象。

9. 空气是否确有重量，做个简单的试验就可以证明。

10. 他认为，流动性很大的美国社会留给个人的感觉是没有根基、孤立、对社会福利漠不关心和人际关系淡漠。

11. 有必要让年轻人了解我们的社会是如何依赖科技进步的，并认识到科学是现代生活的基本组成部分。

12. 我们不知道人体会通过疼痛这种方式通知大脑我们的行为出了差错，而不一定是健康有问题。

13. 蒸汽机的发明使得机械力代替了人力。

14. 这就是症结所在。

15. 人与兽的区别就在于人有思维而且会说话。

16. 我们的实践证明，感知到的东西我们不能立即理解，只有理解了的东西我们才能更深刻地感知。

17. 能量守恒和转换定律说明：能量是不灭的，宇宙间能量的总和是不变的。

18. 他表示希望能再来中国访问。

19. 她不明白自己为什么突然想到了他。

20. 地球引力把一切东西都吸向地心这一事实解释了许多现象。

21. 不久以前，科学家们有了一个令人振奋的发现：可以把这种废物变为塑料。

22. 虽然中国对"中美能否妥善处理两国关系"的问题有明确的答案，但解决问题的关键在美国。

23. 据上所述，我们至少可以得出这样一个结论：世界处于永恒的变化和运动中。

24. "温度计是测量冷热的工具"这一定义是否完美呢？

25. 再发现许多新元素的可能性不大。

26. 上级已下命令，要求将目前在航天实验室里的研究人员送回来。

27. 但是现实地考虑一下，我们不得不正视这样一个事实：我们的前景并不妙。

二、将下列语篇译成汉语。

Passage One：

A Nation of Hypochondriacs

—Norman Cousins

The main impression growing out of twelve years on the faculty of a medical school is that the No.1 health problem in the U.S. today, even more than AIDS or cancer, is that Americans don't know how to think about health and illness. Our reactions are formed on the terror level. We fear the worst, expect the worst, and thus invite the worst. The result is that we are becoming a nation of weaklings and hypochondriacs, a self-medicating society incapable of distinguishing between casual everyday symptoms and those that require professional attention.

Somewhere in our early education we become addicted to the notion that pain means sickness. We fail to learn that pain is the body's way of informing the mind that we are doing something wrong, not necessarily that something is wrong. We don't understand that pain may be telling us that we are eating too much or the wrong things; or that we are smoking too much or drinking too much; or that there is too much emotional congestion in our lives; or that we are being worn down by having to cope daily with overcrowded streets and highways, the pounding noise of garbage grinders, or the cosmic distance between the entrance to the airport and the departure gate. We get the message of pain all wrong. Instead of addressing ourselves to the cause, we become pushovers for pills, driving the pain underground and inviting it to return with increased authority.

参考译文

一个疑病症患者的国度

——诺曼·克森斯

在一所医学院校任教十二年来我获得的主要印象是：当今美国的头号健康问题甚至比艾滋病或癌症都更为严重——美国人不知道如何去认识健康与疾病。我们的反应是建立在恐惧这个尺度之上的。我们怕最坏的事，准备迎接最坏的事，而恰恰就招来了最坏的事。结果我们的社会变得人人虚弱，自疑有病，许多人因为分不清哪些是日常偶发症状、哪些是需要医生医治的症状而擅自用药。

在我们早期教育的某个阶段，我们对"疼痛即疾病"这一观念深信不疑。我们不知道人体会通过疼痛这种方式通知大脑我们的行为出了差错，而不一定是健康有问题。我们不明白，疼痛可能是一种警示：我们已吃得太饱或吃得不当；或吸烟太多或饮酒过度；或生活中未宣泄的情绪太多；或因每天都得面对拥挤的大街和公路、忍受垃圾粉碎机的撞击声和奔波于从机场入口到登机口之间的长距离而疲惫不堪。我们把疼痛传达的信息全理解错了。我们不去探查其缘由却擅自用药把疼痛压下去，致使它以更大的威力再次发作。

Passage Two：

First impressions are often lasting ones. Indeed, if you play your cards right, you can enjoy the benefits of what sociologists call the "halo effect". This means that if you're viewed positively within the critical first few minutes, the person you've met will likely assume everything you do is positive.

How you move and gesture will greatly influence an interviewer's first impression of you. In a landmark study of communications, psychologists discovered that seven percent of any message about our feelings and attitudes comes from the words we use, 38 percent from our voice, and a startling 55 percent from our facial expressions. In fact, when our facial expression or tone of voice conflicts with our words, the listener will typically put more weight on the nonverbal message.

To make your first encounter a positive one, start with a firm handshake. If the interviewer doesn't initiate the gesture, offer your hand first. Whenever you have a choice of seats, select a chair beside his or her desk, as opposed to one across from it. That way there are no barriers between the two of you and the effect is somewhat less confrontational. If you must sit facing the desk, shift your chair slightly as you sit down, or angle your body in the chair so you're not directly in front of your interviewer.

Monitor your body language to make sure you don't seem too desperate for the job, or too eager to please. Keep a Poker face in business situations. Inappropriate smiling is the most common example of a nonverbal behavior that undercuts verbal messages—making you appear weak and unassertive. Good eye contact is also important. One study found that job applicants who make more eye contact are perceived as more alert, dependable, confident, and responsible.

参考译文

第一印象常常是持久的印象。的确，如果处理得当，你就能有幸获得社会学家所说的"光环效应"带来的种种好处。这就是说，要是在一开始关键的几分钟里你就给人留下好的印象，初遇者就可能认为你办的事件件都好。

你的一举一动都会大大影响你给面试者的第一印象。在有关人际交流的一项意义重大的研究中，心理学家发现，关于情绪和态度的信息有7%来自我们的语言文字，有38%来自我们的语音，而惊人的是，竟有55%来自我们的面部表情。事实上，如果面部表情或说话语调与我们所说的话发生矛盾，听者通常会更加看重那些非语言信息。

为了使第一次面试成功，一开始的握手要坚定有力。如果面试者没有主动伸出手来，你就先把手伸出来。要是可以选择座位的话，要坐在面试者桌子的侧面，而不要坐在正对面。这样一来你们中间就没有障碍了，而且在一定程度上起到减少对立的作用。如果你只能坐在桌子对面，那么坐下的时候把椅子稍微挪一下或者把身体斜靠在椅子上，这样你就不是正对着面试者了。

要注意你的形体语言，千万不要表现得对这份工作迫不及待，也不要表现得急于讨好别人。在商务场合要保持一本正经的神态。非语言行为可削弱语言信息的力量，从而使你显得优柔寡断，缺乏自信，而不合时宜的微笑就是一个最为常见的例子。良好的目光交流也非常重要。有一项研究发现，多用目光进行交流的求职者被认为是更机警、可靠、自信、负责的。

第12章

翻译技巧(八)状语从句译法

　　状语从句是英汉两种语言中都存在的语言现象。英语状语从句根据功能的不同可分为时间、地点、原因、条件、让步、目的等状语从句，在翻译成汉语时一般比较容易处理，不会构成翻译的主要障碍，关键在于怎样将其放入恰当的位置，以及怎样处理好句与句之间的连接关系。本章举例说明了各种英语状语从句的翻译方法。

在将英语状语从句译成汉语时，应注意以下几点。第一，应注意各类状语从句在英汉两种语言中的位置差异，在译文中适当调整语序，相应地将其译成符合译入语表达习惯的状语从句。第二，应注意连接词，分清主句和从句之间的逻辑关系，因为汉语造句多用意合法，一些连接词往往被省略。第三，尽量避免机械地照搬连接词的汉语对应词或译义，在准确理解主句和从句间的逻辑关系后，进行相应的句型转换，如将英语的时间状语从句译为汉语的并列句或条件句，将地点状语从句译为汉语的条件句，等等。第四，应注意主语的使用。状语从句的翻译方法主要遵循以下4个原则。

1 状语从句前置

英语中的时间、地点、条件、原因等状语从句既可以前置，也可以后置，而汉语中的这类状语从句一般前置；英语中表示条件的状语从句一般位于句首，尤其是虚拟条件句，对于此类从句，常常采用顺译法，将其置于句首；英语中的让步状语从句置于句首或句尾均可，而在汉语中则前置为多。

2 状语从句后置

汉语中表示原因、时间、条件、让步的从句一般前置，但有时也可放在主句后面，此时，从句有补充说明的作用。英语中表示比较、结果、方式和目的的状语从句在译成汉语时可后置。

3 状语从句的转换

有些状语从句从形式上看是某种状语从句，但从其主句和从句的逻辑意义来看，却不属于该种状语从句，而属于另一种从句。对此，翻译时可根据主句和从句的逻辑意义，进行适当的转换，将其翻译成另一种句型，如将时间状语从句译为条件句或让步状语从句，将地点状语从句译为条件句或结果状语从句，等等。

4 省略连词

由于汉语造句采用意合法，汉语的复合句常常省略连词。因此，翻译英语中某些状语从句中的连词时，不防将其省略，这样更符合汉语表达习惯。此时从句和主句之间可能为并列关系，或与主句紧缩为一个句子。

12.1　时间状语从句译法

英语时间状语从句一般译成与汉语完全对应的表示时间的状语。有些英语状语从句虽然形式上是由表示时间的引导词(如when、before、until等)引导，但根据句子的逻辑意义来判断，应灵活翻译成表因果关系的从句，或者翻译为表条件的状语从句或表目的的状语从句。例如：

When it comes to using personal information on the ads, such as using portraits, we must obtain the individual's authorization.

如果要在广告上使用个人信息，例如使用肖像，我们必须获得个人的授权。

Every time you try to answer a question that asks why, you engage in the process of causal analysis—you attempt to determine a cause or series of causes for a particular effect.

每当你试图回答一个问及为什么的问题时，你就是在进行因果分析了。也就是说，你正努力寻找决定某个结果的某个原因或一系列原因。

Not until we have detailed studies of the present movement of traffic and have a clearer idea of how many people wish to travel, where they want to go, at what time of day and how quickly—not until then can we begin to plan a proper transportation system for the future.

只有详细地研究当前的交通流量，比较清楚地了解有多少人想去旅行，要到哪里去，在一天中的什么时候上路，希望以多快的速度旅行——只有到那时，我们才能开始对未来的运输系统进行合理的规划。

When winds blow particles against a large rock for a long time, the softer layers of the rock are slowly worn away.

由于风把砂粒刮起来，碰撞大岩石，久而久之，较松软的岩石层就被慢慢地磨损。

Before manned spacecraft could be sent to space, the problem of getting the spacecraft safely back to earth had to be solved.

为了把载人的宇宙飞船送到太空上去，就必须先解决使飞船安全返回地球的问题。

Where it is dry so much of the time that few plants can live, the destructive waters have their own way when the occasional rains come.

结构分析：句子的框架是Where it is dry..., the destructive waters have...。where it is dry...是地点状语从句。it是无人称代词，表示自然现象。这个从句中包含一个由that引导的结果状语从句，与so相呼应。主句中包含一个由when引导的时间状语从句。the destructive waters不能直译为"具有破坏性的水"，而应与谓语结合转译成"雨水泛滥，造成灾害"。

参考译文：在长期干旱以致植物稀少的地方，偶尔降雨便会泛滥，造成灾害。

12.2　地点状语从句译法

地点状语从句表示地点、方位，在英语中，这类从句通常由where、wherever等词引导。地点状语从句可置于句首、句中或句尾。地点状语从句通常采用顺译法进行翻译，即如果地点状语从句在英语原文中位于句首，则其译文也应位于句首；反之，若英语从句位于句尾，则其译文也应位于句尾。但有时根据需要，翻译过程中也可对英语中位于主句后的地点状语从句进行语序调整，使其出现在汉语译文的句首。此外，英语地点状语从句除译作汉语的地点状语外，有时还可译作汉语的条件句。例如：

So I sincerely hope that all Chinese compatriots, wherever you come from, no matter which part of China you come from, can stay united in a joint pursuit for the eventual reunification of our motherland and for the rejuvenation of the Chinese nation.

因此，我衷心希望所有的中国同胞，无论你从哪里来，无论你来自中国的哪个地区，都能团结起来，为祖国的最终统一，为中华民族的伟大复兴而共同奋斗。

Make a mark where you have any doubts or questions.

在有疑问的地方做个记号。

Where water resources are plentiful, hydroelectric power stations are being built in large numbers.

哪里水源充足，就在哪里修建大批的水电站。

The materials are excellent for use where the value of the workpieces is not high.

如果零件价位不高，使用这些材料是最好不过的了。

12.3　原因状语从句译法

英语原因状语从句通常由从属连词 as、because、since 引导。由because引导的原因状语从句一般置于句末，也可位于句首，通常用来表示直接原因。由as引导的原因状语从句通常位于句首；若置于句末，其前应有逗号。as表示的原因或理由一般是说话的对方所知道的，它通常译为"由于"。since引出的原因状语从句通常位于句首，把已知的事实作为推理的依据，说明的原因或理由是说话的双方所明知的事实，因此，since往往译为"既然"。英语的原因状语从句一般译为汉语的原因状语从句，有时可视情况译作汉语主句。英语原因状语从句在汉语译文中通常位于句首，偶尔置于句末。例如：

Because we are both prepared to proceed on the basis of equality and mutual respect, we meet at a moment when we can make peaceful cooperation a reality.

由于我们双方都准备在平等和相互尊重的基础上开展合作，我们在这个时刻会晤就能够使和平合作成为现实。

It also plays an important role in making the earth more habitable, as warm ocean currents bring milder temperatures to places that would otherwise be quite cold.

由于温暖的洋流能把温暖的气候带给那些本来十分寒冷的地区并使之变暖，因此，海洋在使地球变得更宜居方面也起着重要的作用。

12.4　条件状语从句译法

条件状语从句是英语语法中的一部分，用来描述主句动作发生的条件或可能性。常见引导词有if、unless、as/so long as、on condition that、provided that/providing that、suppose that/supposing that等。条件状语从句又分为真实条件句和虚拟条件句两大类。真实条件句用于表达真实条件，一般有可能实现；虚拟条件句用于表达与客观事实完全相反的条件或假设，一般不可能实现。通常情况下，条件状语从句可译作汉语的假设句或补语，译为"假如……""如果……""只要……"等。例如：

Whatever its underlying reasons, there is no doubt that much of the pollution caused could be controlled if only companies, individuals, and governments would make more efforts.

结构分析：句子的主干是Whatever its underlying reasons, there is no doubt that...if only companies, ...。whatever引导让步状语从句，谓语may be省略。该从句的主语为reasons，whatever是may be的表语。its指代pollution's。主句中that引导的是doubt的同位语从句。过去分词caused作pollution的定语。同位语从句中包含由if only引导的条件状语从句。整个同位语从句用虚拟语气，表示这种可能性很小。

参考译文：不论污染的根本原因是什么，毫无疑问，只要各公司、个人和各级政府都能做出较大的努力，所造成的大部分污染是可以控制的。

If developing countries feel that industrialized countries are trying to divert attention from their problems by focusing on the problems of poorer countries, we risk wrestling endlessly over these issues rather than solving our common problems.

结构分析：句子的主干是If developing countries feel that..., we risk wrestling endlessly over...。if引导条件状语从句，而此从句中又套了一个由that引导的宾语从句。介词短语by focusing on...作状语。对于这样长的条件句，应采用分译法。we指代前文中的developing countries。wrestle不能直译为"搏斗"，应转译为"争论"。

参考译文：如果发展中国家认为工业化国家正试图通过关注较贫穷国家的问题来转移人们对其问题的注意力，那么我们有可能面临为这些问题纠缠不休的风险，而不是去解决我们的共同问题。

12.5　让步状语从句译法

让步状语从句的主句通常是肯定句，而从句本身可以是肯定句或否定句。从句的主语和谓语与主句的主语和谓语之间没有必然的联系。让步状语从句表示某种与主句所述内容相反的条件或情况，但从句所表示的这些不利因素并不能阻止主句动作的发生，即在相反的条件下，主句的情况依然存在。英语中的让步状语从句可由although、though、even if、even though、no matter、despite、in spite of等词引导，相当于汉语中表示"让步"的状语，一般译为"尽管……"或"即使……"等。例如：

Although the prices of Chinese new energy vehicles exported to Europe are lower than those of similar local models, they are still one to two times higher than their prices in China, ensuring significant profits and dispelling any concerns about dumping.

虽然中国新能源汽车出口欧洲的价格低于当地同类车型，但仍比其在中国的价格高出一到两倍，从而确保了可观的利润，并消除了人们对倾销的担忧。

While it is true that this competition may induce efforts to expand territory at the expense of others, and thus lead to conflict, it cannot be said that war-like conflict among other nations is inevitable, although competition is.

结构分析：该句可拆分为三大部分，即(While it is true that this competition may induce efforts to expand territory at the expense of others, and thus lead to conflict,) (it cannot be said that war-like conflict among other nations is inevitable,) (although competition is.)。第一部分是While引导的让步状语从句，第二部分是主句，第三部分是although引导的让步状语从句。第一部分的主语是it(形式主语)，指代后面的that从句，实际上，While it is true that已形成固定结构，that从句的主语是this competition，谓语是may induce，宾语是efforts，不定式to expand territory作efforts的后置定语，at the expense of others作expand的状语，and之后的lead to是谓语，与前面的induce并列，conflict是lead to的宾语；主句中的主语是it(形式主语)，指代后面的that从句，该从句的主语是conflict，谓语动词是is，表语是inevitable，复合形容词war-like作conflict的定语，among other nations作conflict的后置定语；第三部分中although从句的主语是competition，谓语是is，表语inevitable被省略了。该句的主句运用了被动语态，在翻译时要译为汉语的主动语态，这是常用的一条

原则，因为英文多用被动句，汉语多用主动句。

参考译文：虽然这种竞争会引发以他人利益为代价的领土扩张行动，因此也会引发冲突，但却不能认为类似于战争的国家间冲突不可避免，尽管竞争是不可避免的。

Although humans are the most intelligent creature on earth, anything humans can do, Nature has already done better and in far, far less space.

虽然人类是地球上最聪明的生物，但人能创造的一切，大自然都能创造，而且造得更好，所占空间也小得多。

Lifts stopped working, so that even if you were lucky enough not to be trapped between two floors, you had the unpleasant task of finding your way down hundreds of flights of stairs.

电梯停了，因此即使你运气好，没有被困在两个楼层中间，你也得去完成一项不愉快的任务，即摸黑往下走百级楼梯。

让步状语从句有时译成表示"无条件"的条件分句。汉语里有一种复句，前一分句排除某一方面的一切条件，后一分句说出在任何条件下都会产生同样的结果，也就是说结果的产生没有什么条件限制。这种复句里的前一部分，称为"无条件"的条件分句，通常以whatever、wherever、whoever、whenever、no matter wh-为引导词，通常翻译为"不论""无论""不管"等关联词。例如：

No matter what you buy, shoes, pants, or big-ticket items such as appliances and furniture, if you find some problems with them or simply do not like them any longer, you can return them within 30 days.

无论你买的是什么，鞋子、裤子或者像家电、家具这样的大件物品，如果发现有问题或者单纯不想要了，都可以在30天内退货。

When anyone does something for you, no matter how small and no matter whether he's a superior or servant, it's proper to say "Thank you".

只要有人替你做了一件事，不管事情多么微不足道，也不管这个人是你的上司还是仆人，你都应该说声"谢谢"。

No matter how carefully you move your hand toward a fly, the insect will dart off almost every time.

不管你多么小心翼翼地把手伸向一只苍蝇，差不多每次它都会飞走。

12.6　目的状语从句译法

目的状语从句是指在复杂句中表示主句动作发生目的的状语从句，用于补充说明主句中谓语动词发生的目的，可置于句首或句尾。常用引导词有so that、in order that、for fear that、in case(that)、for the purpose that等。英语目的状语从句一般译成汉语中表示目的的前置分句，常用"为了""省(免)得""以免""以便""生怕"等词引导。例如：

A rocket must attain a speed of about five miles per second so that it may put a satellite in orbit.

火箭必须达到每秒约5英里的速度，才能把卫星送入轨道。

We do not read history simply for pleasure, but in order that we may discover the laws of political growth and change.

我们读历史不单是为了娱乐，还为了从中发现政治发展和政治演变的规律。

Electricity is such a part of our everyday lives and so much taken for granted nowadays that we rarely think twice when we switch on the light or turn on the computer.

如今，电已成为我们日常生活的一部分，被认为是理所当然的事。因此，我们在开灯或开电脑时很少会再去想一想电是怎么来的。

12.7 注意几种状语从句的译法

12.7.1 连词until引导的时间状语从句

(1) until引导的时间状语从句修饰主句中否定形式的瞬间谓语动词，此时汉语译文中常有"直到……才……"的字样。例如：

We can't start the job until we have got the approval from the authority concerned.

没有有关当局的批准，我们不能开始做这项工作。

He didn't appear until the party was over.

他直到聚会结束才来。

He wasn't able to return until the volcano became quiet.

直到火山平息下来，他才得以回去。

(2) until引导的时间状语从句修饰主句中肯定形式的持续性谓语动词，此时汉语译文中常带有"一直……到……"的字样。例如：

He stayed there until the evening was over.

他在那里一直待到晚会结束。

I will wait here until the concert is over.

我会在这里一直等到音乐会结束。

We should continue the struggle until our object is reached.

我们应该继续奋斗，直到达到目的。

(3) 对于will not...until句型，可根据助动词的含义，将until译成"如果"。

A man will not become a fool until he stops asking questions.

人如果停止思考，就会变得愚蠢。

Things will not turn up in the world until somebody turns them up.

世间之事物，如果无人去发掘，是不会自行出现的。

12.7.2　连词since引导的时间状语从句

(1) since引导的时间状语从句中谓语动词为瞬间动词时，常含有"自……以来"的意义。例如：

What have you been doing since I last saw you?

自我上次和你见面以后，你一直在做什么？

It is five years since he joined the army.

他参军已有五年了。

It is two years since we parted.

我们分别至今已有两年了。

(2) since引导的时间状语从句中谓语动词为延续性动词或状态性动词时，常含有"自……结束以来……"的意义。例如：

He has been hunting jobs since he worked in that company.

从那家公司离职后，他一直在找工作。

It is five years since he was a soldier.

他退役已经五年了。

He has been quite well since he smoked.

他戒烟以来身体一直很好。

12.7.3　连词before引导的时间状语从句

(1) before引导的时间状语从句本身意为"在……前"，这种情况下主句与before从句中的两个动作按时间顺序依次发生。例如：

Before the rooster crows, you will say three times that you don't know me.

在公鸡叫之前，你要说三次你不认识我。

You must not count your chickens before they are hatched.

小鸡孵出之前不能算数。/不要过早打如意算盘。

Before they drive any of the buses, they will have to pass a special test.

他们在驾驶公共汽车之前必须通过一项专门的测试。

Before I enter on the subject I have something to say.

在讨论这些问题之前我有些话要说。

(2) before引导的从句可译成"(后)……才"。副词"才"在汉语中表示某事发生得晚或慢。

The train had left before he got to the station.

火车开走后他才到车站。

It seemed a long time before my turn came.

似乎过了好大一会儿才轮到我。

The fire spread four streets before the firefighters could control it.

大火蔓延了四条大街，消防队员们才控制住火势。

(3) 连词before与barely、scarcely、hardly连用时还可译成"刚……就"，在汉语中"就"强调事情发生得早或快。例如：

We had barely run out before the house collapsed.

我们刚跑出来，房子就塌了。

We had scarcely reached the school before it began to rain.

我们刚到学校就下雨了。

(4) 如果原文的目的在于渲染在从句动作发生之前，主句动作已发生，那么before可译成"未……就"或"还没有(来得及)……就"。例如：

The day began to break before we got to the hilltop.

我们还没到达山顶，天就亮了。

The girl was drowned before succors did anything.

救援人员还未能采取措施，那个女孩就已经淹死了。

She rushed out like crazy before I could explain anything.

我还没来得及作任何解释，她就发疯似的冲了出去。

Before we could stop him, he had rushed on to a potato plot and dug up one of the potatoes.

我们还来不及阻止他，他就已经飞奔到一块土豆地里，挖出了一个土豆。

(5) before还作"与其……(宁愿)"解，通常可译为"宁可……(也)不(肯)""宁愿……决不"等。例如：

He would die before he lied.

他宁死也不肯说谎。

He would die before he should disgrace himself.

他宁死也不受辱。

He said he himself would die of hunger before he stole.

他说他本人宁愿饿死也不愿偷他人钱财。

12.7.4 连词because引导的原因状语从句

because引导的原因状语从句本身意为"因为……"，但如语境有变化，也会有不同的译法。例如：

John didn't attend the meeting because he was ill.

约翰没有出席会议，因为他病了。

He does not want to go with us, because he is tired.

他不想和我们一起去，因为他很累。

He doesn't eat because he is hungry, but greedy.

他不是因为饿了，而是因为贪嘴才吃的。

Galileo didn't believe it because Aristotle said so.

伽利略并不因为这是亚里士多德说的，就去相信它。

I didn't criticize him because I hate him but because I love him.

我不是因为恨他，而是因为爱他，才去批评他的。

综合练习

一、将下列句子译成汉语。

1. When censorship laws are relaxed, dishonest people are given a chance to produce virtually anything in the name of "art".

2. Please turn off the light when you leave the room.

3. Mary had scarcely heard the news when she wept aloud.

4. When I reached the beach, I collapsed.

5. They set him free when his ransom had not yet been paid.

6. I was about to speak when Mr. Smith cut in.

7. Turn off the switch when anything goes wrong with the machine.

8. A body at rest will not move till a force is exerted on it.

9. Until all is over, ambition never dies.

10. The crops failed because the season was dry.

11. As the moon's gravity is only about 1/6 of the gravity of the earth, a man of 200 pounds weighs only 33 pounds on the moon.

12. Although its form can be changed, energy can neither be created nor destroyed.

13. Even though robots can do more things than man does, they cannot replace man.

14. Although television was developed for broadcasting, many important uses have been found that have nothing to do with it.

15. Whether the characters portrayed are taken from real life or are purely imaginary, they may become our companions and friends.

16. By many such experiments Galileo showed that, apart from differences caused by air resistance, all bodies fall to the ground at the same speed, whatever their weight is.

17. I still think that you made a mistake while I admit what you said.

18. If one of them dares to lay his little finger on me as we go out, I won't answer for what I'll be doing.

19. If something has the ability to adjust itself to the environment, we say it has intelligence.

20. Granted that this is true, what conclusion can you draw?

21. We won't attack others unless we are attacked.

22. If you get beyond your depth, you'll suffer.

23. A man doesn't know the difficulty of anything unless he does it personally.

24. Some wild animals are not easily tamed unless caught young.

25. No one, unless he be a lunatic, could do that.

26. If we can't do as we could, we must do as we can.

27. If I could relive my life, I would lead quite a different life, leaving less regrets.

28. Should there be urgent situation, press the red button to switch off the electricity.

29. Yet whenever I stopped by his hospital bedside, he was surrounded by visitors from his church, singing and praying.

30. They support the holding of a summit conference no matter whether this sort of conference will make achievement or not.

31. No matter what misfortune befell him, he always squared his shoulders and said, "Never mind. I'll work harder."

32. He got the same result whichever way he did the experiment.

33. No matter how hard it is raining, I am going out for a walk.

34. All living things, whether they are animals or plants, are made up of cells.

35. They were determined to carry out their plan no matter what obstacles they would have to face.

36. We should start early so that we might get there before noon.

37. Steel parts are usually covered with grease for fear that they should rust.

38. He slammed the door so that his mother would know he was home.

39. The murderer ran away as fast as he could, so that he might not be caught red-handed.

40. The bridge was so well built that it lasted for 100 years.

参考译文

1. 当审查放宽时，招摇撞骗之徒就会有机可乘，在"艺术"的幌子下炮制出形形色色的东西来。

2. 离屋时请关电灯。

3. 玛丽一听到这消息就放声大哭。

4. 我一游到海滩，就昏倒了。

5. 他的赎金还没有支付，他们就把他释放了。

6. 我正想讲，史密斯先生就插嘴了。

7. 如果机器发生故障，就关闭开关。

8. 若无外力的作用，静止的物体则不会移动。

9. 不到黄河心不死。

10. 气候干燥，作物歉收。

11. 由于月球的引力只有地球引力的六分之一，所以体重200磅的人在月球上仅重33磅。

12. 尽管能量的形式可以转变，但它既不能被创造，也不能被消灭。

13. 虽然机器人能比人做更多事情，但不能代替人。

14. 虽然电视是为了广播而发明的，但是电视还有许多与广播无关的重要用途。

15. 无论书中描述的角色来自真实生活还是来自纯粹的想象，他们都可能成为我们的伙伴和朋友。

16. 伽利略通过多次这样的实验证明，一切物体，不论其重量如何，除了空气阻力引起的差别外，都是以同样的速度落向地面的。

17. 虽然我承认你所说的那番话，但我还是认为你犯了个错误。

18. 如果我们出去的时候，他们谁敢碰我一根汗毛，我可就要不客气了。

19. 如果某物具有适应环境的能力，我们就说它具有智力。

20. 假设这是实际情况，你又能得出什么结论呢？

21. 人不犯我，我不犯人。

22. 打肿脸充胖子，吃亏的是自己。

23. 事非经过不知难。

24. 一些野生动物，除非在幼小时被捕获，否则是不容易驯养的。

25. 没有人会那样做，除非是狂人。

26. 如果我们不能如愿以偿，则应当尽力而为。

27. 如果生活可以重来，我会过得截然不同，不会留下这么多遗憾。

28. 万一有紧急情况，请按红色按钮以切断电源。

29. 然而，无论我何时来到他的病床边，他总是被来自他奉职的教堂的人所包围，他们又唱又祷告。

30. 他们支持召开首脑会议，不管这种会议是否取得成果。

31. 不管他遭受了什么不幸的事儿，他总是把胸一挺，说："没关系，我再加把劲儿。"

32. 无论用什么方法做实验，他总是得到相同的结果。

33. 不管雨下得多大，我还是要出去散步。

34. 一切生物，不管是动物还是植物，都是由细胞组成的。

35. 无论遇到什么困难，他们都决心实施自己的计划。

36. 为了在正午以前赶到那里，我们应当早点动身。

37. 钢制零件通常会涂上润滑油，以防生锈。

38. 他 "砰" 地关上门，好让母亲知道他回家了。

39. 凶手尽快地跑开，以免被人当场抓住。

40. 桥建得很牢，持续了100年。

二、将下列语篇译成汉语。

Why Measure Life in Heartbeats

Hemingway once wrote that courage is grace under pressure. But I would rather think with the 18th-century Italian dramatist, Vittorio Alfieri, that "often the test of courage is not to die but to live." For living with cancer engenders more than pressure; it begets terror. To live with it and to face up to it—that's courage.

Hope is our most effective "drug" in treating cancer. There is almost no cancer (at any stage) that cannot be treated. By instilling hope in a patient, we can help develop a positive, combative attitude to his disease. Illogical, unproven? Perhaps. But many doctors believe that this must become a part of cancer therapy if the therapy is to be effective.

I have had the joy of two beautiful and wonderful wives, the happiness of parenthood, and the love of eight children. My work was constantly challenging and fulfilling. I have always loved music and books, ballet, and the theater. I was addicted to fitness, tennis, golf, curling, hunting, and fishing. Good food and wine graced my table. My home was a warm and happy place.

But when I became aware of my imminent mortality, my attitudes changed. There was real meaning to the words, "This is the first day of the rest of your life." There was a heightened awareness of each sunny day, the beauty of flowers, and the song of a bird. How often do we reflect on the joy of breathing easily, of swallowing without effort and discomfort, of walking without pain, and of a complete, peaceful night's sleep?

After I became ill, I embarked upon many things I had been putting off before. I read the books I had set aside for retirement and wrote one myself, entitled *The Art of Surgery*. My wife Madeleine and I took more holidays. We played tennis regularly and curled avidly; we took the boys fishing. When I review these past few years, it seems in many ways that I have lived a lifetime since I acquired cancer. On my last holiday in the Bahamas, as I walked along the beach feeling the gentle waves wash over my feet, I felt a part of the universe, even if only a minuscule one, like a grain of sand on the beach.

Although I had to restrict the size of my practice, I felt closer empathy with my patients. When I walked into the Intensive Care Unit there was an awesome feeling knowing I, too, had been a patient there. It was a special satisfaction to comfort my patients with cancer, knowing that it is possible to enjoy life after the anguish of that diagnosis. It gave me a warm feeling to see the sparkle in one patient's eyes—a man with a total laryngectomy—when I asked if he would enjoy a cold beer and went to get him one.

If one realizes that our time on this earth is but a tiny fraction of that within the cosmos, then life calculated in years may not be as important as we think. Why measure life in heartbeats? When life is so dependent on such an unreliable function as the beating of the heart, then it is fragile indeed. The only thing that one can depend upon with absolute certainty is death.

I believe that death may be the most important part of life. I believe that life is infinitesimally brief in relation to the immensity of eternity. I believe that though my life was short in years, it was full in experience, joy, love, and accomplishment; that my own immortality will reside in the memories of my loved ones left behind, mother, brother, wife, children, and dear friends. I believe that I will die with loved ones close by and, as everyone hopes, achieve death in peace, and with dignity.

何必以心跳定生死

海明威曾经写过，勇气就是临危不惧。不过，我更赞同18世纪意大利戏剧家维多利奥·阿尔菲利的观点:"考验一个人的勇气,往往不是看他是否惧死,而是看他是否敢活下去。"身患癌症,不仅带来痛苦,而且引起恐惧。抱病生活,并敢于正视这一现实,这就是勇气。

希望是我们治疗癌症最有效的"药物"。几乎没有什么癌症(无论发展到哪一期)是不能医治的。把希望灌输到病人心里,我们就可以帮助他树立起积极与疾病斗争的观念。也许此话不合逻辑,言之无据,是吗?然而,许多医生认为,要想使疗法有效,这必须成为治疗的一部分。

我有幸先后拥有两位美丽贤惠的妻子所带来的欢乐,体验过为人之父的乐趣,并得到八个子女的爱。过去,我的工作一直富有挑战性,令人有成就感。我一向喜欢听音乐和读书,酷爱芭蕾舞和戏剧。我曾醉心于健身运动、网球、高尔夫球、冰上溜石、打猎和垂钓。我的餐桌摆满美酒佳肴。我的家温馨而又幸福。

可是,当我知道自己大限将至时,生活态度就变了。"这是您余生的开始"这句话对我有了实实在在的含义。对每一个晴天丽日,对鸟语花香,我的感触倍加强烈。平时呼吸轻松,吞食自如,走路毫不费力,一夜安寝到天明,我们几曾回味过其中的乐趣?

患病以后,我着手做以前搁置下来的许多事情。我阅读了几本原计划留到退休后才读的书,而且亲笔写了一本题为《外科术》的书。我与夫人玛德琳度假更频繁了。我们经常去打网球,劲头十足地在冰上溜石,还带儿子们去钓鱼。回顾过去几年,从许多方面来看,自从我得了癌症后,我似乎又活了一辈子。上次到巴哈马度假期间,我沿着海滩漫步,海浪轻轻抚揉着我的双脚,此时此刻我蓦然觉得自己与整个宇宙融为一体,尽管我显得微不足道,就像海滩上的一粒沙子。

虽然我不得不限制自己的医务工作量,我感觉自己与病人更加心灵相通。当我走进特别护理室时,一种敬畏之感油然而生,因为我知道自己也曾是这里的病人。我明白,在经历了被确诊为癌症患者的极度痛苦之后,仍有可能享受生活,因此,安慰癌症患者成了一种特别的乐事。一位病人做了全喉切除术,我问他是否想喝冰镇啤酒,而且为他拿来了一杯,这时我看到他眼里闪现出了火花,一股暖流顿时涌上我的心头。

倘若人们意识到人生在世只不过是宇宙的时间长河中转瞬即逝的一刹那,那么以岁月计算的生命将不会像我们所想象的那样重要。何必以心跳来定生死呢?当生命依赖于心跳这样一种不可靠的功能时,它的确脆弱不堪。而只有死亡才是人们唯一可以绝对确定的。

我想,死亡可能是人生中最重要的一环。我认为,与那漫长的永生相比,生命是极其短暂的。我相信,我以年月计算的生命虽然是短暂的,但经历丰富,充满了欢乐、爱情和成就;我将永远活在我所爱的人——我母亲、兄弟、妻子、儿女及密友的记忆中。我相信,在我弥留之际,我的亲朋好友将陪伴在我身旁并且如大家所愿,我将带着尊严,安详地告别人间。

第13章

翻译技巧(九)被动语态译法

对比汉语和英语,我们会发现英语中的被动句显然多于汉语,因为英语重视形态(形式),而汉语不重视形态,重视语感。以汉语为母语的人自古以来有一种主体思维方式,认为"成事者必在人",施事者"尽在不言中"。所以很多被动关系不必一定用"被"字句。在英语中,语态是动词的一种形式。英语动词有两种语态:主动语态和被动语态。其中,与汉语句子表达方式相比,英语被动语态是使用频率很高的形式,英语被动语态的译法十分灵活,需要结合上下文灵活把握才能翻译出表意准确、流畅通顺的句子。

英语中主客体分明，叙述一件事情时既可以从主体出发，也可以从客体出发，所以英语存在主动句与被动句两种对应的表达形式。与只强调主体意识的汉语相比，英语有一个突出的特点：经常强调客体意识。所以英语被动语态的使用频率远远高于汉语被动句。英语中被动语态的使用范围很广。在不必说出施动者、不愿说出施动者、无从说出施动者等场合，使用被动语态就方便多了，在某些情况下，还能使上下文更连贯。而且，被动语态把要说明的问题放在句子的主语位置上，有两个显著优势：一是不带感情色彩，简洁客观；二是更能引起人们的注意。这在科技作品中更为明显。

汉语中可以表达被动意义的主动句式很多，情况比较复杂。谭卫国先生指出："造成这种汉语被动句使用范围小的原因可能很多，但主要原因有三个：第一个原因是汉语中有许多动词既可以用来表示主动意义，又可用来表达被动意义。第二个原因是汉语是意合语言，即使不用被动句的标志性词语，也可以表达被动意义。第三个原因是汉语大量使用无主句。"中国人很善于通过意义来判断名词与动词之间的施受关系。这里只谈其中一种与被动句关系最密切的形式，就是"意义上的被动句"。这类句子的主语大多表示无生命的事物，是谓语动词支配的对象。汉语中这类句子的数量很大，远远超过被动句，这是由汉语为母语者的思维习惯决定的，可以使语言表达更简洁。以汉语为母语者注重思维形态上的主体性，认为任何行为都只能是人这个行为主体完成的，所以当表示无生命事物的词语充当主语时，以汉语为母语者会自然感觉到它不可能是动作的执行者，动词动作的执行者一定另有其人。这时汉语不必再用"被"字来标明主谓之间的受事关系，用主动句就可以达到表达的目的。这一点在口语中表现得尤为明显。例如，"钱包丢了""饭做好了""煤气用完了"等。正是这种思维习惯使汉语的被动意义具有隐含性，此为汉语句子的重要特点，英语并无此特点，所以这类句子译成英语时要进行语态转换。例如：汉语句子"房间已经打扫干净了"译成英语为"The room has been cleaned."。

汉语的被动句主要用在书面语中，口语中比较少。英语决定(被动语态)出现次数的语体上的主要因素似乎与文章是知识性的还是想象性的有关，而不是与口语或书面语有关。一般来说，被动语态在知识性文章中比想象性文章中用得多，而在纯客观的一般性语体的科学文献和新闻报道中尤其用得多。因此英语被动句形成了其典型的使用场合：科技文章和新闻报道。在科技文章中，科学家们总是力图以客观的态度来说明客观事物的规律，在新闻报道中记者也要注重报道的客观真实性，被动句表义的客观性正好满足了这种要求。汉语常用的则是受事主语句或无主句等表示被动意义的主动句。

英语被动语态译成汉语时，很多情况下都可译成主动句，但也有一些保留了被动形式。这种表达形式上的不同源于以汉语为母语者与母语为英语者思维形式上的差异，强调主体意识是汉语的特点，而英语的特点是主客体分明。受主体意识影响而形成的思维习惯使以汉语为母语者常常从主体出发进行叙述，即使从客体出发，以汉语为母语者也会自然而然地意识到客体与动词间是受事关系，不必依靠"被"这样的形式标志。所以汉语中许多主动句形式的句子表达的却是被动意义，而听话人在理解上也不会出现困难。

了解两种语言在被动语态中的异同，以及英语被动语态的应用特点，可以帮助我们准确把握被动结构的句子，从而获得理想的译文。汉语中虽然有被动句，但其使用范围明显更狭窄，也不像英语那样有固定的或比较统一的构成形式。因此，英译汉中的语态转译现象是一种必然现象。翻译时应注意英汉两种语言在这方面的差别，根据汉语的表达习惯，忠实、通顺地翻译英语被动语态。

13.1　英语被动语态译为汉语的主动语态

英语和汉语都有被动语态，但由于表达习惯上的差异，英语句式中被动语态的使用要广泛得多。同一个意思，英语习惯用被动语态表示，而汉语却往往用主动语态、无主句或判断句。因此，英译汉时，大量被动语态的句子需要通过语态转换的方法加以处理，不能过分拘泥于原文的被动结构，而要根据汉语的习惯，做灵活多样的处理，以保证译文通顺流畅地表达原意。在翻译过程中，英语有很多被动句可以直接转换成汉语的主动句，转换的方法大致有以下几种。

13.1.1　原句中的主语、谓语不变，译文中没有表示被动的标志，以主动句表达被动意义

易词而译是指在译文中用一个表示主动概念的动词代替原文中表示被动概念的动词，例如用"得知"译"are told"，用"得不到"译"aren't given"，用"收入"译"are paid"，等等。这样的译文不仅读起来自然流畅，而且避免了"被告知""被问道"等不符合汉语表达习惯的词。例如：

She didn't expect she should be asked to speak before a big audience.

她没想到会让她在一大群听众前讲话。

If you are asked personal questions you need not answer them.

如果有人问你私人问题，不必回答。

His sense of inferiority that acquired in his youth has never been totally eradicated.

他在青少年时留下的自卑感还没有完全消除。

The money will be used to sustain national parks and reserves within the tropical rain forest belt in countries around the globe.

这笔款将用于维持全世界范围内的国家公园和热带雨林地区保留林的发展。

College students are found to spend too much time on their phones and have a difficult time falling asleep.

大学生花在手机上的时间过多，入睡困难。

13.1.2 原句中的主语译作谓语的宾语

这种译法适合用来翻译英语里无生命名词作主语的句子。英语常用无生命名词作句子的主语，而汉语习惯用有生命的名词作句子的主语。若英语的被动式译成相应的汉语被动式后读出来生硬、不太顺口，翻译时可考虑将原文的主语(即受动者)与原文的宾语(即施事者)互换位置，这样一来，原文的主语成了译文的宾语，而原文的宾语成了译文的主语。例如：

Heat is constantly produced by the body as a result of muscular and cellular activity.

由于肌肉和细胞的活动，身体不断产生**热**。

The *friendship* was tamed to enmity through idle gossips.

流言蜚语使他们之间的**友谊**变成了怨仇。

As China has an increasing number of elderly people, *great attention* has been paid to the senior group.

随着中国老年人口的不断增加，老年群体受到了极大的**关注**。

13.1.3 英语被动语态惯用法的翻译

在英语被动语态中，有一种以"it"作形式主语，以被动语态作谓语，谓语后接由"that"引起的主语从句的表达方法。这类习惯用语可一律译成汉语的主动结构，即将原文中的主语从句置于译文中的宾语位置。译文主语或者略去，或者采用"据"字的结构，或者根据上下文以"人们""我们""有人""大家"等泛指人称代词补充之。

不加主语的：

It is hoped that... 希望

It is reported that... 据报道

It is said that... 据说

It is supposed that... 据推测

It must be admitted that... 必须承认

It must be pointed out that... 必须指出

It may be said without fear of exaggeration that... 可以毫不夸张地说

It will be seen from this that... 由此可见

可以加主语的:

It is asserted that... 有人主张

It is believed that... 有人相信

It was told that... 有人曾经说

It will be said that... 有人会说

It is well known that... 大家知道(众所周知)

It is generally considered that... 大家认为

It was told that... 曾经有人说

例如:

It is generally accepted that the experiences of the child in his first years largely determine his character and later personality.

人们普遍认为,孩子们的早年经历在很大程度上决定了他们的性格及其未来的人品。

It is estimated that more than 30 museums in China, including the National Museum of China and the Dunhuang Academy China, have hosted live broadcasts on online platforms during the epidemic, each gaining over 10 million viewers in one day.

据估计,包括中国国家博物馆和敦煌研究院在内的中国三十多家博物馆在疫情期间在网络平台上进行了直播,每家博物馆日浏览量均超过1000万。

13.1.4　英语被动语态译成汉语中带表语的主动语态

有的英语被动句并非强调被动的动作,而是以被动语态的形式描述事物的过程、性质和状况,实际上与系表结构很相似。这类被动句可译成"是……的"句式。例如:

Rainbows are formed when sunlight passes through small drops of water in the sky.

彩虹是阳光透过天空中的小水滴时形成的。

The women were carefully selected from among many applicants.

这些妇女是从众多的应聘者当中选拔出来的。

How can a series of motionless or still pictures be blended on a screen to produce emotion pictures?

一组不动的(即静止的)图片是怎样在银幕上连到一起合成电影的呢?

13.1.5　英语被动语态译成汉语中带句首词的无主句

与英语相比,汉语有一种独特的句式:无主句。英语的许多被动句不需要或无法讲出动作的发出者,因此往往可译成汉语的无主句而把原句中的主语译成宾语。一般说来,描述什么地方发生、存在什么事物的英语被动句以及表示观点、态度、告诫、要求、号召等的被动句译成汉语时往往采用无主句,有时还可在动词前加上"把""使""将""对"等词。例如:

New sources of energy must be found to avoid causing energy shortages in the world.

必须找到新能源,以免造成世界性的能源短缺。

Methods are found to take these materials out of the rubbish and use them again.

现在已经找到了从垃圾中提取这些材料并加以利用的方法。

Great efforts should be made to inform young people especially the dreadful consequence of taking up the habit.

应该尽最大努力告诫年轻人吸烟的危害,特别是上瘾后的可怕后果。

此外,英语中有些固定的动词短语,如make use of、pay attention to、take care of、put an end to等,变成被动语态时可以其中名词作主语,翻译时可译成无主句,把主语和谓语合并译出。

The legitimate security interests of all countries should *be taken care of* and a balanced approach should be adopted.

应**照顾**所有国家的合法安全利益,并采取平衡的做法。

Special *attention has been paid to* the country's sparsely populated and remote regions to improve their capability to fight against the disease.

尤其要**关注**该国人口稀少和偏远地区,以提高其抗击该疾病的能力。

13.2　英语被动语态译为汉语的被动语态

英译汉时,汉语也有用被动形式来表达的情况。这时通常看重被动的动作,有时,可以说出动作的发出者,有时则没有这种必要。在把英语被动句译成汉语被动句时,我们常常使用下述几种方法。

(1) 将英语的被动语态译为汉语中带"被"或"给"字的句子。例如:

Except in times of drought, water has never been regarded as a valuable natural resource.

除了干旱时期，水从未被视为宝贵的自然资源。

In 2006, Shanxi Opera (or Jinju) was recognized as one of the first national intangible cultural heritages.

2006年，晋剧被认定为首批国家级非物质文化遗产之一。

A mess had been made of the house.

房子被弄得一片狼藉。

Vitamin C is destroyed when it is overheated.

维生素C受热过度就会被破坏。

(2) 将英语的被动语态译为汉语中带"遭""受"或"挨"字的句子。例如：

Last year the region was hit by the worst drought in 100 years.

去年该地区遭受了百年来最严重的旱灾。

Laureates are recognized for their scientific achievements and contributions to global research.

获奖者因其科学成就和对全球研究的贡献而受到认可。

He was set upon by two masked men.

他遭到两个蒙面人的袭击。

(3) 将英语的被动语态译为汉语中带"把""使"或"由"字的句子。例如：

He was obsessed with fear of poverty.

对贫困的担心使他忧虑重重。

Despite their countless capabilities, the miracle chips must be programmed by human beings.

尽管这些神奇的集成线路有数不清的性能，但还需要由人为它们编程。

Rivers are controlled by dams.

拦河坝把河水控制住了。

(4) 将英语的被动语态译为汉语中带"得到、受到……的""为……所"等结构的句子。例如：

Such conduct will be looked down upon by all with sense of decency.

这种行为将会为一切有良知的人所蔑视。

All the buildings were destroyed in a big fire.

所有的建筑物均为一场大火所焚毁。

Our vision is becoming a Chinese brand respected by the whole world.

我们的愿景是成为受全世界尊敬的中国品牌。

(5) 英语原文中的主语在译文中仍作主语。在采用此方法时，我们往往在译文中使用"予以""加以""经过" "用……来"等词来体现原文中的被动含义。例如：

Mistakes must not be covered up. They must be exposed before you can correct them.

错误不应当加以掩饰，而必须予以揭露，才能得以改正。

Nuclear power's danger to health safety, and even life itself can be summed up in one word: radiation.

核能对健康、安全，乃至对生命本身构成的危险可以用"辐射"一词加以概括。

13.3　英语双重被动句的常见译法

英语双重被动句的译法类似于一般被动句的译法，但英语双重被动句在译成汉语时不能生搬硬套，需要根据汉语的表达习惯采取一些综合、辅助的办法，因为英语中有双重被动句，而汉语中没有相应的句式。

(1) 英语双重被动句译成含有泛指主语的汉语主动句。译句前通常加上"人们""大家" "我们"等泛指人称代词。原句第一个被动结构中的过去分词译为泛指人称代词的谓语动词，原句的主语与第二个被动结构扩展为一个新的分句。例如：

The river is known to have been polluted.

众所周知，这条河已经受了污染。

The problem is believed to be settled sooner or later.

大家相信这个问题迟早会解决的。

The meeting is suggested to be put off till next Friday.

有人建议会议推迟到下周五举行。

(2) 英语双重被动句译成以动词开头的汉语无主句，第一个被动结构中的过去分词译为句首的动词，第二个被动结构中的过去分词与原句中的主语译为动宾结构。例如：

These books weren't permitted to be taken out of the room.

不许将这些书带出房间。

No building is permitted to be built here.

此处不准盖房。

Cars are allowed to be parked over there.

可以把车停在那边。

The mayor was arranged to be met at the airport.

安排在机场接见市长。

(3) 有些英语双重被动句在译成汉语时，可将第一个被动结构译成"据……"，原句中的主语与第二个被动结构扩展为一个新的分句。例如：

The child is reported to have been found.

据报道，孩子已经找到了。

He is said to have been sent to Switzerland.

据说他被派到瑞士去了。

The result is supposed to be announced soon.

据估计，成绩不久就宣布。

一般来说，英语被动语态是由"be+及物动词的过去分词"构成的。但是，这并不是被动语态的唯一表示方式。除了助动词be外，还有些动词可以用来构成被动语态。弄清这一问题，有利于翻译英语被动句。"动词get、become或feel的一定形式+及物动词的过去分词"可表示被动语态。这一结构通常表示动作的结果并非动作本身，也常用来表示突然发生、未曾料到的势态。这类句子常译成汉语被动句或汉语主动句。例如：

I think we may make it unless we get held up.

我想如果不被耽搁的话，我们能按时到达。

We all felt worried about the complication.

我们都为此事的复杂性而感到烦恼。

总而言之，英语被动语态的用法比较复杂，翻译方法又是灵活多样的。随着英语语言的发展和科学技术的不断进步，被动语态会更多地出现在语言实践中，我们应进一步细微观察，认真研究它的结构、用法及其翻译，力求把被动语态用好、译好。

综合练习

一、将下列英语句子译成汉语。

1. We hold these truths to be self-evident that all men are created equal.

2. He was seen to enter the house.

3. He was thrown into confusion by the return of his wife.

4. He has been wedded to translation.

5. The news was passed on by word of mouth.

6. Her husband has been made Mayor, and Mayra herself had got a medal for her work for the aged.

7. He was told that two of them seemed unlikely to pass the exam.

8. The jacket was creased, but the creases will wear out.

9. Many streets have been widened.

10. I hoped I may be pardoned by all of you.

11. The subway was completed by the end of last year.

12. The compass was invented in China four thousand years ago.

13. The performance was fully appreciated by the audience, mostly college students.

14. A truly elegant taste is generally accompanied with excellence of heart.

15. To whom nothing is given, of whom nothing is required.

16. The virtue of a man should be measured not by his extraordinary exertions, but by his everyday conduct.

17. It is believed that the future will be better than the present.

18. It was announced that there will be a new film tomorrow.

19. It is said that the meeting will not be held.

20. It is decided that I will meet them at the airport.

21. It is known that matter is in constant motion.

22. History is made by the people.

23. My first thirty years were spent in Western America.

24. Coffee stains can soon be washed out.

25. The response of the premature to certain drugs should be thoroughly understood.

26. In many countries/regions, authority is seldom, if ever, questioned.

27. The traffic regulations served are to be observed.

28. Smoking is not allowed in the office.

29. A telephone was fitted up in the pavilion.

30. Three hundred thousand Yuan has been raised for the village children to build a school.

31. The doctor should be sent for right away.

32. Beethoven and Mozart are both rated among the greatest composers of the world.

33. Those young trees were washed away by the flood.

34. The success of the Chinese people is continually lauded.

35. Our foreign policy is supported by the people all over the world.

36. The boy was criticized yesterday.

37. The translation technique should be paid enough attention to.

38. Other questions will be discussed briefly.

参考译文

1. 我们认为这些真理是不言而喻的：人人生而平等。

2. 有人看见他进了那所房子。

3. 他由于妻子归来而陷入惶惑不安中。

4. 他与翻译结下不解之缘。

5. 众口相传，消息不胫而走。

6. 迈拉的丈夫当上了市长，她自己也由于悉心为老年人工作而获得了一枚奖章。

7. 他已得知他们中有两个人好像不能及格。

8. 衣服起褶了，但会慢慢消失的。

9. 许多街道都拓宽了。

10. 我希望能得到你们大家的原谅。

11. 这条地铁于去年年底完工。

12. 中国在四千年前发明了指南针。

13. 观众对演出十分欣赏，他们中大多数是大学生。

14. 真正的审美力与心灵美通常是分不开的。

15. 有舍才有得。

16. 要衡量一个人的品德，不能看他一时的努力，而要看他的日常行为。

17. 人们相信明天会更好。

18. 有人通知明天放映新影片。

19. 据说会不开了。

20. 决定让我去机场接他们。

21. 大家知道，物质处于不断运动中。

22. 历史是人民创造的。

23. 我的前三十年是在美国西部度过的。

24. 咖啡渍是可以很快洗掉的。

25. 应该全面了解早产儿对某些药物的反应。

26. 在许多国家/地区，人们很少向权威提出质疑。

27. 必须遵守交通规则。

28. 办公室内不许抽烟。

29. 亭子里装了一部电话。

30. 已经筹集了三十万元为村里的孩子们建一所学校。

31. 得马上请医生来。

32. 贝多芬和莫扎特都被视为世界上最伟大的作曲家。

33. 那些小树被大水冲走了。

34. 中国人民的胜利不断受到人们的赞扬。

35. 我们的对外政策受到全世界人民的支持。

36. 这男孩昨天挨了一顿批评。

37. 翻译技巧应引起足够的重视。

38. 其他问题将简单地加以讨论。

二、将下列语篇译成汉语。

What are the keys to a successful life?

No matter what your goals are in life, there is one great law that you need to obey in order to be successful: No one else is going to climb the ladder of success for you. No one else is responsible for your health, wealth, happiness, or success. From the day you leave your parents' house and start to make your own choices, you are responsible for your life and the choices you make.

You choose the job you work in, the person you live with, and how much you exercise every day. Only you can choose how you spend your time, and the decisions you make on a consistent basis will make or break your life.

If you want a better life, you need to make better decisions. You can blame other people for your lack of results or happiness all life long, but it doesn't change anything. Only you can change your life by changing the choices you make. Take responsibility for everything in your life, even if you can't directly influence it. Even if it's not in your direct control, you can always choose how you respond.

According to motivational speaker Brian Tracy, the biggest enemy to success is the path of least resistance. If you choose what is fun and easy over what is necessary, you will never reach the levels of success and happiness you are capable of achieving in your life. That's because every great victory requires great sacrifice.

If success was easy, everybody would be successful. But because success in any area of your life requires hard work and sacrifices, most people will never reach their full potential.

Whenever you decide not to do what you should be doing, you not only waste your opportunity to grow as a person, but you also lose confidence in yourself. You start to see yourself as lazy and unsuccessful, and that self-image will become a successful prophecy.

To achieve any goal you have, there are only three things you need: A clear vision for what it is you want, a plan to get there, and massive action consistently repeated over time! While the first two parts are the easy parts of the equation, most people struggle with the last part: Hard work.

There is nothing that you can't achieve with hard work, so it is necessary that you build the habit of choosing what is hard and necessary over what is fun and easy to do. Doing this is probably the surest way to succeed in life.

参考译文

成功的关键是什么？

无论你的人生目标是什么，要想获得成功，都必须遵守一条伟大的法则：没有人会替你攀登成功的阶梯。没有人能为你的健康、财富、幸福或成功负责。从你离开父母的家，开始做出自己的选择的那一天起，你就要对自己的人生和所做出的选择负责。

你可以选择自己工作，选择与你生活在一起的人，选择每天锻炼多少。只有你自己可以选择如何分配自己的时间，而你不断做出的选择将决定你一生的成败。

如果你想要更好的生活，就需要做出更好的决定。你可以将自己的一无所成或终生不幸归咎于他人，但这并不能改变什么。你只能通过改变自己的选择来改变生活。对生活中的每件事负责，即使你不能直接影响它，即使这件事不在你的直接控制之下，你也可以选择如何应对。

励志演说家布莱恩·特雷西说过，通往成功的最大敌人是阻力最小的道路。如果你选择做轻松有趣之事，而非必要之事，你将永远无法到达你本能够达到的成功和幸福的人生境界，因为每一次伟大的胜利都需要做出巨大的牺牲。

如果成功很容易，那么每个人都会成功。但正因为生活中任何领域的成功都需要努力付出，做出牺牲，因此大多数人永远无法充分发挥其潜力。

每当你决定逃避本应做的事情时，你不仅浪费了一个成长的机会，也失去了对自己的信心。你开始认为自己懒惰、失败，然后便会自暴自弃。

要实现任何目标，你只需要做三件事：清楚自己想要什么，制订目标与计划，付诸大量行动，长期坚持不懈！前两件事很简单，但大多数人都很难做到第三件：付诸行动。

没有什么是无法通过努力来实现的，因此你有必要养成习惯，选择做艰难且必要的事，而不是有趣而简单的事。这可能是你通向成功最可靠的途径。

第14章

翻译技巧(十)英语长句译法

　　潘文国先生在《汉英语言对比纲要》一书中讲到汉英句子结构的对比,指出英语句子是树式结构,而汉语句子是竹式结构。"树式结构的背后是以整驭零的封闭性结构,竹式结构的背后是以零驭整的开放性结构。"也就是说,英语句子犹如一棵枝叶繁茂的参天大树,有树干,有枝叶,枝叶以树干为核心。因此,英语中各种长句、难句比比皆是;长句主要由基本句型扩展而成,其方式包括:增加修饰成分,如定语、状语,用各种短语(如介词、分词、动名词或不定式短语)充当句子成分,也可通过关联词将两个或两个以上的句子组合成并列复合句或主从复合句。在处理英语句子的时候,我们需要剔除枝叶对我们的干扰,把握好句子基本的主干结构。而汉语句子就不同了,在表情达意时,往往要借助动词,按照动作的发生顺序或逻辑顺序,逐步交代,层层铺开,结构犹如竹子,一节一节连下去,表义不完,句子不止。因此,在英译汉时,往往要先分析句子结构、形式,才能确定句子的功能、意义。

汉语注重隐性连贯(covert coherence)，是意合(parataxis)语言。所谓"意合"是指句子之间不用关联词作纽带而靠内涵意义和语序表明关系，词语之间的关系常在不言之中，词法意义和逻辑关系常隐含在字里行间。而英语句子偏重形合(hypotaxis)。所谓"形合"是指句中的词语或分句之间用语言形式手段(如连接代词、关系代词、连接副词或关系副词)连接起来，表达语法意义和逻辑关系，因此句子注重显性接应(overt cohesion)，注重句子形式和结构完整，以形显义来表达一定的语法关系和逻辑关系。这些语言形式手段的运用增加了英语复合句的长度。另外，汉语句子句首开放，句尾收缩，多用松散句、省略句等。这些特征大大地限制了句子的长度。正如王力先生指出的："西洋人做文章把语言化零为整，中国人做文章几乎可以说是化整为零。"

与汉语句子相比，英语复合句长而复杂，这是英语自身在发展中形成的特点。F. Crews 认为：从句子深层语义结构而论，英语句子喜欢头轻脚重而避免头重脚轻，使句子的重心置于句尾，形成尾重(end-weight)。正如刘宓庆先生所言："英语句首封闭，句尾开放，定语修饰语可以后置。句子多用包孕式主从复合句，句子可以不断向句尾扩展延伸。"这样就形成了复杂的主从复合句。由此可知，汉英两种语言差别很大。在翻译主从复合句时，首先要弄清原文的句法结构，找出主句与从句，确定主句的主语、谓语和宾语。然后分析从句结构，在理解原文内容的基础上分清主次，分清几层意思之间的逻辑关系(时间、因果关系等)，再按照汉语特点和表达方式正确地译出原文的意思。一般来说，造成长句的原因有三方面：①修饰语过多；②并列成分多；③语言结构层次多。英语长句都是由基本结构扩展而来的，所以了解英语基本结构的扩展是分析长句的基础。英语句子扩展的主要方式有以下三种。

(1) 增加句子的修饰语。

(2) 增加并列成分或并列句。

(3) 由短语或从句充当句子成分。

在分析语法所表达的意思时，要注意逻辑上的联系，语法不能脱离逻辑。随后，在弄清句子结构的基础上可以运用各种处理方法进行翻译。

长句的翻译应分两步走：第一步为理解阶段，第二步为表达阶段。理解是翻译的第一步，也是最重要的一步，是正确翻译的基础。所谓"理解"，就是从语法上区分主句和从句，从语义上找出这个句子有几层含义以及各个层次之间的逻辑关系。弄清楚一个长句的结构后，第一步，也是关键的一步就是尽可能正确地把整个句子的意思表达出来。如上所述，英语和汉语是两种完全不同的语言，在句子结构和表达方式上都有所不同。因此，我们在翻译中要把这些因素考虑进来。除了译者对原文的理解之外，译文的成功与否很大程度上取决于译者对母语的驾驭能力以及对翻译技巧的运用。如果译者对一个句子的理解是错误的，那么译文也绝不可能正确。

英译汉中的长句处理一般可分为6个具体的步骤。

理解阶段的三个步骤为：①扼要拟出全句的轮廓；②辨清主从结构，并根据上下文领会全句的要旨；③划出句与句之间的从属关系，弄清每句原文的意思。

表达也分三步：①尝试性译出每层的意思；②各层意思之间的重组与综合；③润色。在熟悉了长句的处理步骤后，我们就可以运用不同的方法翻译不同类型的长句。在分析长句时可以采用下面的方法。

(1) 找出全句的主语、谓语和宾语，从整体上把握句子的结构。

(2) 找出句中所有的谓语结构、非谓语动词、介词短语和从句的引导词。

(3) 分析从句和短语的功能，例如，它是否为主语从句、宾语从句、表语从句等；若是状语，它是表示时间、原因、结果，还是表示条件等。

(4) 分析词、短语和从句之间的相互关系，例如，定语从句所修饰的先行词是哪一个，等等。

(5) 注意插入语等其他成分。

(6) 注意分析句子中是否有固定词组或固定搭配。

下面结合一些实例来进行分析。

Behaviorists suggest that the child who is raised in an environment where there are many stimuli which develop his or her capacity for appropriate responses will experience greater intellectual development.

结构分析：①该句的主语为behaviorists，谓语为suggest，宾语为一个从句，因此整个句子为Behaviorists suggest that-clause结构。②该句共有5个谓语结构，它们的谓语动词分别为suggest、is raised、are、develop、experience，这5个谓语结构之间的关系为：Behaviorists suggest that-clause 结构为主句；who is raised in an environment为定语从句，所修饰的先行词为child；where there are many stimuli为定语从句，所修饰的先行词为environment；which develop his or her capacity for appropriate responses为定语从句，所修饰的先行词为stimuli；在suggest的宾语从句中，主语为child，谓语为experience，宾语为greater intellectual development。在做了如上的分析之后，我们就会对该句有一个较为透彻的理解，然后根据上面所讲述的各种翻译方法进行翻译。

参考译文：行为主义者认为，如果儿童的成长环境里有许多刺激因素，这些因素又有利于其适当反应能力的发展，那么，儿童的智力会发展到较高的水平。

总结一下，长句的翻译方法主要有4种：顺译法、逆译法、分译法和综合法。

14.1　顺译法

在一个长句中，如果所叙述的一连串动作是按照动作发生的时间先后安排的，或是按照逻辑关系排列的，这与汉语表达方式基本一致，因此可按照原文顺序译出。例如：

For a family of four, for example, it is more convenient as well as cheaper to sit comfortably at home, with almost unlimited entertainment available, than to go out in search of amusement elsewhere.

结构分析：①该句的主干为it is more...to do sth. than to do sth. else，这是一个比较结构，而且是在两个不定式之间进行比较。②该句中共有三个谓语结构，它们之间的关系为：it is more convenient as well as cheaper to... 为主体结构，但it是形式主语，真正的主语为第二个谓语结构(to sit comfortably at home)，并与第三个谓语结构(to go out in search of amusement elsewhere)作比较。③句首的for a family of four作状语，表示条件。另外，还有两个介词短语作插入语：for example和with almost unlimited entertainment available，其中第二个介词短语作伴随状语，修饰to sit comfortably at home。

参考译文：譬如，对于一个四口之家来说，舒舒服服地在家中看电视，就能看到几乎数不清的娱乐节目，这比到外面别的地方去消遣要便宜、方便得多。

Achieving these will depend, in very large measure, upon the mobilization and education of the entire population, in particular, on improving the education of girls and women who are, at once, the most educational deprived part of the population, and that with the greatest unexploited potential and talent.

结构分析：这是一个结构复杂而又不流散的英语复合句。谓语动词depend后接两个介词(短语upon...与on...)，第二个介词短语在语义上是第一个的具体与深化，起强调作用。这与汉语的表达习惯相一致。另外，who 引导的定语从句是对girls and women的补充说明。该从句又有两个并列表语：the...part 和that... (即the part)。

参考译文：要达到这些目的，在很大程度上依赖于动员和教育全体人民，尤其依赖于改善女童和妇女的教育。在所有的人中，她们既是在教育权利上受剥夺最严重的一部分，又是具有最大的尚未发掘的潜力和才能的一部分。

What begins as penny-ante dishonesty in elementary school—glancing at a neighbor's spelling test—snowballs into more serious cheating in middle and high school, as enrollments swell and students start moving class to class, teacher to teacher.

结构分析：本句是一个结构复杂的句子。它有两个从句，其中由what引导的从句即名词性从句中的主语从句，谓语是snowballs into，另外，破折号之间的分词短语是对

what引导的主语从句的补充说明，也应译出；另一个从句为由as引导的伴随状语从句，它由两个并列分句组成。

参考译文：小学时的不诚实行为只是小打小闹，比如偷看一眼邻桌的拼写试卷。到了初中、高中，随着招生人数的增加，学生不断更换班级、更换老师，那些"小打小闹"逐渐发展成更为严重的作弊行为。

Dying patients especially—who are easiest to mislead and most often kept in the dark—can then not make decisions about the end of life; about whether or not they should enter a hospital or to have surgery; about where and with whom they should spend their remaining time; about how they should bring their affairs to a close and leave.

结构分析：本句结构复杂，句中出现了三个同位语从句，与汉语的句序、内在逻辑关系及表达法基本相似，因而可用顺译法直接翻译。

参考译文：特别是临终病人——最易受骗，也最易被人蒙在鼓里——因而不能作出临终前的种种抉择：是否要住进医院或进行手术；在何处与何人度过剩下的日子；如何处理完自己的后事然后与世长辞。

14.2　逆译法

事物发展顺序是先有因后有果，先有假设后有可能，先有条件后有结果。汉语正是按照这种先后、因果、由假设到推论、由事实到结论的事物发展逻辑顺序逐层叙述、层层推进的。汉语信息焦点(即说话人认为最重要的内容)往往出现在后面，越靠后越显得重要，句子语义结构是"头轻脚重"。汉语通常称复合句为"偏正句"，偏句是指从句，常在句首，而正句是指主句，多在句末，起总结作用。相反，英语在表达多层逻辑思维时，句子语义结构往往是"头重脚轻"，将重要信息放在句首，次要的在句末。翻译英语长句时，不能拘泥于原文形式机械地翻译，必须破句重组，逆着原文的顺序翻译以达到译文与原文的"动态对等"，这就是逆译法。在许多情况下，英语长句的表达次序与汉语表达习惯不同，有时甚至完全相反。在这种情况下，我们必须改变原文的句序，从原文后面译起，逆着原文的顺序进行翻译，使译文符合汉语的表达习惯。例如：

It remains to be seen whether the reserves of raw materials would be sufficient to supply world economy which would have grown by 500 percent.

结构分析：句中whether the reserves of...by 500 percent 部分为主语从句，it 是形式主语，形成了It remains to be seen whether...的结构。此句如果按照自然顺序翻译，就无法正确表达，而如果先翻译which would have grown by 500 percent这一定语从句，并根据其

逻辑意思，将其译成条件状语从句，译文就变得通顺流畅。

参考译文：如果世界经济真的以5倍于现有的速度在增长，那么原材料的储备是否能充分满足其需求，尚不得而知。

It therefore becomes more and more important that, if students are not to waste their opportunities, there will have to be much more detailed information about courses and more advice.

结构分析：该句由一个主语从句、一个条件状语从句和一个主句组成。"It therefore becomes more and more important"是主句，也是全句的中心内容。全句共有三个谓语结构：becomes more and more important、are not to waste their opportunities，以及 have to be much more detailed information about courses and more advice。包含三层含义：变得越来越重要；不浪费他们的机会；得为他们提供更为详尽的信息并予以更多的指导。为了使译文符合汉语的表达习惯，该句的翻译宜采用逆序法。

参考译文：因此，如果要使学生充分利用其(上大学的)机会，就得为他们提供关于课程的更为详尽的信息并予以更多的指导。这个问题显得越来越重要了。

14.3　分译法

在英语长句中，如果主句与从句或主句与修饰语之间的关系不是很密切，那么翻译时可按汉语多短句的习惯，把长句中的从句或短语化为句子，分开来叙述；有时，也可以适当增加词语以使语义连贯。在下列情况下，我们常采用分译法翻译英语长句。

He poured into his writing all the pain of his life and the conviction it had brought to him that the world could be made a better place to live in if the people became the masters of their fate.

结构分析：这句中的宾语很长，从all the pain of his life 开始，直至句末people became the masters of their fate为止；宾语conviction受定语从句it had brought to him的修饰，后跟一个较长的同位语从句that...of their fate。将这句话译成汉语时可将定语从句"这种痛苦给他带来的"移在"信念"之前，但无法将这么长的同位语从句放在"信念"之前，在此只需要将conviction和同位语从句分译，将其译为"这种信念认为……"，译文就会变得通顺达意。

参考译文：他在作品里倾诉了自己一生的痛苦给他带来的一种信念，认为如果人民成为自己命运的主人，世界就会变得更美好。

The president said at a press conference dominated by questions on yesterday's election results that he could not explain why the Republicans had suffered such a widespread defeat, which in the end would deprive the Republican Party of long-held superiority in the House.

结构分析：本句含有两个宾语从句和一个非限制性定语从句。全句共有三层意思：在一次关于选举结果的记者招待会上，总统发了言；他说他不能解释为什么共和党遭到了这样大的失败；这种情况最终会使共和党失去在众院中长期享有的优势。三层意思都具有相对的独立性，因此，在译文中拆成三个单句分别叙述。

参考译文：一次记者招待会上，问题集中于昨天的选举结果，总统就此发了言。他说他不能解释为什么共和党遭到了这样大的失败。这种情况最终会使共和党失去在众院中长期享有的优势。

Television, it is often said, keeps one informed about current events, allows one to follow the latest developments in science and politics, and offers an endless series of programmes which are both instructive and entertaining.

结构分析：在此长句中，有一个插入语"it is often said"、三个并列谓语结构，还有一个定语从句。这三个并列的谓语结构尽管在结构上属于同一个句子，但都有独立的意义，因此在翻译时，可以采用分句法，按照汉语的习惯把整个句子分解成几个独立的分句。

参考译文：人们常说，通过电视可以了解时事、掌握科学和政治的最新动态。从电视里还可以看到层出不穷、既有教育意义又有娱乐性的新节目。

Trendy, young Internet users, who see themselves as the opposite of Tuhao—not wealthy, but well-educated and cultured—have further popularized the term by using it in various comic situations, at prominent news events, or coining new catchphrases with it.

结构分析：这是一个复杂句，句子的主干是"Trendy, young Internet users...have further popularized the term"，定语从句"who see themselves as the opposite of Tuhao"用来修饰"Trendy, young Internet users"。破折号中间的成分是对定语从句的补充。

参考译文：新潮的青年网民们将自己视为与"土豪"相反的一类人——没钱，却有文化有教养。他们将该词运用到各种爆笑场景以及新闻头条中，并创造出一系列新流行语，这下，"土豪"一词大火特火。

At a time of increasing global challenges and threats, such as inequality, exclusion, violence and sectarianism worsened by local tensions and conflicts which undermine humanity's cohesion, learning to live together and fostering rights, inclusion and non-discrimination among all members of the global community become more topical than ever before.

结构分析：该句摘自 2022 年 6 月 CATTI 英语二级笔译实务真题，是典型的长难句，包含一个定语从句和一个分词短语(作后置定语)。句子的主干是 learning to...become more topical than ever before. 其中 learning to live together and fostering rights, inclusion and non-discrimination 是主语, 后面还跟了修饰成分 among all members of the global community, 这么一大串确实很令人迷惑。遇到这种情况时, 首先要把句子的主、谓、宾找出来, 再对其他修饰成分进行分析, 这样就会清晰很多。翻译时需要对原文语序进行调整, 并对原句进行切分, 将 at a time 放到中间以衔接前后文, 即先把背景交待好, 然后提及 "在此形势下, 学习……变得更加重要"。

参考译文: 不平等、排外、暴力和宗派主义等全球性挑战和威胁日益加剧, 而地方紧张局势和冲突使之愈演愈烈, 这破坏了人类的凝聚力。在此形势下, 学会共处, 保障全球社会所有成员的权利, 促进人们之间的包容, 消除歧视, 比以往任何时候都更加重要。

14.4 综合法

我们常常会遇到一些英语长句, 翻译时既不能只用顺译法, 也不能只用逆译法和分译法。这时就应仔细推敲, 或按时间先后, 或按逻辑顺序, 有顺有逆、有主有次地对全句进行综合处理。例如:

One teacher writes that instead of drawing students' compositions in critical red ink, the teacher will get far more constructive results by finding one or two things which have been done better than last time, and commenting favorably on them.

结构分析: 这个长句含有一个宾语从句, 宾语从句中又有一个定语从句(which have been done better than last time)修饰它前面的中心词things。由介词by和instead of引导的短语作方式状语修饰句子the teacher will get...results。翻译这个句子时不能单纯使用顺译法、逆译法或拆分法, 而应综合运用分译、逆译等几种技巧。

参考译文: 一位老师写道, 如果老师能从学生的作文中找出一两处比上次做得更好的地方加以表扬, 而不是用红墨水把学生的作文改得一塌糊涂, 将会取得更积极的效果。

As regards health, I have nothing useful to say since I have little experience of illness. I eat and drink whatever I like, and sleep when I cannot keep awake. I never do anything on the ground that it is good for health, though in actual fact the things I like doing are mostly wholesome.

结构分析: 原文有三个句子, 但翻译时可根据前后文间的逻辑关系将其合并为两句。原文第一句用顺译法, 第三句用逆译法, 按照目的语的表达习惯先说原因。因此,上文翻译采用了综合译法。也就是说翻译时经过仔细推敲，或按照时间先后，或按照逻辑顺序，有顺有逆、有主有次地对全句进行综合处理，英语和汉语的字面意思不完全对应，但是内涵是相同的。

参考译文：谈到健康问题，我就没有什么可说的了，因为我没怎么生过病。我想吃什么就吃什么，眼睛睁不开了就睡觉，从不以对身体有益为理由做任何事，但实际上我喜欢做的事大都是对身体健康有益的。

People were afraid to leave their houses, for although the police had been ordered to stand by in case of emergency, they were just as confused and helpless as anybody else.

结构分析：该句共有三层含义。①人们不敢出门；②尽管警察已接到命令，要准备好应付紧急情况；③警察和其他人一样不知所措和无能为力。在这三层含义中，②表示让步，③表示原因，而①则表示结果，应按照汉语习惯顺序进行翻译。

参考译文：尽管警察已接到命令，要准备好应付紧急情况，但人们不敢出门，因为警察和其他人一样不知所措、无能为力。

综合练习

一、翻译下列长句。

(一) 用顺译法翻译下列长句。

1. The global economy that boomed in the 1960s, growing at an average of 5.5 percent a year and pushed ahead at a 4.5 percent-a-year rate in the mid-1970s, simply stopped growing in 1981–1982.

2. All services in business such as gift wrapping, delivery, and credit have some amount of costs associated with them, and these costs must be covered by higher prices.

3. Her first impulse was to go round all the rooms looking for the thieves, but then she decided that at her age it might be more prudent to have someone with her, so she went to fetch the porter from his basement.

4. As I lie awake in bed, listening to the sound those sharp rain drops pounding on the pavement, my mind goes reeling down dark corridors teeming with agonizing flashbacks, and a chill from within fills me with dread.

5. One widely held belief is that a sharp fright will end a troublesome bout of hiccups, but many people prefer just waiting for them to go away as this "cure" is often worse than the ailment itself.

6. So, as well as being overworked, a detective has to be out at all hours of the day and night interviewing his witnesses and persuading them, usually against their own best interests,

to help them.

7. She could always reflect that all parties concerned had married according to their stations, a prerequisite for their true happiness.

8. When Torvald gave her money for new dress and such things, she never spent more than half of it, and she found other ways to earn money.

9. We hear what they said and view what they did; we see them as if they were really alive; we sympathize with them, enjoy with them, and grieve with them; their experience becomes ours, and we feel as if we were in a measure actors with them in the scenes which they described.

10. The world is undergoing profound changes: the integration of economy with science and technology is increasing, the restructuring of the world economy is speeding up, and economic prosperity depends not only on the total volume of resources and capital, but also directly on the accumulation and application of technological knowledge and information.

11. Power politics and hegemony still exist in international political, economic, and security realms, and have further asserted themselves; regional conflicts have erupted one after another; the gap in development between North and South countries continues to widen. Mankind is plagued by transnational problems such as environmental degradation, arms proliferation, international crimes, and terrorism.

12. Working for President Ronald Reagan, Mr. Bush was a silent and subservient vice president, a former rival who gave himself the task of proving his loyalty by staying in the background and never speaking out when his beliefs differed from those of his boss.

13. Increasing labor force participation, record nationalasset, surging consumer confidence and spending, near record levels of immigration, and urban renewal are all anecdotal evidences that hopes are high.

14. In such cases, the public and its political decision-makers get information only of a certain kind, because there is no private, well-funded foundation call "The Consortium of Single Mothers on Welfare" that bestows similar massive funding to discover the efforts of poverty on the development of children.

15. Even when we turn off the bedside lamp and are fast asleep, electricity is working for us, driving our refrigerators, heating our water, or keeping our rooms air-conditioned.

16. In Africa I met a boy, who was crying as if his heart would break and said when I spoke to him, that he was hungry because he had had no food for two days.

17. Prior to the twentieth century, women in novels were stereotypes of lacking any

features that made them unique individuals and were also subject to numerous restrictions imposed by the male-dominated culture.

18. It begins as a childlike interest in the grand spectacle and exciting event; it grows as a mature interest in the variety and complexity of the drama, the splendid achievements and terrible failures; it ends as deep sense of the mystery of man's life of all the dead, great and obscure, who once walked the earth, and of wonderful and awful possibilities of being a human being.

19. Owing to the remarkable development in mass-communications, people everywhere are feeling new wants and are being exposed to new customs and ideas, while governments are often forced to introduce still further innovations for the reasons given above.

参考译文

1. 世界经济在20世纪60年代很繁荣，年平均增长率为5.5%，到了70年代中期，年平均增长率仍高达4.5%，但是在1981年到1982年间，世界经济完全停止增长了。

2. 所有商业服务，如礼品包装、货物配送和信用贷款，都有一定的成本。这些成本必须通过提高价格来弥补。

3. 她的第一反应是逐一搜查所有的房间以寻找窃贼，但她接着又想，自己上了年纪，若有人来帮着一起干，那就更为稳妥，所以她从地下室那里找了守门人来。

4. 我躺在床上，睡不着，听着雨点儿在路面上啪啪作响。我思绪万千，恍恍惚惚进入了一条幽暗的通道。回想起许多痛苦的往事，心里一阵冰凉，不禁感到毛骨悚然。

5. 一种普遍为人们接受的观点是，猛然的惊吓会止住一阵讨厌的打嗝。但是许多人宁愿等打嗝自然过去，因为这种"治嗝的方法"常常比打嗝本身更糟。

6. 所以除了过度操劳外，警探还须没日没夜地在外面找证人谈话，而且往往要说服他们违背自身的利益来帮助他。

7. 她总可以这样回首往事，她周围的人全都门当户对地婚配成亲，这才是他们真正幸福的必要条件。

8. 每当托伐给她钱买新衣服和其他东西时，她起码要省下一半，而且要想别的路子去挣钱。

9. 我们如闻其声，如观其行，如见其人；我们赞同、支持他们，和他们悲喜与共；他们的感受成为我们自己的感受，我们觉得仿佛自己是在他们所描绘的场景中与他们同台扮演着角色。

10. 世界正在发生深刻的变化：经济与科学技术的结合与日俱增；世界经济的重组加快步伐；经济繁荣不仅取决于资源和资本的总量，而且直接有赖于技术知识和信息的积累及其应用。

11. 强权政治和霸权主义在国际政治、经济和安全领域中依然存在并有新的发展，地区冲突此起彼伏，南北发展差距继续扩大，环境恶化、武器扩散、国际犯罪、恐怖主义等跨国问题困扰着人类。

12. 布什先生为里根总统效力时，是一个缄默而顺从的副总统，他以前曾是里根的竞争对手，当了副总统以后，他要证实自己对里根的忠诚：他尽量不抛头露面突出自己，在自己的观点与上司相左时，他总是把话放到肚子里。

13. 劳动阶层越来越多地致力于发展经济、国有资产达到创纪录的水平、消费者信心高涨、消费增长、移民数量接近新高纪录以及城市不断更新、改造，这些都是栩栩如生的证据，表明人们充满了希望。

14. 在这些事例中，公众和决策者只能获得一种类别的信息，因为根本没有名为"单身母亲福利协会"的私人基金会：有雄厚的资金，足以拿出相近数额的巨额资金来资助关于贫困对于儿童成长影响的研究。

15. 即使在我们关掉了床头灯并深深地进入梦乡时，电仍在为我们工作：让电冰箱维持低温，把水加热，或使室内空调机继续运转。

16. 在非洲，我遇到了一个男孩，他哭得伤心极了，我问他时，他说他饿了，两天没有吃饭了。

17. 在20世纪以前，小说中的妇女都是模式化的形象。她们没有任何特点，因而无法成为具有个性的人；她们还要屈从于由男性主宰的文化传统强加给她们的种种束缚。

18. 我们对历史的爱好起源于孩童般的兴趣——我们最初仅对一些历史上的宏伟场面和激动人心的事件感兴趣；其后，这种爱好变得成熟起来，我们开始对历史这出"戏剧"的多样性和复杂性，对历史上的辉煌成就和悲壮失败也感兴趣；对历史的爱好，最终以我们对人类生命的一种深沉的神秘感而宣告结束。逝去者，无论是伟人还是平庸之人，所有在这个地球上走过而已逝的人，都有能取得伟大成就或制造可怕事件的潜力。

19. 大众通信技术的显著发展使各地的人们不断感到有新的需求，不断接触到新的习俗和思想，由于上述原因，政府常常得推出更多的革新。

(二) 用逆译法翻译下列长句。

1. We were most impressed by the fact that even those patients who were not told of their serious illness were quite aware of its potential outcome.

2. He knew how ashamed he would have been if she had known his mother and the kind of place in which he was born, and the kind of people among whom he was born.

3. A lion had long watched them in the hope of making prize of them, but found that there was little chance for him so long as they kept all together.

4. Such is human nature in the West that a great many people are often willing to sacrifice higher pay for the privilege of becoming white-collar workers.

5. It should be the pressing task in international postal cooperation to actively help developing countries overcome difficulties in their development of postal services and to energetically narrow the gap between the developing and the developed countries in this field.

6. Fourth, severe punishment shall be imposed on those who make use of or instigate minors to smuggle, traffic, transport, or manufacture drugs, sell drugs to minors, or lure, instigate, deceive, or force them into taking or injecting drugs, and on those who have again committed drug-related crimes after having been convicted of the crime of smuggling, trafficking, transporting, manufacturing, or i1legally holding drugs.

7. A great number of graduate students were driven into the intellectual slum when in the United States the intellectual poor became the classic poor, the poor under the rather romantic guise of the "Beat Generation", a real phenomenon in the late fifties.

8. Insects would make it impossible for us to live in the world; they would devour all our crops and kill our flocks and herds, if it were not for the protection we get from insect-eating animals.

9. Any man on the street scarcely realizes that whereas the disappearance, or even what we see in some quarters, the continuous neglect and degradation of the teaching profession, must mean a disaster to the entire nation.

参考译文

1. 即使那些病人没有被告知患了重病，他们也十分清楚潜在的后果，这一点给我们留下了深刻的印象。

2. 他有这样的母亲，出生在这样的地方、这样的人中间，要是这些都让她知道的话，他知道该有多丢人。

3. 一头狮子盯了它们许久，想抓住它们，但又发觉，如果它们老是凑在一起，那就很难如愿以偿。

4. 许多人常常宁愿牺牲比较高的工资以换取白领工人的社会地位，这在西方倒是人之常情。

5. 积极帮助发展中国家克服邮政建设中面临的困难，努力缩小发展中国家与发达国家在邮政领域的差距，应成为国际邮政合作的当务之急。

6. 其四，对利用、教唆未成年人走私、贩卖、运输、制造毒品，或者向未成年人出售毒品的，引诱、教唆、欺骗或者强迫未成年人吸食、注射毒品的，因走私、贩卖、运输、制造、非法持有毒品罪被判过刑又有毒品罪行的,从重处罚。

7. 20世纪50年代后期的美国出现了一个任何人都不可能视而不见的现象——穷知识分子以"垮掉的一代"这种颇为浪漫的姿态出现而成为美国典型的穷人,正是这个时候大批大学生被赶进了知识分子的贫民窟。

8. 假如没有那些以昆虫为食的动物保护我们,昆虫将吞噬我们所有的庄稼,害死我们的牛羊家畜,使我们不能生存于世。

9. 如果没有教师这一职业,或者像在某些地区那样,教育事业长期不受重视并且每况愈下,那么就整个国家而言,这必将是一场灾难。这一点一般人很少认识到。

(三)用分译法翻译下列长句。

1. A spirited discussion springs up between a young girl who insists that women have outgrown the jumping-on-the-chair-at-the-sight-of-a-mouse era and a colonel who says they haven't.

2. Tardiness in rising is punished by extra haste in eating breakfast or in walking to catch the train: in the long run, it may even mean the loss of a job or of advancement in business.

3. The mother might have spoken with understandable pride of her child.

4. Her complete happiness was marred only by the fact that she knew her marriage would upset her father who disliked change of any kind and that she had unknowingly prepared Harriet for another disappointment.

5. Human beings have distinguished themselves from other animals, and in doing so ensured their survival, by the ability to observe and understand their environment, and then either to adapt to that environment, or to control and adapt it to their own needs.

6. The number of the young people in the United States who cannot read is incredible—about one in four.

7. All they have to do is to press a button, and they can see plays, films, operas, and shows of every kind, not to mention political discussions and the latest exciting football match.

8. A conflict between the generations—between youth and age—seems the most stupid of all conflicts, for it is one between oneself as one is and oneself as one will be, or between oneself as one was and oneself as one is.

9. There is a tide taken at the flood in the affairs not only of men but of women too, which leads on to fortune.

10. Some men have been virtuous blindly, others have speculated fantastically, and others have been shrewd to bad purposes.

参考译文

1. 一位年轻的女子和一位上校展开了一场热烈讨论。女士坚持认为，妇女已有进步，看见老鼠就吓得跳上椅子的时代已经过去了，上校则认为没有。

2. 爱懒床的人会得到惩罚：他们得赶着吃早餐，跑着赶火车。从长远来看，这可能意味着失去工作或升职的机会。

3. 母亲在谈到自己的孩子时，也许有些自豪感，这是可以理解的。

4. 但她的圆满幸福也有美中不足。她知道自己的婚事会使父亲很不高兴，因为老人不愿生活有丝毫的改变。而且她在不知不觉中又一次使哈里特面临失望的打击。

5. 人类具有观察和了解周围环境的能力，要么适应环境，要么控制环境，或根据自身的需要改造环境。人类就这样把自己和其他动物区别开来并一代代地生存下来。

6. 大约有四分之一的美国青年人没有阅读能力，这简直令人难以置信！

7. 他们只需要按一下开关。开关一开，就可以看到电视剧、电影、歌剧，以及其他各种各样的文艺节目。至于政治问题的辩论、最近的激动人心的足球赛，更是不在话下。

8. 一代人与一代人之间的冲突，也就是年轻人与老年人之间的冲突，似乎是最可笑的。因为这就是现在与将来的自己，或者是过去与现在的自己之间的冲突。

9. 人生在世，有时会走运，抓住时机，就能飞黄腾达，不但男性如此，女性也一样。

10. 有些人品行端正，却趋于盲目；有些人勤于思考，却脱离现实；有些人非常精明，却不走正道。

(四) 用综合法翻译下列长句。

1. As far as sight could reach, I feasted my eyes on a vastness of infinite charm, which presents itself in a profusion of color, in verdant luxuriance, in dulcet warbling, in pervading perfume, in rippling undulation, in cataract sprays, in hilly waves, in field crisscross, and verily in vitality and variety.

2. What the New Yorker would find missing is what many outsiders find oppressive and distasteful about New York—its rawness, tension, urgency; its bracing competitiveness; the rigor of its judgment; and the congested, democratic presence of so many other New Yorkers encased in their own world.

3. Countless others have written on this theme, and it may be that I shall pass unnoticed among them; if so I must comfort myself with the greatness and splendor of my rivals, whose work will rob my own of recognition.

4. Modern scientific and technical books, especially textbooks, require revision at short intervals if their authors wish to keep pace with new ideas, observations, and discoveries.

5. The principal of a great Philadelphia high school is driven to cry for help in combating

the notion that it is undemocratic to run a special program of studies for outstanding boys and girls.

6. It was an old woman, tall and shapely still, though withered by time, on whom his eyes fell when he stopped and turned.

7. Law-and-order is the longest-running and probably the best-loved political issue in U.S. history. Yet it is painfully apparent that millions of Americans who would never think of themselves as lawbreakers, let alone criminals, are increasingly taking liberties with the legal codes that are designed to protect them and their society.

参考译文

1. 纵目眺望，我饱览了一片无限娇艳的风光：万紫千红，郁郁葱葱。鸟语悦耳，花香袭人，涟漪荡漾，瀑布飞流，层峦起伏，阡陌纵横。真可谓生机勃勃，气象万千。

2. 纽约的粗犷、紧张，那种急迫感和催人奋发的竞争性，其是非观念之严酷无情，市内各色人等熙熙攘攘、兼容并蓄于各自的天地之中，这一切都使那些非纽约人感到厌恶和窒息；而这一切，又正是纽约人所眷恋的。

3. 有关这个题目的其他著作数不胜数，我写的书可能淹没其间，无人垂顾；倘若如此，那是因为我的竞争对手博大精深，才华横溢，所以他们的著作才会使我的作品默默无闻，我必须借此安慰自己。

4. 对于现代科技类书籍，特别是教科书，如果作者希望自己书中的内容能与新概念、新观察到的事实和新发现同步发展，就应该每隔较短的时间更新书中的内容。

5. 费城的一所名牌中学为一些出类拔萃的男女学生开设一套特别课程，有人认为这种做法不民主，结果校长不得不大声疾呼求助人们同这种观念作斗争。

6. 他站住，转过身来，看见个年迈妇女，她个子很高，依然一副好身材，虽然受岁月折磨而显得憔悴。

7. 法律和秩序是美国历史上持续时间最长、也可能是政治上最热门的话题。然而，如今数以百万计的美国人尽管从来不认为自己会违反法律，更不用说会成为罪犯，却在越来越随意地践踏那些专为保护他们和他们的社会而制定的法规。显而易见，这不能不使人痛心疾首。

二、翻译下列语篇。

Companionship of Books

A man may usually be known by the books he reads as well as by the company he keeps; for there is a companionship of books as well as of men; and one should always live in the best company, whether it be of books or of men.

A good book may be among the best of friends. It is the same today that it always was, and it will never change. It is the most patient and cheerful of companions. It does not turn its back upon us in times of adversity or distress. It always receives us with the same kindness; amusing and instructing us in youth, and comforting and consoling us in age.

Men often discover their affinity to each other by the mutual love they have for a book just as two people sometimes discover a friend by the admiration which both entertain for a third. There is an old proverb, "Love me, love my dog." But there is more wisdom in this: "Love me, love my book." The book is a truer and higher bond of union. Men can think, feel, and sympathize with each other through their favorite author. They live in him together, and he in them.

A good book is often the best urn of a life enshrining the best that life could think out; for the world of a man's life is, for the most part, but the world of his thoughts. Thus, the best books are treasuries of good words, the golden thoughts, which, remembered and cherished, become our constant companions and comforters.

Books possess an essence of immortality. They are by far the most lasting products of human effort. Temples and statues decay, but books survive. Time is of no account with great thoughts, which are as fresh today as when they first passed through their author's minds, ages ago. What was then said and thought still speaks to us as vividly as ever from the printed page. The only effect of time has been to sift out the bad products; for nothing in literature can long survive but what is really good.

Books introduce us into the best society; they bring us into the presence of the greatest minds that have ever lived. We hear what they said and did; we see them as if they were really alive; we sympathize with them, enjoy with them, and grieve with them; their experience becomes ours, and we feel as if we were in a measure actors with them in the scenes which they described.

The great and good do not die, even in this world. Embalmed in books, their spirits walk abroad. The book is a living voice. It is an intellect to which we still listens.

参考译文

以书为伴

通常看一个人读些什么书就可知道他的为人，就像看他同什么人交往就可知道他的为人一样，因为有人以人为伴，也有人以书为伴。无论是书友还是朋友，我们都应该以最好的为伴。

好书就像是你最好的朋友。它始终不渝，过去如此，现在如此，将来也永远不变。

它是最有耐心、最令人愉悦的伴侣。在我们穷愁潦倒、临危遭难时，它也不会抛弃我们，对我们始终很亲切。在我们年轻时，好书陶冶我们的情操，增长我们的知识；到我们年老时，它又给我们以慰藉和勉励。

人们常常因为喜欢同一本书而结为知已，就像有时两个人因为敬慕同一个人而成为朋友一样。有句古谚说道："爱屋及乌。"其实"爱我及书"这句话蕴涵更多的哲理。书是更为真诚而高尚的情谊纽带。人们可以通过共同喜爱的作家沟通思想，交流感情，彼此息息相通，并与自己喜欢的作家思想相通，情感相融。

好书常如最精美的宝器，珍藏着人生的思想精华，因为人生的境界主要就在于其思想的境界。因此，最好的书是金玉良言和崇高思想的宝库，这些良言和思想若铭记于心并多加珍视，就会成为我们忠实的伴侣和永恒的慰藉。

书籍具有不朽的本质，是目前为止人类努力创造的最为持久的成果。寺庙会倒坍，神像会朽烂，而书却经久长存。对于伟大的思想来说，时间的更移无关紧要。多年前初次闪现于作者脑海的伟大思想今日依然清新如故。时间惟一的作用是淘汰不好的作品，因为只有真正的佳作才能经世长存。

书籍使我们能与最优秀的人为伍，使我们置身于历代伟人巨匠之间，如闻其声，如观其行，如见其人，同他们情感交融，悲喜与共，感同身受。我们觉得自己仿佛在作者所描绘的舞台上和他们一起扮演着角色。

纵然在今世，伟人亦长存。他们的精神被载入书册，传于四海。书是人生至今仍在聆听的智慧之声，永远充满着活力。

参考文献

[1] 张丽华. 文体协商：翻译中的语言、文类与社会[M]. 北京：北京大学出版社，2023.

[2] 杨朝燕，曾文华. 文化与翻译[M]. 北京：清华大学出版社，2022.

[3] 李运兴. 英汉语篇翻译[M]. 4版. 北京：清华大学出版社，2020.

[4] 叶子楠. 高级英汉翻译理论与实践[M]. 4版. 北京：清华大学出版社，2020.

[5] 朱华. 非文学翻译——应用与方法[M]. 北京：北京大学出版社，2024.

[6] 陈德彰. 英汉翻译入门[M]. 2版. 北京：外语教学与研究出版社，2020.

[7] 彭萍. 英汉笔译[M]. 北京：外语教学与研究出版社，2022.

[8] 外宣微记. 笔尖上的文化碰撞：对外话语与翻译[M]. 北京：外文出版社，2022.

[9] 张震久，孙建民. 英汉互译简明教程[M]. 2版. 北京：外语教学与研究出版社，2021.

[10] 何刚强. 笔译理论与技巧[M]. 北京：外语教学与研究出版社，2022.

[11] 纪蓉琴，黄敏. 新编文体与翻译教程[M]. 北京：清华大学出版社，2018.

[12] 陈德彰. 英汉翻译入门[M]. 北京：外语教育与研究出版社，2005.

[13] 陈宏薇. 新编汉英翻译教程[M]. 上海：上海外语教育出版社，2004.

[14] 程镇球. 翻译论文集[D]. 北京：外语教学与研究出版社，2002.

[15] 陈菁，雷天放. 口译教程[M]. 上海：上海外语教育出版社，2006.

[16] 陈小慰. 新编实用翻译教程[M]. 北京：经济科学出版社，2006.

[17] 方梦之. 英汉—汉英应用翻译教程[M]. 上海：上海外语教育出版社，2005.

[18] 方梦之，毛忠明. 英汉—汉英应用翻译综合教程[M]. 上海：上海外语教育出版社，2008.

[19] 冯庆华，穆雷. 英汉翻译基础教程[M]. 北京：高等教育出版社，2008.

[20] 郭著章，李庆生. 英汉互译实用教程[M]. 武汉：武汉大学出版社，2003.

[21] 何刚强. 笔译理论与技巧[M]. 北京：外语教学与研究出版社，2009.

[22] 贾文波. 应用翻译功能论[M]. 北京：中国对外翻译出版公司，2004.

[23] 李昌拴. 非文学翻译理论与实践[M]. 北京：中国对外翻译出版公司，2004.

[24] 连淑能. 英译汉教程[M]. 北京：高等教育出版社，2006.

[25] 刘重德. 英汉语比较与翻译[M]. 青岛：青岛出版社，1998.

[26] 刘和平. 口译理论与教学[M]. 北京：中国对外翻译出版公司，2005.

[27] 刘季春. 实用翻译教程(修订版)[M]. 广州：中山大学出版社，2007.

[28] 刘宓庆. 文体与翻译[M]. 北京：中国对外翻译出版公司，1998.

[29] 罗进德. 非文学翻译理论与实践[M]. 北京：中国对外翻译出版公司，2004.

[30] 潘红. 商务英语英汉翻译教程[M]. 北京：中国商务出版社，2004.

[31] 钱钟书. 文学翻译的最高标准[A]. 翻译理论与翻译技巧论文集[C]. 北京：中国对外翻译出版公司，1985.

[32] 申雨平，戴宁. 实用英汉翻译教程[M]. 北京：外语教学与研究出版社，2002.

[33] 思果. 翻译新究[M]. 北京：中国对外翻译出版公司，2001.

[34] 孙致礼. 再谈文学翻译的策略问题[J]. 中国翻译，2003(1)：51.

[35] 孙致礼. 新编英汉翻译教程[M]. 上海：上海外语教育出版社，2003.

[36] 王恩冕. 大学英汉翻译教程[M]. 3版. 北京：对外经贸大学出版社，2009.

[37] 王振国，李艳琳. 新英汉翻译教程[M]. 北京：高等教育出版社，2007.

[38] 王治奎，等. 大学英汉翻译教程[M]. 济南：山东大学出版社，1995.

[39] 魏志成. 英汉比较翻译教程[M]. 北京：清华大学出版社，2004.

[40] 伍锋，何庆机. 应用文体翻译理论与实践[M]. 杭州：浙江大学出版社，2008.

[41] 谢群. 英汉互译教程[M]. 武汉：华中科技大学出版社，2010.

[42] 许建平. 英汉互译实践与技巧[M]. 北京：清华大学出版社，2007.

[43] 杨士焯. 英汉翻译教程[M]. 北京：北京大学出版社，2006.

[44] 叶子南. 高级英汉翻译理论与实践[M]. 北京：清华大学出版社，2001.

[45] 曾诚. 实用汉英翻译教程[M]. 北京：外语教学与研究出版社，2002.

[46] 张培基，等. 英汉翻译教程[M]. 上海：上海外语教育出版社，1998.

[47] 张培基. 英汉翻译教程[M]. 上海：上海外语教育出版社，2009.

[48] 张新红. 商务英语翻译[M]. 北京：高等教育出版社，2003.

[49] 赵萱，郑仰成. 科技英语翻译[M]. 北京：外语教学与研究出版社，2006.

[50] 仲伟合. 英语口译教程[M]. 北京：高等教育出版社，2007.

[51] 钟述孔. 英汉翻译手册[M]. 北京：商务出版社，1997.

[52] 庄绎传. 英汉翻译简明教程[M]. 北京：外语教学与研究出版社，2002.

[53] 张林影. 英语翻译教学中的文化因素及其恰当处理[J]. 教育探索，2013(2)：49-51.

[54] Baker M. Routledge Encyclopedia of Translation Studies[M]. Shanghai: Shanghai

Foreign Language Education Press, 2004.

[55] Bassnett S. Translation Studies[M]. 3rd ed. Shanghai: Shanghai Foreign Language Education Press, 2010.

[56] Jin Di, Nida E A. On Translation[M]. Beijing: China Translation & Publishing Corporation, 1984.

[57] Lefevere A. Translation, Rewriting and the Manipulation of Literary Fame[M]. Shanghai: Shanghai Foreign Language Education Press, 2010.

[58] Newmark P. About Translation[M]. Beijing: Foreign Language Teaching and Researching Press, 2006.

[59] Nida E A. L anguage, Culture, and Translating[M]. Shanghai: Shanghai Foreign Language Education Press, 1993.

[60] Tytler A F. Essay on the Principles of Translation[M]. Philadelphia: John Benjamins Publishing Co, 1970.

[61] Venuti L. The Translator's Invisibility[M]. London and New York: Routledge, 1995: 20, 132.

[62] Venuti L. Translator's Invisibility: A History of Translation[M]. London & New York: Routledge, 1995.